ONE NATION
UNDEREMPLOYED
JOBS REBUILD AMERICA

2014 STATE OF BLACK AMERICA®

// CONTRIBUTORS

Vanessa Allen, M.D., Ph.D.

Margarita "Maggie" Anderson

Donna Jones Baker

The Honorable Alvin Brown

Lindsay D. Brown

Ursula M. Burns

The Honorable Donna M. Christensen

The Honorable Mignon L. Clyburn

The Honorable Michael B. Hancock

Chanelle P. Hardy, Esq.

Hill Harper

Wade Henderson, Esq.

Rufina A. Hernández, Esq.

The Honorable Rubén Hinojosa

The Honorable Mike Honda

Tanya Clay House, Esq.

Sherrilyn Ifill, Esq.

Michael L. Lomax, Ph.D.

Tanya Leah Lombard

Wynton Marsalis

Erika McConduit-Diggs, Esq.

Marc H. Morial

Randal D. Pinkett, Ph.D.

The Honorable Stephanie Rawlings-Blake

Jonathan C. Ray

Jeffrey A. Robinson, Ph.D.

The Honorable Kathleen Sebelius

Thomas M. Shapiro, Ph.D.

J. Marshall Shepherd, Ph.D.

The Honorable Jabar Shumate

Joseph A. Slash

Elnora Watson

The Honorable AC Wharton

Valerie Rawlston Wilson, Ph.D.

A **NATIONAL URBAN LEAGUE** PUBLICATION

WWW.NUL.ORG / #JOBS4ALL

2014 STATE OF BLACK AMERICA®

ONE NATION UNDEREMPLOYED: JOBS REBUILD AMERICA

PUBLISHER

Marc H. Morial

EDITORIAL DIRECTOR

Latraviette D. Smith-Wilson

EDITOR-IN-CHIEF

Chanelle P. Hardy, Esq.

EXECUTIVE EDITORS

Hazeen Y. Ashby, Esq.,
Pamela Rucker Springs

CREATIVE DIRECTOR

Rhonda Spears Bell

STAFF EDITORS

Suzanne Bergeron, MSW, Shree Chauhan,
Susie Saavedra, Kyle R. Williams, Esq.,
Valerie Rawlston Wilson, Ph.D.

DESIGN

Untuck Design

CONTENTS

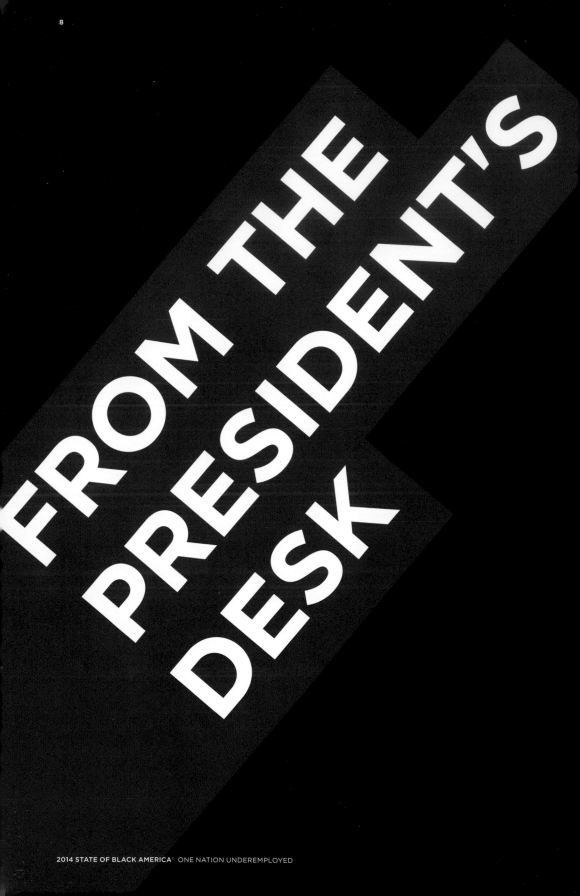

FROM THE PRESIDENT'S DESK

2014 RANG IN WITH A CHORUS OF INTERNATIONAL VOICES RAISED IN PERFECT PITCH AROUND ONE SUBJECT—INCOME INEQUALITY. FROM PRESIDENT BARACK OBAMA TO POPE FRANCIS AND NEW YORK MAYOR BILL DE BLASIO TO THE WORLD ECONOMIC FORUM, INCOME INEQUALITY HAS BEEN IDENTIFIED AS ONE OF THE MOST CRITICAL ISSUES THREATENING OUR FUTURE ON BOTH A GLOBAL AND DOMESTIC SCALE.

MARC H. MORIAL

PRESIDENT & CEO, NATIONAL URBAN LEAGUE

While each country, state and city has its own story to tell, the refrain is all-too-familiar and consistent: there is an urgent and growing disparity between what a very few have and what many are losing hope to ever achieve.

Here in the United States, our story is rife with examples indicating that despite being five years out of the Great Recession, we have yet to realize a great recovery. Instead, what we see emerging is indisputable clarity of what I refer to as "The Great Divide." Whether it is termed income inequality, loss of social mobility, the eroding middle class or opportunity inequality, at its core is a great divide between the people who have homes, secure jobs, savings and retirement and the people who have only some—or worse yet, none—of these.

Conservative voices including Marco Rubio and Rand Paul have also entered the inequality conversation, not as one of income inequality but of the inextricably linked opportunity inequality. This further underscores that although political leanings, semantics and proposed solutions may differ, no one can curse, dismiss, avoid or hide the fact that the very essence of 20th century America—the possibility of upward mobility for all—is becoming elusive and distant in the 21st century.

The theme of this year's *State of Black America, "One Nation Underemployed: Jobs Rebuild America,"* conveys the essence of this widening inequality gap between our country's richest and poorest citizens. Through its straight-talk, insightful essays from leading voices and the revealing Equality Index, our 2014 publication looks at the great divide nationally—and for the first time city-by-city—between the few who are reaping the rewards of economic recovery and the majority who are still reeling from the aftershocks of the Great Recession. While "too big to fail" corporations went into

the bail-out emergency room and recovered to break earnings and stock market records, most Americans have been left in ICU with multiple diagnoses of unemployment, underemployment, home losses and foreclosures, low or no savings and retirement accounts, credit denials, cuts in education and school funding—and the list of maladies continues.

As this divide increases, our nation's fragile economic recovery and growth and our ability to continue to successfully compete in a global marketplace are at heightened risk. An Oxfam report released in January confirmed what the Urban League Movement has posited for the last few years: in the U.S., where the gap between rich and poor has grown at a faster rate than

> WHILE "TOO BIG TO FAIL" CORPORATIONS WENT INTO THE BAIL-OUT EMERGENCY ROOM AND RECOVERED TO BREAK EARNINGS AND STOCK MARKET RECORDS, MOST AMERICANS HAVE BEEN LEFT IN ICU WITH MULTIPLE DIAGNOSES OF UNEMPLOYMENT, UNDEREMPLOYMENT, HOME LOSSES AND FORECLOSURES, LOW OR NO SAVINGS AND RETIREMENT ACCOUNTS, CREDIT DENIALS, CUTS IN EDUCATION AND SCHOOL FUNDING—AND THE LIST OF MALADIES CONTINUES.

any other developed country, the richest one percent of Americans have received 95 percent of the wealth created since 2009—after the economic crisis—while the bottom 90 percent of Americans have become poorer.

When we overlay that with the disproportionate impact of unemployment on African Americans and other people of color, as well as the impact of the twin terrors of racial income and wealth gaps, we see an even direr situation.

Our 2013 Equality Index included a 50-year retrospective which definitively showed that despite tremendous progress of African Americans in education, the two-to-one, Black–white unemployment gap—a catalyst for the Civil Rights Movement of the 1960s—persisted. This year's Equality Index indicates that unemployment inequality between Blacks and whites has widened, with the white unemployment rate dropping below 7 percent, and the Black unemployment rate remaining above 13 percent. Perhaps most troubling and ominous about this trend is that the widening gap is most pronounced for women, many of whom have children and are the sole household income earners.

We are not challenged by a mass unwillingness to work. We are stifled by massive un- and under-employment that undermines our nation's principles of economic mobility. With a Black–white income equality of only 60 percent and with Black households having just $6 in wealth for every $100 in wealth of white households, the situation is clear. The recovery has simply been insufficient in the job and wealth creation necessary to revive and restore all that was lost as the financial markets shook and progress began to crack. What we see emerging from the rubble is a State of Black America in crisis—in severe economic crisis.

We must speak to this crisis. We must speak to it despite a climate in Washington acculturated and underscored by fake filibuster, obstructionism, and a zeal to cut people programs that emanates in our body politic. We must speak against the focus on public policies that have benefited a select few at the top, while investments in policies and programs that could support and drive economic mobility and job growth for those hit hardest have all but dried up.

The National Urban League has always stood for economic empowerment. Our latest scale-efforts, including our Jobs Rebuild America initiative and our focus on "One Nation Underemployed" in the *State of Black America*, underscore that we are doubling down not only to raise our voices, but to do everything we can to help people achieve economic survival, sustainability and mobility in these very difficult times.

We launched Jobs Rebuild America in May 2013 as a solutions-based approach to the nation's employment and education crisis, bringing together federal government, business,and nonprofit resources to create economic opportunity in 50 communities across the country through the Urban League affiliate network. This $100 million, five-year effort is designed to reach job-seekers, vulnerable youth and entrepreneurs using a comprehensive community development model that includes program offerings such as job-training for youth (18-24) and mature workers (55+); college preparation; a jobs network; entrepreneurship support; tax credits; and small business financing and other resources through the Urban Empowerment Fund—our Community Development Financial Institution (CDFI).

Jobs Rebuild America also includes grassroots advocacy focusing on federal legislative action to ensure a responsible fiscal plan and support for efforts that spur job creation. The National

Urban League has recently championed bills and issues including the reintroduction and passage of the Urban Jobs Act and Project Ready STEM Act to spotlight the urgency of job creation and the need to invest in the education and skills enhancement of disadvantaged young people; the transportation bill; and the Harkin-Miller Fair Minimum Wage Act, which proposes a minimum wage increase to $10.10 for all workers, with an index to inflation thereafter.

An increase in the minimum wage alone would result in almost 30 million people receiving a raise—nearly half of whom would be people of color—and a reduction in poverty. However, as evidenced by the majority of credible studies on the topic, it would not lead to higher unemployment or less job creation. Women working a minimum of 20 hours per week disproportionately make up the majority of those who would benefit. Contrary to the inaccurate stereotypes often perpetuated about these women, many of them work full-time jobs, but still cannot earn enough to cover basic needs of shelter, food and clothing—and keep their families out of poverty. Earning a living wage should not be a luxury in America.

That is why we are determined—even against the backdrop of grinding political gridlock and polarization—to continue our tripod effort between the government, corporate and nonprofit sectors to bring about substantive change in our nation. The problems we face are too big for any one entity to solve alone. But together, in earnest effort, we can get beyond the limitations of ideology and focus on the strength of partnership and solutions.

In his January 2014 State of the Union address, President Obama spoke poignantly about the link between opportunity, jobs and our national character, saying, "Opportunity is who we are. And the defining project of our generation must be to restore that promise. We know where to start: The best measure of opportunity is access to a good job."

We agree, and the Urban League Movement is on the ground and in our communities every day helping to ensure that while stark employment, income and wealth divides threaten our nation, they will not defeat our spirit. We each have a role in putting our country on the right track toward employment, equality and empowerment.

What is your part? ★

INTRODUCTION TO THE 2014
EQUALITY
INDEX

VALERIE RAWLSTON
WILSON, PH.D.

*NATIONAL URBAN
LEAGUE WASHINGTON
BUREAU*

"THE LOWEST UNEMPLOYMENT RATE IN OVER FIVE YEARS. A REBOUNDING HOUSING MARKET. A MANUFACTURING SECTOR THAT'S ADDING JOBS FOR THE FIRST TIME SINCE THE 1990S. MORE OIL PRODUCED AT HOME THAN WE BUY FROM THE REST OF THE WORLD— THE FIRST TIME THAT'S HAPPENED IN NEARLY TWENTY YEARS. OUR DEFICITS—CUT BY MORE THAN HALF."

—*President Barack Obama*

President Obama opened his January 2014 State of the Union address citing evidence of an American economy gaining strength.

At the same time, he also acknowledged the growing income inequality and diminished opportunities for upward economic mobility that threaten to stall or even derail this progress. Consider the following U.S. labor market statistics. At the end of 2013, the unemployment rate dipped below 7 percent for the first time since November 2008.[1] Average job growth for 2013 was 194,000 jobs per month.[2] The private sector has added jobs for the last 46 consecutive months.[3] The economy has grown at an annual rate of nearly 2 percent or better for the last four years.[4]

While all of these factors indicate an economy in recovery, beneath the surface of these numbers are some troubling facts about the ongoing challenges facing American workers. More than one-third of unemployed workers have been out of work for six months or longer and one in four has been jobless for a year or longer.[5] Though the unemployment rate declined by 1.2 percentage points from January to December 2013—the largest decline over a single year since the recovery began—labor force participation also reached a 35-year low in December.[6] This downward trend in labor force participation raises concerns about underutilization of America's labor capacity, or underemployment. If we factored in the number of people who want and are available for work (but are not actively looking for a job) along with the number of unemployed workers actively looking for a job, and those who are working part-time out of necessity (but would prefer full-time work), the actual rate of underemployment was 13.1 percent at the end of 2013, nearly double the official unemployment rate.[7]

For African Americans, these challenges are even greater. Though the Black unemployment rate briefly and narrowly dipped below 12 percent for the first time since 2008 at the end of last year,[8] 42 percent of Black unemployed workers are long-term unemployed and 28 percent have been jobless for at least a year.[9] The rate of underemployment for African Americans was 20.5 percent, compared to 11.8 percent for white workers and 18.4 percent for Hispanic workers.[10]

In addition to these weaknesses in the labor market, income inequality has increased over the last 30 years as the gap between low, middle and high incomes has widened.[11] Since the recession,

MORE THAN ONE-THIRD OF UNEMPLOYED WORKERS HAVE BEEN OUT OF WORK FOR SIX MONTHS OR LONGER AND ONE IN FOUR HAS BEEN JOBLESS FOR A YEAR OR LONGER.

this trend has continued to worsen. Between 2007 and 2012, average household income for those in the bottom and middle quintiles has fallen at an annual rate of 2.1 percent and 1.5 percent, respectively.[12] Over this same period of time, average household income for those in the highest quintile fell by less than half a percent per year while that of the top five percent of households has remained unchanged.[13] The top 20 percent of households now receive a greater share of aggregate income than the other 80 percent of households combined.[14]

These income or class schisms also influence racial and ethnic income disparities as African American and Latino households are more skewed toward the lower end of the income distribution. Over half of African American (56.5%) and Latino (50.8%) households in this country are less than middle income compared to 35.5 percent of white households.[15] By contrast, 23 percent of white households are in the highest income quintile, but only 10 percent of African American and 11 percent of Latino households are among the highest income earners in the country.[16] As a result, as overall income inequality has grown, so has racial and ethnic income inequality. According to this year's Equality Index, Black median household income is about 60 percent of that of whites (down from 62 percent before the recession) and Latino median household income is 71 percent of that of white households (down from 74 percent before the recession).

As the National Urban League continues to press the case for closing the growing divide in economic opportunity and mobility, the 2014 National Urban League Equality Index is the tenth edition of this important tool for tracking Black–white racial equality in America and the fifth edition of the Hispanic–White Index.

New to the 2014 Equality Index is a special feature on racial and ethnic disparities in unemployment and income across the country through rankings of Black–white and Hispanic–white unemployment and income equality for about 80 metropolitan statistical areas ("metro areas" or "metros") in America.[17]

In addition to the metro area rankings based specifically on unemployment and income equality, the 2014 Equality Index also features index values for 21 key indicators of economic, education, health and social justice equality for 26 metro areas with large African American and/or Hispanic populations.

Also featured in this new section are commentaries from the mayors of four of these cities—Stephanie Rawlings-Blake in Baltimore, MD; Michael B. Hancock in Denver, CO; Alvin Brown in Jacksonville, FL and AC Wharton in Memphis, TN—focused on how they are driving job creation and helping to narrow the divide between the haves and have-nots.

// OVERVIEW OF 2014 NATIONAL URBAN LEAGUE EQUALITY INDEX

The 2014 Equality Index of Black America stands at 71.2 percent compared to a revised 2013 index of 71.0 percent. Revisions to the previous year's index are done for greater comparability across years and reflect data points that have been corrected, removed from the current year's index or re-weighted so that less emphasis is placed on older data. Relative to last year's Equality Index, there was little change in 2014 because improvements in the civic engagement index (from 99.9% to 104.7%), which is weighted at only ten percent of the overall index, were offset by a loss of ground or no change in the other more heavily weighted areas—economics (from 56.3% to 55.5%), social justice (from 56.9% to 56.8%), health (unchanged at 76.8%) and education (unchanged at 76.8%).

The 2014 Equality Index of Hispanic America stands at 75.8 percent compared to a revised 2013 index of 74.6 percent. The increase in the Hispanic–white index was driven by improvements in all categories, except for economics. The greatest gains were in civic engagement (from 68% to 71.2%), followed by social justice (from 63.4% to 66.1%), education (from 71.8% to 73.2%) and health (from 101.1% to 102.3%). The economics index declined modestly from 60.8% to 60.6%.

Gains in both civic engagement indices came from increased registration and voter participation by African Americans and Latinos in the 2012 election. The growing racial and ethnic divide in employment, homeownership and mortgage and home improvement loan denials drove losses in the economics index for both groups.

// METROPOLITAN AREA RANKINGS OF UNEMPLOYMENT EQUALITY

Nationally, both African Americans and Latinos lost economic ground relative to whites. Yet, beneath these national trends are various local dynamics. Aligned with the National Urban League's focus on policies and programs aimed at closing employment and income gaps, the 2014 Equality Index provides a ranking of unemployment and income equality in the nation's largest metropolitan areas. The full list of rankings can be found in the tables immediately following the national Black–White Equality Index and Hispanic–White Equality Index.

Black-White Unemployment Equality

Compared to the national Black–white unemployment index of 50 percent—indicating that on average, African Americans are twice as likely as whites to be unemployed—there are 23 (out of 77) ranked metro areas with smaller unemployment gaps (or a higher unemployment index) than the nation.[18] At 63.9 percent, the smallest Black–white unemployment gap was in the Augusta, GA metro area. However, a closer look at unemployment rates in the metros with the greatest unemployment equality reveals that they are not the metros with the lowest unemployment rates for both Blacks and whites. For example, none of the top ten metros with the smallest Black–white unemployment gaps (highest unemployment indices) are among the top ten metros with the lowest Black or white unemployment rates (Table 1). Additionally, these metros were among the hardest hit by the recession, have experienced weaker recoveries[19] and with the exception of two, all have Black and white unemployment rates that exceed the national averages for each group.

There are, however, three metros that top both lists of the lowest Black and white unemployment rates—Oklahoma City, OK, Washington, D.C. and Harrisburg, PA—but Oklahoma City, OK is the only one with a smaller unemployment gap than the nation. The common thread among these three metros is the fact that the government is a major employer and the severity of the recession was relatively mild, compared to other major metro areas.[20]

Oklahoma City, OK, continues to be among the metro areas with the best performance in output (GDP), unemployment and job growth.[21] The fact that there is little overlap of metros where whites and Blacks both have their best employment outcomes suggests the existence of "dual" labor markets for Blacks and whites within metro areas.

Hispanic-White Unemployment Equality

For Latinos, 33 (out of 83) ranked metro areas have smaller unemployment gaps than the nation, and in four of these metros—Memphis, TN, Madison, WI, Indianapolis, IN and Nashville, TN—Latinos actually have lower unemployment rates than whites (Table 2). These were also metro areas where the educational attainment of whites was at or slightly below national averages, while in two metros, attainment for Latinos was above national averages. According to *The State of Black America 2013*, educational attainment accounts for roughly three-quarters of the average difference in Hispanic and white unemployment rates. Whereas there was no overlap in the top ten metro areas with the smallest Black–white unemployment gaps and the top ten metros with the lowest Black and white unemployment rates, there was one metro area among the top ten metros for all three Hispanic–white unemployment measures. Coincidentally, that metro—Madison, WI—also ranked last in Black–white unemployment rate equality, further driving the point that labor markets produce winners and losers for different groups of workers. In addition to Madison, WI, Oklahoma City, OK and Provo, UT also topped both lists of the lowest Hispanic and white unemployment rates. Madison, WI and Oklahoma City, OK both experienced milder recessions relative to the metros with the smallest Hispanic–white unemployment gaps.[22]

// METROPOLITAN AREA RANKINGS OF INCOME EQUALITY

Black-White Income Equality

Compared to the national Black–white income index of 60 percent—indicating that on average, the median African American household has less than two-thirds the income of the white median household—there are 18 (out of 77) ranked metro areas with smaller income gaps (or a higher income index) than the nation. At 77.9 percent, the smallest Black–white income gap was in the Riverside, CA metro area. Still, consistent with the pattern for Black–white unemployment equality, the greatest income equality is not necessarily happening in the same metro areas where median household income for both Blacks and whites

is the highest, or where local economies are strongest. With the exception of San Antonio, TX, all of the metros with the lowest Black–white income gaps were among the hardest hit by the recession and, consequently, have recovered least.[23] There are no metros in the top ten for both Black–white income equality and highest median household incomes for Blacks and whites *(Table 3)*. While there are four metro areas on both the Black and white top ten lists for highest median household income— Washington, D.C., New York, NY, Baltimore, MD and Boston, MA—none of them have Black–white income equality that is above the national average. They are, however, high cost of living areas that employ a significant number of professionals, either in universities, the federal government or major business industries, which contributes to higher than average incomes at the top of the scale and drives greater income inequality.[24] In fact, all of the areas where white households have their ten highest median incomes nationally have Black–white income equality below the national average. On the other hand, six of the top ten metros with the highest Black median household income have Black–white income equality that is higher than the national average. Yet, even in metro areas where there is above average income equality and median Black household income is highest, that income is still well below the highest median white household income and in fact is lower than the metro area with the 26th highest white median household income.

Hispanic–White Income Equality

For Latinos, only 13 (out of 83) ranked metro areas have smaller Hispanic–white income gaps than the national average of 71 percent. At 89.6 percent, the smallest income gap is in the Lakeland, FL metro area. Similar to the pattern of income equality between Blacks and whites, the greatest income equality is not necessarily

TABLE 1

Top Ten Metro Areas: Highest Black-White Unemployment Index, Lowest Black Unemployment Rate and Lowest White Unemployment Rate
★ *Featured Metro Area*   **Bold:** *Higher than U.S. Black-White Index*

	HIGHEST BLACK-WHITE UNEMPLOYMENT INDEX (Index in Parentheses)	LOWEST BLACK UNEMPLOYMENT RATE (Index in Parentheses)	Black Unemployment Rate	LOWEST WHITE UNEMPLOYMENT RATE (Index in Parentheses)	White Unemployment Rate
1	**Augusta-Richmond County, GA-SC (63.9%)**	**Oklahoma City, OK (52.2%)**	9.0%	Baton Rouge, LA (32.0%)	4.1%
2	**Riverside-San Bernardino-Ontario, CA (63.5%)**	**Knoxville, TN (54%)**	11.3%	Washington-Arlington-Alexandria, D.C.-VA-MD-WV (35.0%)	4.2%
3	**Palm Bay-Melbourne-Titusville, FL (63.1%)**	**Durham-Chapel Hill, NC (56.1%)**	11.4%	Des Moines-West Des Moines, IA (31.4%)	4.3%
4	**Las Vegas-Paradise, NV (62.2%)**	**San Antonio-New Braunfels, TX (51.3%)**	11.5%	Madison, WI (23.8%)	4.4%
5	**Chattanooga, TN-GA (61.1%)**	Austin-Round Rock-San Marcos, TX (49.6%)	11.9%	**Oklahoma City, OK (52.2%)**	4.7%
6	**San Diego-Carlsbad-San Marcos, CA (60.7%)**	Washington-Arlington-Alexandria, D.C.-VA-MD-WV (35.0%)	12.0%	Lancaster, PA (27.8%)	4.7%
7	**Providence-New Bedford-Fall River, RI-MA (60.7%)**	**Seattle-Tacoma-Bellevue, WA (57.4%)**	12.2%	Harrisburg-Carlisle, PA (38.7%)	4.8%
8	**Lakeland-Winter Haven, FL (58.5%)**	**Nashville-Davidson-Murfreesboro-Franklin, TN (55.3%)**	12.3%	Omaha-Council Bluffs, NE-IA (38.9%)	5.1%
9	**Seattle-Tacoma-Bellevue, WA (57.4%)**	Harrisburg-Carlisle, PA (38.7%)	12.4%	Minneapolis-St. Paul-Bloomington, MN-WI (28.9%)	5.2%
10	**Durham-Chapel Hill, NC (56.1%)**	**Deltona-Daytona Beach-Ormond Beach, FL (55.6%)**	12.6%	Albany-Schenectady-Troy, NY (41.9%)	5.4%

TABLE 2

Top Ten Metro Areas: Highest Hispanic-White Unemployment Index, Lowest Hispanic Unemployment Rate and Lowest White Unemployment Rate   ★ *Featured Metro Area*   **Bold:** *Higher than U.S. Hispanic-White Index*

	HIGHEST HISPANIC-WHITE UNEMPLOYMENT INDEX (Index in Parentheses)	LOWEST HISPANIC UNEMPLOYMENT RATE (Index in Parentheses)	Hispanic Unemployment Rate	LOWEST WHITE UNEMPLOYMENT RATE (Index in Parentheses)	White Unemployment Rate
1	**Memphis, TN-MS-AR (171.1%)**	**Memphis, TN-MS-AR (171.1%)**	3.8%	Washington-Arlington-Alexandria, D.C.-VA-MD-WV (63.6%)	4.1%
2	**Jacksonville, FL (112.9%)**	**Madison, WI (97.8%)**	4.5%	Ogden-Clearfield, UT (53.2%)	4.2%
3	**Indianapolis-Carmel, IN (111.5%)**	**Indianapolis-Carmel, IN (111.5%)**	6.1%	Des Moines-West Des Moines, IA (51.2%)	4.3%
4	**Nashville-Davidson-Murfreesboro-Franklin, TN (107.9%)**	**Nashville-Davidson-Murfreesboro-Franklin, TN (107.9%)**	6.3%	**Madison, WI (97.8%)**	4.4%
5	**Madison, WI (97.8%)**	Washington-Arlington-Alexandria, D.C.-VA-MD-WV (63.6%)	6.6%	Oklahoma City, OK (68.1%)	4.7%
6	**North Port-Bradenton-Sarasota, FL (96.3%)**	**Tulsa, OK (91.3%)**	6.9%	Lancaster, PA (37.6%)	4.7%
7	**Oxnard-Thousand Oaks-Ventura, CA (96.1%)**	Oklahoma City, OK (68.1%)	6.9%	Harrisburg-Carlisle, PA (51.6%)	4.8%
8	**Poughkeepsie-Newburgh-Middletown, NY (94.4%)**	**Knoxville, TN (87.1%)**	7.0%	Omaha-Council Bluffs, NE-IA (63.0%)	5.1%
9	**Las Vegas-Paradise, NV (92.1%)**	**Columbus, OH (81.9%)**	7.2%	Minneapolis-St. Paul-Bloomington, MN-WI (49.5%)	5.2%
10	**Tulsa, OK (91.3%)**	**Provo-Orem, UT (72.6%)**	7.3%	Provo-Orem, UT (72.6%)	5.3%

happening in the same metro areas where median household income for both Latinos and whites is the highest, or where local economies are strongest. With the exception of Honolulu, HI, all of the metros with the lowest Hispanic-white income gaps were among the hardest hit by the recession and, consequently, have recovered least.[25] Although there are six metros among the ten highest median household incomes for both Latinos and whites—Washington, D.C., Baltimore, MD, San Jose, CA, Oxnard, CA, San Francisco, CA and Bridgeport, CT—none of them exceed national Hispanic-white income equality. *(See Table 4)*. Similar to those metros where both Black and white households have their highest median incomes, these six cities also employ large numbers of professionals.[26] Still, in the metro area with the highest Hispanic median household income, that income is lower than the metro area with the 30th highest white median household income.

Together these data reveal a national divide on economic outcomes that is not only defined along class lines, but also along racial lines. They also reveal how labor markets can produce vastly different outcomes for different groups of workers, but it is the job of local elected officials to work together with community-based organizations and private industry to tackle some of the challenges creating these disparities. Some of the strategies for doing this are highlighted by mayors contributing commentary in the featured metro area section of this chapter. ★

NOTES

[1] Author's analysis based on data available from U.S. Department of Labor, Bureau of Labor Statistics, Current Population Survey.

[2] U.S. Department of Labor, Bureau of Labor Statistics, *The Employment Situation—January 2014* news release. Retrieved from: *http://www.bls.gov/news. release/archives/empsit_02072014.pdf.*

[3] Author's analysis based on data available from U.S. Department of Labor, Bureau of Labor Statistics, Current Employment Statistics.

[4] U.S. Department of Commerce, Bureau of Economic Analysis, National Economic Accounts, Gross Domestic Product.

[5] U.S. Department of Labor, Bureau of Labor Statistics, *The Employment Situation—January 2014* news release. Retrieved from: *http://www.bls.gov/news.release/ archives/empsit_02072014.pdf.*

[6] Author's analysis based on data available from U.S. Department of Labor, Bureau of Labor Statistics, Current Population Survey.

[7] U.S. Department of Labor, Bureau of Labor Statistics, Current Population Survey, December 2013.

[8] Author's analysis based on data available from U.S. Department of Labor, Bureau of Labor Statistics, Current Population Survey.

[9] Author's calculations based on data available from U.S. Department of Labor, Bureau of Labor Statistics, Current Population Survey, December 2013. Estimates are not seasonally adjusted.

[10] Ibid.

[11] Mishel, L., Bivens, J., Gould, E. & Shierholz, H. (2012). *The State of Working America, 12th Edition*. New York, NY: Cornell University Press. Retrieved from: *http:// stateofworkingamerica.org/subjects/income/?reader.*

[12] Author's calculations based on data available from U.S. Census Bureau, Current Population Survey, Annual Social and Economic Supplements.

[13] Ibid.

[14] Ibid.

[15] Ibid.

[16] Ibid.

[17] These metro areas are those for which there were large enough samples of African American and Latino populations to calculate reliable estimates.

[18] It should be noted that the national and metro area unemployment rates come from different sources; therefore, this comparison is only an approximation based on data reported in the current edition of the Equality Index. The national unemployment rates are from the 2013 Current Population Survey, and the metro area unemployment rate statistics are from the 2012 American Community Survey. Based on

TABLE 3

Top Ten Metro Areas: Highest Black-White Income Index, Highest Black Median Household Income, Highest White Median Household Income

★ *Featured Metro Area* **Bold:** *Higher than U.S. Black-White Index*

	HIGHEST BLACK-WHITE INCOME INDEX *(Index in Parentheses)*	HIGHEST BLACK MEDIAN HOUSEHOLD INCOME *(Index in Parentheses)*	*Black Median Household Income (Dollars)*	HIGHEST WHITE MEDIAN HOUSEHOLD INCOME *(Index in Parentheses)*	*White Median Household Income (Dollars)*
1	**Riverside–San Bernardino–Ontario, CA (77.9%)**	Washington–Arlington–Alexandria, D.C.–VA–MD–WV (58.8%)	62,726	Washington–Arlington–Alexandria, D.C.–VA–MD–WV (58.8%)	106,597
2	**San Diego–Carlsbad–San Marcos, CA (72.5%)**	**San Diego–Carlsbad–San Marcos, CA (72.5%)**	**48,161**	Bridgeport–Stamford–Norwalk, CT (40.6%)	97,654
3	**Palm Bay–Melbourne–Titusville, FL (70.0%)**	**Riverside–San Bernardino–Ontario, CA (77.9%)**	**44,572**	San Francisco–Oakland–Fremont, CA (45.1%)	90,452
4	**Greensboro–High Point, NC (68.3%)**	New York–Northern New Jersey–Long Island, NY–NJ–PA (54.3%)	44,474	New York–Northern New Jersey–Long Island, NY–NJ–PA (54.3%)	81,865
5	**Las Vegas–Paradise, NV (68.1%)**	Baltimore–Towson, MD (54.2%)	43,663	**Baltimore–Towson, MD (54.2%)**	80,487
6	**Lakeland–Winter Haven, FL (66.5%)**	Boston–Cambridge–Quincy, MA–NH (55.0%)	43,230	Boston–Cambridge–Quincy, MA–NH (55.0%)	78,551
7	**San Antonio–New Braunfels, TX (64.6%)**	**Austin–Round Rock–San Marcos, TX (61.6%)**	**42,672**	Hartford–West Hartford–East Hartford, CT (51.3%)	75,265
8	**Phoenix–Mesa–Glendale, AZ (64.6%)**	San Antonio–New Braunfels, TX (64.6%)	42,446	Houston–Sugar Land–Baytown, TX (53.4%)	75,201
9	**Providence–New Bedford–Fall River, RI–MA (64.5%)**	**Atlanta–Sandy Springs–Marietta, GA (61.7%)**	**41,463**	Los Angeles–Long Beach–Santa Ana, CA (52.0%)	73,865
10	**Tampa–St. Petersburg–Clearwater, FL (64.2%)**	**Virginia Beach–Norfolk–Newport News, VA–NC (62.8%)**	**40,897**	Minneapolis–St. Paul–Bloomington, MN–WI (40.3%)	71,376

TABLE 4

Top Ten Metro Areas: Highest Hispanic-White Income Index, Highest Hispanic Median Household Income, Highest White Median Household Income   ★ *Featured Metro Area* **Bold:** *Higher than U.S. Hispanic-White Index*

	HIGHEST HISPANIC-WHITE INCOME INDEX *(Index in Parentheses)*	HIGHEST HISPANIC MEDIAN HOUSEHOLD INCOME *(Index in Parentheses)*	*Hispanic Median Household Income (Dollars)*	HIGHEST WHITE MEDIAN HOUSEHOLD INCOME *(Index in Parentheses)*	*White Median Household Income (Dollars)*
1	**Lakeland–Winter Haven, FL (89.6%)**	Washington–Arlington–Alexandria, D.C.–VA–MD–WV (59.8%)	63,779	Washington–Arlington–Alexandria, D.C.–VA–MD–WV (59.8%)	106,597
2	**Palm Bay–Melbourne–Titusville, FL (88.9%)**	**Honolulu, HI (79.1%)**	**58,161**	San Jose–Sunnyvale–Santa Clara, CA (55.4%)	99,899
3	**Jacksonville, FL (84.7%)**	Baltimore–Towson, MD (69.6%)	55,983	Bridgeport–Stamford–Norwalk, CT (50.1%)	97,654
4	**Deltona–Daytona Beach–Ormond Beach, FL (81.5%)**	San Jose–Sunnyvale–Santa Clara, CA (55.4%)	55,302	San Francisco–Oakland–Fremont, CA (56.8%)	90,452
5	**Riverside–San Bernardino–Ontario, CA (80.2%)**	Oxnard–Thousand Oaks–Ventura, CA (69.8%)	54,751	New York–Northern New Jersey–Long Island, NY–NJ–PA (50.2%)	81,865
6	**Honolulu, HI (79.1%)**	San Francisco–Oakland–Fremont, CA (56.8%)	51,420	Baltimore–Towson, MD (69.6%)	80,487
7	**Modesto, CA (75.9%)**	Bridgeport–Stamford–Norwalk, CT (50.1%)	48,968	Boston–Cambridge–Quincy, MA–NH (49.0%)	78,551
8	**Las Vegas–Paradise, NV (75.7%)**	Poughkeepsie–Newburgh–Middletown, NY (66.7%)	47,502	Oxnard–Thousand Oaks–Ventura, CA (69.8%)	78,457
9	**North Port–Bradenton–Sarasota, FL (74.6%)**	**Riverside–San Bernardino–Ontario, CA (80.2%)**	**45,912**	Hartford–West Hartford–East Hartford, CT (42.7%)	75,265
10	**Stockton, CA (74.1%)**	**Jacksonville, FL (84.7%)**	**45,894**	Houston–Sugar Land–Baytown, TX (56.1%)	75,201

national unemployment rates from the 2012 Current Population Survey that were reported in last year's Equality Index, 18 of the 77 ranked metro areas had a higher unemployment index than the nation in 2012.

[19] Brookings, Metro Monitor—September 2013. Retrieved from: *http://www.brookings.edu/research/ interactives/metromonitor#US-recovery-overall-nv.* The severity of the recession and extent of recovery is based on four indicators—total employment, unemployment rate, total output and house prices. Augusta, GA had the best recession ranking of the ten metros with the greatest unemployment equality (21 out of 100). Rankings for the other nine metros range from 58 to 97 out of 100. Seattle, WA had the best amount recovered ranking (20 out of 100). The other nine metros range from 54 to 100 out of 100.

[20] Ibid. According to the Brookings Metro Monitor September 2013 ranking of the 100 largest metro areas in the country, Oklahoma City, OK, Washington, D.C. and Harrisburg, PA were all within the top 20 with regard to the severity of the recession.

[21] Ibid. Based on the extent of recovery, Oklahoma City, OK ranked 10th in employment, 7th in unemployment and 15th in output, out of 100 metros.

[22] Ibid. Oklahoma City, OK and Madison, WI ranked 4th and 5th, respectively, on severity of the recession. Rankings of other metros with the greatest Hispanic-white unemployment equality ranged from 32 to 97 out of 100.

[23] Ibid. San Antonio, TX ranked 3rd on severity of the recession and 4th on the extent of the recovery. All other metros with the greatest Black-white income equality ranged from 60 to 97 on severity of the recession and from 66 to 100 on the extent of the recovery.

[24] Ibid. Based on industries with the highest location quotient, which is a measure of industry specialization within the metro area.

[25] Ibid. Honolulu, HI ranked 15th in severity of the recession and 16th in extent of the recovery. Rankings of the other metro areas with the smallest Hispanic-white income gaps ranged from 83 to 97 in severity of the recession and from 83 to 100 in extent of recovery.

[26] Ibid. Based on industries with the highest location quotient, which is a measure of industry specialization within the metro area.

UNDERSTANDING THE
EQUALITY
INDEX

VALERIE RAWLSTON WILSON, PH.D.

NATIONAL URBAN LEAGUE WASHINGTON BUREAU

// WHY DOES NUL PUBLISH AN EQUALITY INDEX?

Economic empowerment is the central theme of the National Urban League's mission. The Equality Index gives us a way to document progress toward this mission.

// WHAT IS THE EQUALITY INDEX TRYING TO DO?

Imagine if we were to summarize how well African Americans and Hispanics are doing, compared to whites, in the areas of economics, health, education, social justice and civic engagement, and represent that by a pie.

The Equality Index measures the share of that pie which African Americans and Hispanics get.

Whites are used as the benchmark because the history of race in America has created advantages for whites that continue to persist in many of the outcomes being measured.

// 2014 EQUALITY INDEX OF BLACK AMERICA IS 71.2%. WHAT DOES THAT MEAN?

That means that rather than having a whole pie (100%), which would mean full equality with whites in 2014, African Americans are missing about 29% of the pie *(Figure 1)*.

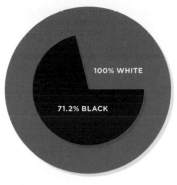

FIGURE 1
2014 Equality Index is 71.2%

// HOW IS THE EQUALITY INDEX CALCULATED?

The categories that make up the Equality Index are economics, health, education, social justice and civic engagement. In each, we calculate how well African Americans and Hispanics are doing relative to whites and add them to get the total Equality Index.

Each category is weighted, based on the importance that we give to each *(Figure 2)*.

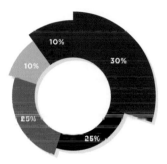

FIGURE 2
Different Categories that Make Up the Equality Index
★ *Economics* **30%** ★ *Health* **25%** ★ *Education* **25%**
★ *Social Justice* **10%** ★ *Civic Engagement* **10%**

// IS IT POSSIBLE TO SEE HOW WELL AFRICAN AMERICANS AND HISPANICS ARE DOING IN EACH OF THE CATEGORIES?

Yes. We show this in the tables included with the Equality Index.

Each category can be represented by a mini-pie and interpreted in the same way as the total Equality Index. So, an index of 55.5% for the economics category for African Americans in 2014 means that African Americans are missing close to half of the economics mini-pie.

FIGURE 3
Equality Index for 2014

CATEGORY	2014
EQUALITY INDEX	71.2%
Economics	55.5%
Health	76.8%
Education	76.8%
Social Justice	56.8%
Civic Engagement	104.1%

// IS IT POSSIBLE TO SEE HOW WELL AFRICAN AMERICANS AND HISPANICS ARE DOING OVER TIME?

Yes. The National Urban League has published the Equality Index and all the variables used to calculate it annually since 2005. We have noted the ones for 2006, 2010 and 2014.

FIGURE 4
Equality Index for 2006, 2010 and 2014

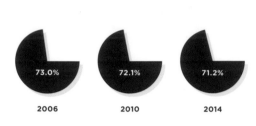

CATEGORY	2006	2010	2014
EQUALITY INDEX	**73.0%**	**72.1%**	**71.2%**
Economics	56.1%	57.9%	55.5%
Health	75.9%	76.7%	76.8%
Education	77.6%	78.3%	76.8%
Social Justice	74.2%	57.8%	56.8%
Civic Engagement	103.7%	102.2%	104.7%

2006   2010   2014

// IT DOESN'T LOOK LIKE THERE'S BEEN MUCH IMPROVEMENT IN THE EQUALITY INDEX—WHAT'S THE POINT?

Since the Equality Index is made up of a lot of different parts, improvements in one area are sometimes offset by losses in another area, leaving the overall index unchanged.

Change often happens slowly. The Equality Index offers solid evidence of just how slowly change happens, making it an important tool for driving policies needed in the ongoing fight against inequality.

// NOT ALL AFRICAN AMERICANS ARE DOING POORLY AND NOT ALL WHITES ARE DOING WELL. WHY DOESN'T THE EQUALITY INDEX CAPTURE CLASS DIFFERENCES?

The national data used to calculate the Equality Index is reported in averages for each of the racial groups. An average includes both people who are doing well and people who are not. An average is the easiest way to summarize a large amount of information, but can mask other important differences. We provide a local perspective on inequality this year by featuring a condensed version of the Equality Index for 26 metro areas with large African American and/or Latino populations.

// WHAT SHOULD I DO NEXT?

Support the work of the National Urban League as we continue to advance policies and programs to empower African American and other urban communities. ★

WHAT CAN YOU DO NEXT TO HELP? SUPPORT THE WORK OF THE NATIONAL URBAN LEAGUE AS WE CONTINUE TO ADVANCE POLICIES AND PROGRAMS TO EMPOWER AFRICAN AMERICAN AND OTHER URBAN COMMUNITIES.

NATIONAL URBAN LEAGUE

2014 BLACK-WHITE

EQUALITY

INDEX

IHS GLOBAL INSIGHT

✦ Updated ★ History Revised ✦ Removed Weight in 2013 ★ New Series 2014 ★ No New Data

2014 EQUALITY INDEX OF BLACK AMERICA	Source	Year	Black	White	Index	Diff. ('14-'13)
Total Equality Weighted Index					**71.2%**	**0.002**
ECONOMICS (30%)						
MEDIAN INCOME (0.25)						
Median Household Income (Real), Dollars	ACS	2012	33,764	56,565	60%	(0.00)
Median Male Earnings, Dollars	ACS	2012	37,526	52,148	72%	(0.00)
Median Female Earnings, Dollars	ACS	2012	33,251	40,558	82%	(0.01)
POVERTY (0.15)						
Population Living Below Poverty Line, %	ACS	2012	28.1	11.0	39%	0.00
Population Living Below 50% of Poverty Line, %	ACS	2012	13.5	4.9	36%	0.00
Population Living Below 125% of Poverty Line, %	ACS	2012	34.8	14.6	42%	(0.00)
Population Living Below Poverty Line (Under 18), %	CPS ASEC	2012	37.9	12.3	32%	0.00
Population Living Below Poverty Line (18–64), %	CPS ASEC	2012	23.9	9.7	41%	(0.00)
Population Living Below Poverty Line (65 and Older), %	CPS ASEC	2012	18.2	6.8	37%	(0.01)
EMPLOYMENT ISSUES (0.20)						
Unemployment Rate, %	BLS	2013	13.1	6.5	50%	(0.03)
Unemployment Rate: Male, %	BLS	2013	14.2	6.8	48%	(0.01)
Unemployment Rate: Female, %	BLS	2013	12.1	6.2	51%	(0.03)
Unemployment Rate Persons Ages 16–19, %	BLS	2013	38.8	20.3	52%	(0.04)
Percent Not in Workforce: Ages 16–19, %	BLS	2013	72.0	63.1	88%	0.01
Percent Not in Workforce: Ages 16 and Older, %	BLS	2013	38.8	36.5	94%	0.00
Labor Force Participation Rate, %	BLS	2013	61.2	63.5	96%	0.00
LFPR 16–19, %	BLS	2013	28.0	36.9	76%	0.03
LFPR 20–24, %	BLS	2013	65.3	73.1	89%	(0.02)
LFPR Over 25: Less Than High School Grad., %	BLS	2013	38.2	46.3	83%	0.05
LFPR Over 25: High School Grad., No College, %	BLS	2013	59.6	58.3	102%	(0.03)
LFPR Over 25: Some College, No Degree, %	BLS	2013	60.8	64.0	109%	0.03
LFPR Over 25: Associate's Degree, %	BLS	2013	73.6	71.9	102%	(0.01)
LFPR Over 25: Some College or Associate Degree, %	BLS	2013	71.1	67.0	106%	0.02
LFPR Over 25: College Grad., %	BLS	2013	78.6	75.0	105%	0.00
Employment to Pop. Ratio, %	BLS	2013	53.2	59.4	90%	0.00
HOUSING & WEALTH (0.34)						
Home Ownership Rate, %	Census	2012	43.9	73.5	60%	(0.01)
Mortgage Application Denial Rate (Total), %	HMDA	2012	39.6	13.2	33%	(0.05)
Mortgage Application Denial Rate (Male), %	HMDA	2012	36.8	15.5	42%	(0.05)
Mortgage Application Denial Rate (Female), %	HMDA	2012	42.0	15.3	36%	(0.05)
Mortgage Application Denial Rate (Joint), %	HMDA	2012	38.6	10.8	28%	(0.05)
Home Improvement Loans Denials (Total), %	HMDA	2012	64.2	30.5	48%	(0.02)
Home Improvement Loans Denials (Male), %	HMDA	2012	64.4	37.2	58%	(0.02)
Home Improvement Loans Denials (Female), %	HMDA	2012	67.6	38.8	57%	(0.00)
Home Improvement Loans Denials (Joint), %	HMDA	2012	52.4	21.7	41%	(0.03)

2014 EQUALITY INDEX OF BLACK AMERICA	Source	Year	Black	White	Index	Diff. ('14–'13)
Percent of High-Priced Loans (More Than 3% Above Treasury)	HMDA	2012	6.7	3.2	47%	(0.02)
Median Home Value, 2000 Dollars	Census	2000	80,600	123,400	65%	0.00
Median Wealth, 2010 Dollars	Census SIPP	2011	6,314	110,500	6%	0.01
Equity in Home, Dollars	Census SIPP	2011	50,000	85,000	59%	0.03
Percent Investing in 401(K), %	EBRI	2009	27.8	36.9	75%	0.00
Percent Investing in IRA, %	EBRI	2009	10.1	25.6	39%	0.00
U.S. Firms By Race (% Compared to Employment Share)	Census	2007	7.1	83.4	9%	0.00
DIGITAL DIVIDE (0.05)						
Households With Computer at Home, %	Census	2011	68.3	84.8	81%	(0.01)
Households With the Internet, %	Census	2011	56.9	76.2	75%	(0.03)
Adult Users With Broadband Access, %	Census	2011	54.6	72.9	75%	(0.02)
TRANSPORTATION (0.01)						
Car Ownership, %	Census	2011	70.5	88.3	80%	0.02
Means of Transportation to Work: Drive Alone, %	ACS	2012	71.8	79.7	90%	0.00
Means of Transportation to Work: Public Transportation, %	ACS	2012	11.2	3.0	26%	(0.00)
Economic Weighted Index					**55.5%**	**(0.008)**

HEALTH (25%)						
DEATH RATES & LIFE EXPECTANCY (0.45)						
Life Expectancy at Birth	CDC	2010	74.7	78.8	95%	0.00
Male	CDC	2010	71.4	76.4	93%	0.00
Female	CDC	2010	77.7	81.1	96%	0.00
Life Expectancy at 65 (Additional Expected Years)	CDC	2010	17.7	19.1	93%	0.00
Male at 65	CDC	2010	15.8	17.7	89%	0.00
Female at 65	CDC	2010	19.1	20.3	94%	0.00
Age-Adjusted Death Rates (Per 100,000): All Causes	CDC	2010	920.4	755.0	82%	0.00
Age-Adjusted Death Rates (Per 100,000): Male	CDC	2010	1,131.7	892.5	79%	0.00
Age-Adjusted Death Rates (Per 100,000): Female	CDC	2010	770.8	643.3	83%	0.00
Age-Adjusted Death Rates (Per 100,000): Heart Disease	CDC	2010	229.5	179.9	78%	0.00
Ischemic Heart Disease	CDC	2010	133.4	115.0	86%	0.00
Age-Adjusted Death Rates (Per 100,000): Stroke (Cerebrovascular)	CDC	2010	54.3	37.8	70%	0.00
Age-Adjusted Death Rates (Per 100,000): Cancer	CDC	2010	208.8	176.5	85%	0.00
Trachea, Bronchus, and Lung	CDC	2010	52.6	50.8	97%	0.00
Colon, Rectum, and Anus	CDC	2010	22.4	15.5	69%	0.00
Prostate (Male)	CDC	2010	49.0	20.3	41%	0.00
Breast (Female)	CDC	2010	31.3	22.1	71%	0.00
Age-Adjusted Death Rates (Per 100,000): Chronic Lower Respiratory	CDC	2010	29.6	46.6	157%	0.00

2014 EQUALITY INDEX OF BLACK AMERICA	Source	Year	Black	White	Index	Diff. ('14-'13)
Age-Adjusted Death Rates (Per 100,000): Influenza and Pneumonia	CDC	2010	17.1	14.9	87%	0.00
Age-Adjusted Death Rates (Per 100,000): Chronic Liver Disease and Cirrhosis	CDC	2010	6.9	9.4	136%	0.00
Age-Adjusted Death Rates (Per 100,000): Diabetes	CDC	2010	39.6	18.2	46%	0.00
Age-Adjusted Death Rates (Per 100,000): HIV	CDC	2010	12.0	1.1	9%	0.00
Unintentional Injuries	CDC	2010	32.4	42.4	131%	0.00
Motor Vehicle-Related Injuries	CDC	2010	11.4	11.9	104%	0.00
Age-Adjusted Death Rates (Per 100,000): Suicide	CDC	2010	5.4	15.0	278%	0.00
Age-Adjusted Death Rates (Per 100,000): Suicide Males	CDC	2010	9.4	24.2	257%	0.00
Death Rates (Per 100,000): Suicide Males Ages 15–24	CDC	2010	11.5	20.4	177%	0.00
Age-Adjusted Death Rates (Per 100,000): Suicide Females	CDC	2010	1.9	6.2	326%	0.00
Death Rates (Per 100,000): Suicide Females Ages 15–24	CDC	2010	2.1	4.4	210%	0.00
Age-Adjusted Death Rates (Per 100,000): Homicide	CDC	2010	18.6	2.5	13%	0.00
Age-Adjusted Death Rates (Per 100,000): Homicide Male	CDC	2010	33.1	3.3	10%	0.00
Death Rates (Per 100,000): Homicide Males Ages 15–24	CDC	2010	74.9	4.1	5%	0.00
Age-Adjusted Death Rates (Per 100,000): Homicide Female	CDC	2010	5.2	1.8	35%	0.00
Death Rates (Per 100,000): Homicide Females Ages 15–24	CDC	2010	7.9	1.8	23%	0.00
Death Rates (Per 100,000) By Age Cohort: < 1 Male	CDC	2010	1,281.5	575.9	45%	0.00
Death Rates (Per 100,000) By Age Cohort: 1–4 Male	CDC	2010	45.4	27.5	61%	0.00
Death Rates (Per 100,000) By Age Cohort: 5–14 Male	CDC	2010	20.7	14.3	69%	0.00
Death Rates (Per 100,000) By Age Cohort: 15–24 Male	CDC	2010	150.8	93.4	62%	0.00
Death Rates (Per 100,000) By Age Cohort: 25–34 Male	CDC	2010	230.8	143.6	62%	0.00
Death Rates (Per 100,000) By Age Cohort: 35–44 Male	CDC	2010	321.1	219.1	68%	0.00
Death Rates (Per 100,000) By Age Cohort: 45–54 Male	CDC	2010	739.1	508.1	69%	0.00
Death Rates (Per 100,000) By Age Cohort: 55–64 Male	CDC	2010	1,705.0	1,046.2	61%	0.00
Death Rates (Per 100,000) By Age Cohort: 65–74 Male	CDC	2010	3,274.7	2,256.9	69%	0.00
Death Rates (Per 100,000) By Age Cohort: 75–84 Male	CDC	2010	6,849.1	5,770.3	84%	0.00
Death Rates (Per 100,000) By Age Cohort: 85+ Male	CDC	2010	14,974.2	15,816.6	106%	0.00
Death Rates (Per 100,000) By Age Cohort: <1 Female	CDC	2010	1,055.7	480.4	46%	0.00
Death Rates (Per 100,000) By Age Cohort: 1–4 Female	CDC	2010	34.8	21.8	63%	0.00
Death Rates (Per 100,000) By Age Cohort: 5–14 Female	CDC	2010	15.5	10.9	70%	0.00
Death Rates (Per 100,000) By Age Cohort: 15–24 Female	CDC	2010	45.6	38.4	84%	0.00
Death Rates (Per 100,000) By Age Cohort: 25–34 Female	CDC	2010	99.1	66.8	67%	0.00
Death Rates (Per 100,000) By Age Cohort: 35–44 Female	CDC	2010	209.1	133.1	64%	0.00
Death Rates (Per 100,000) By Age Cohort: 45–54 Female	CDC	2010	497.4	307.7	62%	0.00
Death Rates (Per 100,000) By Age Cohort: 55–64 Female	CDC	2010	996.9	631.5	63%	0.00
Death Rates (Per 100,000) By Age Cohort: 65–74 Female	CDC	2010	2,068.1	1,535.9	74%	0.00
Death Rates (Per 100,000) By Age Cohort: 75–84 Female	CDC	2010	4,675.5	4,232.6	91%	0.00
Death Rates (Per 100,000) By Age Cohort: 85+ Female	CDC	2010	12,767.7	13,543.5	106%	0.00

☆ Updated ★ History Revised ☆ Removed Weight in 2013 ☆ New Series 2014 ★ No New Data

2014 EQUALITY INDEX OF BLACK AMERICA	Source	Year	Black	White	Index	Diff. ('14-'13)
PHYSICAL CONDITION (0.10)						
Overweight: 18+ Years, % of Population	CDC	2011	34.8	35.7	103%	0.00
Overweight: Men 20 Years and Over, % of Population	CDC	2007–2010	31.2	39.5	127%	0.00
Overweight: Women 20 Years and Over, % of Population	CDC	2007–2010	26.0	27.8	107%	0.00
Obese, % of Population	CDC	2011	36.7	26.3	72%	0.00
Obese: Men 20 Years and Over, % of Population	CDC	2007–2010	37.7	33.8	90%	0.00
Obese: Women 20 Years and Over, % of Population	CDC	2007–2010	53.7	32.7	61%	0.00
Diabetes: Physician Diagnosed in Ages 20+, % of Population	CDC	2007–2010	15.0	6.7	45%	0.00
AIDS Cases Per 100,000 Males Ages 13+	CDC	2011	72.9	8.6	12%	(0.00)
AIDS Cases Per 100,000 Females Ages 13+	CDC	2011	32.2	1.4	4%	(0.00)
SUBSTANCE ABUSE (0.10)						
Binge Alcohol (5 Drinks in 1 Day, 1X a Year) Ages 18+, % of Population	CDC	2011	14.1	26.2	186%	0.00
Use of Illicit Drugs in the Past Month Ages 12 +, % of Population	SAMHSA	2012	11.3	9.2	81%	(0.10)
Tobacco: Both Cigarette & Cigar Ages 12+, % of Population	SAMHSA	2012	27.2	29.2	107%	(0.04)
MENTAL HEALTH (0.02)						
Students Who Consider Suicide: Male, %	CDC YRBS	2011	9.0	12.8	142%	0.08
Students Who Carry Out Intent and Require Medical Attention: Male, %	CDC YRBS	2011	2.4	1.5	63%	0.27
Students That Act on Suicidal Feeling: Male, %	CDC YRBS	2011	7.7	4.6	60%	(0.02)
Students Who Consider Suicide: Female, %	CDC YRBS	2011	17.4	18.4	106%	0.17
Students Who Carry Out Intent and Require Medical Attention: Female, %	CDC YRBS	2011	2.4	2.2	92%	(0.08)
Students That Act on Suicidal Feeling: Female, %	CDC YRBS	2011	8.8	7.9	90%	0.12
ACCESS TO CARE (0.05)						
Private Insurance Payment for Health Care: Under 65 Years Old, % of Distribution	CPS ASEC	2012	51.1	74.6	68%	0.01
People Without Health Insurance, % of Population	CPS ASEC	2012	19.0	11.1	58%	0.01
People 18 to 64 Without a Usual Source of Health Insurance, % of Adults	CPS ASEC	2012	25.8	15.3	59%	0.01
People 18 to 64 and in Poverty Without a Usual Source of Health Insurance, % of Adults	CPS ASEC	2012	40.3	37.6	93%	(0.04)
Population Under 65 Covered By Medicaid, % of Population	CPS ASEC	2012	28.9	12.2	42%	0.00
ELDERLY HEALTH CARE (0.03)						
Population Over 65 Covered By Medicaid, % of Population	CPS ASEC	2012	15.1	5.6	37%	0.02
Medicare Expenditures Per Beneficiary, Dollars	CDC	2009	19,211	15,938	83%	0.00
ISSUES (0.04)						
Prenatal Care Begins in 1st Trimester	CDC	2007	75.0	87.7	86%	0.00
Prenatal Care Begins in 3rd Trimester	CDC	2007	6.0	2.3	38%	0.00
Percent of Births to Mothers 18 and Under	CDC	2010	4.9	1.7	35%	0.00
Percent of Live Births to Unmarried Mothers	CDC	2010	72.5	29.0	40%	0.00
Infant Mortality Rates Among Mothers with Less Than 12 Years of Education	CDC	2005	14.8	9.3	63%	0.00

☆ Updated ★ History Revised ☆ Removed Weight in 2013 ☆ New Series 2014 ★ No New Data

2014 EQUALITY INDEX OF BLACK AMERICA	Source	Year	Black	White	Index	Diff. ('14–'13)
Infant Mortality Rates Among Mothers with 12 Years of Education	CDC	2005	14.2	7.1	50%	0.00
Infant Mortality Rates Among Mothers with 13 or More Years of Education	CDC	2005	11.4	4.1	36%	0.00
Mothers Who Smoked Cigarettes During Pregnancy, %	CDC	2007	7.7	12.7	165%	0.00
Low Birth Weight, % of Live Births	CDC	2010	13.5	7.1	53%	0.00
Very Low Birth Weight, % of Live Births	CDC	2010	3.0	1.2	39%	0.00
REPRODUCTION ISSUES (0.01)						
Abortions, Per 1,000 Live Births	CDC	2007	447.0	159.0	36%	0.00
Women Using Contraception, % of Population	CDC	2006-2010	54.2	65.6	83%	(0.02)
DELIVERY ISSUES (0.10)						
All Infant Deaths: Neonatal and Post, Per 1,000 Live Births	CDC	2008	12.7	5.5	43%	0.00
Neonatal Deaths, Per 1,000 Live Births	CDC	2008	8.3	3.5	42%	0.00
Postneonatal Deaths, Per 1,000 Live Births	CDC	2008	4.4	2.0	45%	0.00
Maternal Mortality, Per 100,000 Live Births	CDC	2007	23.8	8.1	34%	0.00
CHILDREN'S HEALTH (0.10)						
Babies Breastfed, %	CDC	2007	58.1	76.2	76%	0.00
Children Without a Health Care Visit in Past 12 Months (up to 6 Years Old), %	CDC	2010-2011	5.9	3.5	59%	0.00
Vaccinations of Children Below Poverty: Combined Vacc. Series 4:3:1:3:1:4, % of Children 19–35 Months	CDC	2011	61.0	60.0	102%	0.13
Uninsured Children, %	CPS ASEC	2012	9.3	6.5	70%	0.04
Overweight Boys 6-11 Years Old, % of Population	CDC	2007-2010	23.3	18.6	80%	0.00
Overweight Girls 6-11 Years Old, % of Population	CDC	2007-2010	24.5	14.0	57%	0.00
AIDS Cases Per 100,000 All Children Under 13	CDC	2011	0.2	0.0	7%	(0.03)
Health Weighted Index					**76.8%**	**(0.000)**

EDUCATION (25%)						
(0.25)						
TEACHER QUALITY (0.10)						
Middle Grades: Teacher Lacking at Least a College Minor in Subject Taught (High Vs. Low Minority Schools), %	ET	2000	49.0	40.0	85%	0.00
HS: Teacher Lacking An Undergraduate Major in Subject Taught (High Vs. Low Poverty Secondary Schools), %	ET	2007-2008	21.9	10.9	88%	0.00
Per Student Funding (High [30%] Vs. Low [0%] Poverty Districts), Dollars	SFF	2009	10,948	10,684	102%	0.00
Teachers With <3 Years Experience (High Vs. Low Poverty Schools), %	NCES	2007-2008	13.0	10.0	77%	0.00
Distribution of Underprepared Teachers (High Vs. Low Minority Schools), % (California Only)	SRI	2008-2009	5.0	1.0	20%	0.00
COURSE QUALITY (0.15)						
College Completion, % of All Entrants	NCES	2004	39.5	61.5	64%	(0.02)
% of ACT Test Takers with Strong HS Curriculum (Core Curriculum)	ACT	2013	69.0	76.0	91%	(0.03)

2014 EQUALITY INDEX OF BLACK AMERICA	Source	Year	Black	White	Index	Diff. ('14–'13)
HS Students: Enrolled in Chemistry, %	NCES	2009	65.3	71.5	91%	(0.03)
HS Students: Enrolled in Algebra II, %	NCES	2009	70.5	77.1	91%	(0.06)
Students Taking: Precalculus, %	CB	2009	22.7	37.9	60%	0.04
Students Taking: Calculus, %	CB	2009	6.1	17.5	35%	(0.01)
Students Taking: Physics, %	CB	2009	26.9	37.6	72%	(0.02)
Students Taking: English Composition, %	CB	2009	31.0	43.0	72%	0.00
ATTAINMENT (0.30)						
Graduation Rates, 2-Year Institutions Where Students Started As Full Time, First Time Students, %	NCES	2006	27.1	32.0	85%	0.00
Graduation Rates, 4-Year Institutions Where Students Started As Full Time, First Time Students, %	NCES	2003	37.7	59.3	64%	0.00
NCAA Div. I College Freshmen Graduating Within 6 Years, %	NCAA	2005	33.0	52.0	63%	0.00
Degrees Earned: Associate, % of Population Aged 18–24 Yrs	NCES	2011–2012	3.0	3.6	85%	0.02
Degrees Earned: Bachelor's, % of Population Aged 18–29 Yrs	NCES	2011–2012	2.5	4.0	62%	0.02
Degrees Earned: Master's, % of Population Aged 18–34 Yrs	NCES	2011–2012	0.8	1.1	75%	0.04
Educational Attainment: at Least High School (25 Yrs. and Over), % of Population	Census	2012	85.0	92.5	92%	0.00
Educational Attainment: at Least Bachelor's (25 Yrs. and Over), % of Population	Census	2012	21.2	34.5	62%	0.00
Degrees Conferred, % Distribution, By Field						
Agriculture/Forestry	NCES	2012	0.4	1.7	24%	(0.00)
Art/Architecture	NCES	2012	0.3	0.7	47%	(0.01)
Business/Management	NCES	2012	25.7	18.9	136%	0.02
Communications	NCES	2012	3.8	3.9	99%	0.02
Computer and Information Sciences	NCES	2012	2.5	2.1	119%	(0.01)
Education	NCES	2012	10.3	12.6	82%	(0.00)
Engineering	NCES	2012	2.4	4.9	49%	(0.02)
English/Literature	NCES	2012	1.7	2.7	62%	0.01
Foreign Languages	NCES	2012	0.4	1.0	39%	0.00
Health Sciences	NCES	2012	11.8	11.9	99%	0.00
Liberal Arts/Humanities	NCES	2012	2.5	1.9	134%	(0.06)
Mathematics/Statistics	NCES	2012	0.4	0.9	47%	0.01
Natural Sciences	NCES	2012	3.6	5.4	67%	(0.02)
Philosophy/Religion/Theology	NCES	2012	0.4	0.6	66%	0.01
Psychology	NCES	2012	6.3	5.2	121%	(0.02)
Social Sciences/History	NCES	2012	6.7	7.5	89%	(0.01)
Other Fields	NCES	2012	20.8	18.1	115%	0.00
SCORES (0.25)						
PRESCHOOL 10% OF TOTAL SCORES (0.015)						
Children's School Readiness Skills (Ages 3–5), % With 3 or 4 Skills* *Recognizes all letters, counts to 20 or higher, writes name, reads or pretends to read	NCES	2005	44.1	46.8	94%	0.00

☆ Updated ★ History Revised ☆ Removed Weight in 2013 ☆ New Series 2014 ☆ No New Data

2014 EQUALITY INDEX OF BLACK AMERICA	Source	Year	Black	White	Index	Diff. ('14–'13)
ELEMENTARY 40% OF TOTAL SCORES (0.06)						
Average Scale Score (out of 500) in U.S. History, 8th Graders	NCES	2010	250	274	91%	0.00
Average Scale Score (out of 500) in U.S. History, 4th Graders	NCES	2010	198	224	88%	0.00
Average Scale Score (out of 500) in Math, 8th Graders	NCES	2013	263	294	89%	0.00
Average Scale Score (out of 500) in Math, 4th Graders	NCES	2013	224	250	90%	(0.00)
Average Scale Score (out of 500) in Reading, 8th Graders	NCES	2013	250	276	91%	(0.00)
Average Scale Score (out of 500) in Reading, 4th Graders	NCES	2013	206	232	89%	0.00
Average Scale Score (out of 300) in Science, 8th Graders	NCES	2011	129	163	79%	0.010
Average Scale Score (out of 300) in Science, 4th Graders	NCES	2009	127	163	78%	0.00
Average Scale Score (out of 300) in Writing, 8th Graders	NCES	2011	132	158	84%	0.00
Science Proficiency at or Above Proficient, 8th Graders, % of Students	NCES	2011	10	43	23%	0.03
Science Proficiency at or Above Proficient, 4th Graders, % of Students	NCES	2009	11	47	22%	0.00
Reading Proficiency at or Above Proficient, 8th Graders, % of Students	NCES	2013	17	48	35%	0.01
Reading Proficiency at or Above Proficient, 4th Graders, % of Students	NCES	2013	17	45	38%	(0.00)
Math Proficiency at or Above Proficient, 8th Graders, % of Students	NCES	2013	14	44	32%	0.02
Math Proficiency at or Above Proficient, 4th Graders, % of Students	NCES	2013	18	54	33%	0.01
Writing Proficiency at or Above Proficient, 8th Graders, % of Students	NCES	2011	11	34	32%	(0.07)
Writing Proficiency at or Above Proficient, 4th Graders, % of Students	NCES	2013	17	45	30%	(0.00)
HIGH SCHOOL 50% OF TOTAL SCORES (0.075)						
Writing Proficiency at or Above Basic, 12th Graders, % of Students	NCES	2011	61	86	71%	0.00
Average Scale Score (out of 300) in Science, 12th Graders	NCES	2005	120	156	77%	0.00
Average Scale Score (out of 500) in U.S. History, 12th Graders	NCES	2010	268	296	91%	0.00
Average Scale Score (out of 500) in Reading, 12th Graders	NCES	2009	269	296	91%	0.00
High School GPAs for Those Taking the SAT	CB	2009	3.00	3.40	88%	0.00
SAT Reasoning Test: Mean Scores	CB	2013	1,278	1,576	81%	0.00
Mathematics, Joint	CB	2013	429	534	80%	0.00
Mathematics, Male	CB	2013	436	552	79%	0.00
Mathematics, Female	CB	2013	423	519	82%	0.00
Critical Reading, Joint	CB	2013	431	527	82%	0.01
Critical Reading, Male	CB	2013	427	530	81%	0.00
Critical Reading, Female	CB	2013	433	525	82%	0.01
Writing, Joint	CB	2013	418	515	81%	0.00
Writing, Male	CB	2013	408	508	80%	0.00
Writing, Female	CB	2013	426	521	82%	0.00
ACT: Average Composite Score	ACT	2013	16.9	22.2	76%	0.00

2014 EQUALITY INDEX OF BLACK AMERICA	Source	Year	Black	White	Index	Diff. ('14–'13)
ENROLLMENT (0.10)						
School Enrollment: Ages 3–34, % of Population	Census	2012	58.3	55.6	105%	0.02
Preprimary School Enrollment	Census	2012	63.7	66.7	95%	0.02
3 and 4 Years Old	Census	2012	53.1	56.5	94%	(0.04)
5 and 6 Years Old	Census	2012	91.5	93.8	98%	0.02
7 to 13 Years Old	Census	2012	98.2	97.8	100%	0.01
14 and 15 Years Old	Census	2012	97.3	98.2	99%	(0.01)
16 and 17 Years Old	Census	2012	94.2	96.4	98%	(0.02)
18 and 19 Years Old	Census	2012	68.6	68.8	100%	(0.03)
20 and 21 Years Old	Census	2012	49.4	55.9	88%	0.15
22 to 24 Years Old	Census	2012	27.9	30.2	92%	(0.02)
25 to 29 Years Old	Census	2012	16.1	14.6	110%	(0.09)
30 to 34 Years Old	Census	2012	12.2	6.6	185%	0.39
35 and Over	Census	2012	3.2	1.6	197%	(0.29)
College Enrollment (Graduate or Undergraduate): Ages 14 and Over, % of Population	Census	2012	9.7	7.1	138%	0.64
14 to 17 Years Old	Census	2012	1.1	1.6	66%	(0.72)
18 to 19 Years Old	Census	2012	39.1	49.8	79%	(0.05)
20 to 21 Years Old	Census	2012	43.6	54.4	80%	0.09
22 to 24 Years Old	Census	2012	27.5	29.4	94%	0.02
25 to 29 Years Old	Census	2012	16.0	14.4	111%	(0.07)
30 to 34 Years Old	Census	2012	12.1	6.6	183%	0.38
35 Years Old and Over	Census	2012	3.0	1.6	190%	(0.31)
College Enrollment Rate As a Percent of All 18- to 24-Year-Old High School Completers, %	NCES	2011	37.1	44.7	83%	0.00
Adult Education Participation, % of Adult Population	NCES	2004–2005	46.0	46.0	100%	0.00
STUDENT STATUS & RISK FACTORS (0.10)						
High School Dropouts: Status Dropouts, % (Not Completed HS and Not Enrolled, Regardless of When Dropped Out)	Census	2009	11.6	9.1	78%	0.00
Children in Poverty, %	Census	2012	37.9	12.3	32%	0.00
Children in All Families Below Poverty Level, %	Census	2012	37.5	11.8	31%	0.01
Children in Families Below Poverty Level (Female Householder, No Spouse Present), %	Census	2012	53.3	36.5	68%	0.03
Children With No Parent in The Labor Force, %	AECF	2012	49.0	24.0	49%	(0.02)
Children (Under 18) With a Disability, %	Census	2012	5.1	4.1	80%	0.01
Public School Students (K-12): Repeated Grade, %	NCES	2007	20.9	8.7	42%	0.00
Public School Students (K-12): Suspended, %	NCES	2003	19.6	8.8	45%	0.00
Public School Students (K-12): Expelled, %	NCES	2003	5.0	1.4	28%	0.00
Center-Based Child Care of Preschool Children, %	NCES	2005	66.5	59.1	89%	0.00
Parental Care Only of Preschool Children, %	NCES	2005	19.5	24.1	81%	0.00
Teacher Stability: Remained in Public School, High Vs. Low Minority Schools, %	NCES	2009	83.4	85.6	97%	0.05
Teacher Stability: Remained in Private School, High Vs. Low Minority Schools, %	NCES	2009	77.0	78.9	98%	0.10

☆ Updated ★ History Revised ☆ Removed Weight in 2013 ☆ New Series 2014 ★ No New Data

2014 EQUALITY INDEX OF BLACK AMERICA	Source	Year	Black	White	Index	Diff. ('14–'13)
Zero Days Missed in School Year, % of 10th Graders	NCES	2002	28.3	12.1	234%	0.00
3+ Days Late to School, % of 10th Graders	NCES	2002	36.4	44.4	122%	0.00
Never Cut Classes, % of 10th Graders	NCES	2002	68.9	70.3	98%	0.00
Home Literacy Activities (Age 3 to 5)						
Read to 3 or More Times a Week	NCES	2007	78.0	90.6	86%	0.00
Told a Story at Least Once a Month	NCES	2005	54.3	53.3	102%	0.00
Taught Words or Numbers Three or More Times a Week	NCES	2005	80.6	75.7	107%	0.00
Visited a Library at Least Once in Last Month	NCES	2007	24.6	40.8	60%	0.00
Education Weighted Index					**76.8%**	**0.000**

SOCIAL JUSTICE (10%)

EQUALITY BEFORE THE LAW (0.70)

	Source	Year	Black	White	Index	Diff.
Stopped While Driving, %	BJS	2008	8.8	8.4	95%	0.00
Speeding	BJS	2002	50.0	57.0	114%	0.00
Vehicle Defect	BJS	2002	10.3	8.7	84%	0.00
Roadside Check for Drinking Drivers	BJS	2002	1.1	1.3	118%	0.00
Record Check	BJS	2002	17.4	11.3	65%	0.00
Seatbelt Violation	BJS	2002	3.5	4.4	126%	0.00
Illegal Turn/Lane Change	BJS	2002	5.1	4.5	88%	0.00
Stop Sign/Light Violation	BJS	2002	5.9	6.5	110%	0.00
Other	BJS	2002	3.7	4.0	108%	0.00
Mean Incarceration Sentence (In Average Months)	BJS	2006	42	37	88%	0.00
Average Sentence for Incarceration (All Offenses): Male, Months	BJS	2006	45	40	89%	0.00
Average Sentence for Murder: Male, Months	BJS	2006	266	265	100%	0.00
Average Sentence for Sexual Assault	BJS	2006	125	115	92%	0.00
Average Sentence for Robbery	BJS	2006	101	89	88%	0.00
Average Sentence for Aggravated Assault	BJS	2006	48	42	88%	0.00
Average Sentence for Other Violent	BJS	2006	41	43	105%	0.00
Average Sentence for Burglary	BJS	2006	50	41	82%	0.00
Average Sentence for Larceny	BJS	2006	23	24	104%	0.00
Average Sentence for Fraud	BJS	2006	27	27	100%	0.00
Average Sentence for Drug Possession	BJS	2006	25	21	84%	0.00
Average Sentence for Drug Trafficking	BJS	2006	40	39	98%	0.00
Average Sentence for Weapon Offenses	BJS	2006	34	34	100%	0.00
Average Sentence for Other Offenses	BJS	2006	25	26	104%	0.00
Average Sentence for Incarceration (All Offenses): Female, Months	BJS	2006	25	26	104%	0.00
Average Sentence for Murder	BJS	2006	175	225	129%	0.00
Average Sentence for Sexual Assault	BJS	2006	32	72	225%	0.00
Average Sentence for Robbery	BJS	2006	54	61	113%	0.00

☆ Updated   ★ History Revised   ☆ Removed Weight in 2013   ☆ New Series 2014   ★ No New Data

2014 EQUALITY INDEX OF BLACK AMERICA	Source	Year	Black	White	Index	Diff. ('14–'13)
Average Sentence for Aggravated Assault	BJS	2006	29	30	103%	0.00
Average Sentence for Other Violent	BJS	2006	17	55	324%	0.00
Average Sentence for Burglary	BJS	2006	34	29	85%	0.00
Average Sentence for Larceny	BJS	2006	19	17	89%	0.00
Average Sentence for Fraud	BJS	2006	23	22	96%	0.00
Average Sentence for Drug Possession	BJS	2006	15	17	113%	0.00
Average Sentence for Drug Trafficking	BJS	2006	27	26	96%	0.00
Average Sentence for Weapon Offenses	BJS	2006	24	24	100%	0.00
Average Sentence for Other Offenses	BJS	2006	20	22	110%	0.00
Convicted Felons Sentenced to Probation, All Offenses, %	BJS	2006	25	29	86%	0.00
Probation Sentence for Murder, %	BJS	2006	3	4	75%	0.00
Probation Sentence for Sexual Assault, %	BJS	2006	16	16	100%	0.00
Probation Sentence for Robbery, %	BJS	2006	12	15	80%	0.00
Probation Sentence for Burglary, %	BJS	2006	20	25	80%	0.00
Probation Sentence for Fraud, %	BJS	2006	35	35	100%	0.00
Probation Sentence for Drug Offenses, %	BJS	2006	25	34	74%	0.00
Probation Sentence for Weapon Offenses, %	BJS	2006	25	23	109%	0.00
Incarceration Rate: Prisoners Per 100,000	BJS	2012	1,423	253	18%	0.01
Incarceration Rate: Prisoners Per 100,000 People: Male	BJS	2012	2,841	463	16%	0.00
Incarceration Rate: Prisoners Per 100,000 People: Female	BJS	2012	115	49	43%	0.03
Prisoners as a % of Arrests	FBI, BJS	2012	20.9	7.7	37%	0.00
VICTIMIZATION & MENTAL ANGUISH (0.20)						
Homicide Rate Per 100,000	BJS	2011	17.3	2.8	16%	0.00
Homicide Rate Per 100,000: Firearm	NACJD	2011	14.1	1.6	11%	(0.01)
Homicide Rate Per 100,000: Stabbings	NACJD	2011	1.8	0.5	25%	(0.05)
Homicide Rate Per 100,000: Personal Weapons	NACJD	2011	0.6	0.2	38%	(0.00)
Homicide Rate Per 100,000: Male	CDC	2010	33.4	3.3	10%	(0.00)
Homicide Rate Per 100,000: Female	CDC	2010	5.1	1.7	33%	(0.01)
Murder Victims, Rate Per 100,000	USDJ	2012	15.7	2.4	15%	(0.00)
Hate Crimes Victims, Rate Per 100,000	USDJ	2012	5.7	0.3	6%	0.02
Victims of Violent Crimes, Rate Per 1,000 Persons Age 12 or Older	BJS	2012	34.2	25.2	74%	(0.08)
Delinquency Cases, Year of Disposition, Rate Per 100,000	NCJJ	2010	2,368.4	808.4	34%	0.02
Prisoners Under Sentence of Death, Rate Per 100,000	BJS	2011	4.4	0.9	21%	(0.03)
High School Students Carrying Weapons on School Property	CDC	2011	4.6	5.1	111%	0.00
High School Students Carrying Weapons Anywhere	CDC	2011	14.2	17.0	120%	0.00
Firearm-Related Death Rates Per 100,000: Males, All Ages	CDC	2007	40.4	16.1	40%	0.00
Ages 1–14	CDC	2007	2.4	0.7	29%	0.00
Ages 15–24	CDC	2007	91.5	13.4	15%	0.00
Ages 25–44	CDC	2007	64.8	18.3	28%	0.00
Ages 25–34	CDC	2007	88.1	18.0	20%	0.00
Ages 35–44	CDC	2007	40.7	18.7	46%	0.00

☆ Updated ★ History Revised ☆ Removed Weight in 2013 ☆ New Series 2014 ★ No New Data

2014 EQUALITY INDEX OF BLACK AMERICA	Source	Year	Black	White	Index	Diff. ('14–'13)
Ages 45–64	CDC	2007	20.1	19.5	97%	0.00
Age 65 and Older	CDC	2007	11.4	27.3	241%	0.00
Firearm-Related Death Rates Per 100,000: Females, All Ages	CDC	2007	4.1	2.9	70%	0.00
Ages 1–14	CDC	2007	0.9	0.3	34%	0.00
Ages 15–24	CDC	2007	7.3	2.5	34%	0.00
Ages 25–44	CDC	2007	6.7	4.1	61%	0.00
Ages 25–34	CDC	2007	7.2	3.4	47%	0.00
Ages 35–44	CDC	2007	6.2	4.6	75%	0.00
Ages 45–64	CDC	2007	2.9	3.9	136%	0.00
Age 65 and Older	CDC	2007	1.3	2.2	172%	0.00
Social Justice Weighted Index					**56.8%**	**(0.001)**

CIVIC ENGAGEMENT (10%)

DEMOCRATIC PROCESS (0.4)

	Source	Year	Black	White	Index	Diff.
Registered Voters, % of Citizen Population	Census	2012	73.1	73.7	99%	0.07
Actually Voted, % of Citizen Population	Census	2012	66.2	64.1	103%	0.14

COMMUNITY PARTICIPATION (0.3)

	Source	Year	Black	White	Index	Diff.
Percent of Population Volunteering for Military Reserves, %	USDD	2010	0.8	1.0	80%	0.00
Volunteerism, %	BLS	2012	21.1	27.8	76%	0.04
Civic and Political	BLS	2012	4.5	5.7	79%	0.23
Educational or Youth Service	BLS	2012	24.6	25.1	98%	0.05
Environmental or Animal Care	BLS	2012	1.2	2.8	43%	0.35
Hospital or Other Health	BLS	2012	5.3	8.2	65%	(0.15)
Public Safety	BLS	2012	0.4	1.3	31%	(0.26)
Religious	BLS	2012	40.7	32.3	126%	(0.13)
Social or Community Service	BLS	2012	13.4	14.3	94%	0.03
Unpaid Volunteering of Young Adults	NCES	2000	40.9	32.2	127%	0.00

COLLECTIVE BARGAINING (0.2)

	Source	Year	Black	White	Index	Diff.
Members of Unions, % of Employed	BLS	2012	13.4	11.1	121%	0.00
Represented By Unions, % of Employed	BLS	2012	14.8	12.3	120%	0.00

GOVERNMENTAL EMPLOYMENT (0.1)

	Source	Year	Black	White	Index	Diff.
Federal Executive Branch (Nonpostal) Employment, % of Adult Population	OPM	2008	1.2	0.8	145%	0.00
State and Local Government Employment, %	EEOC	2009	4.0	2.5	158%	0.00
Civic Engagement Weighted Index					**104.7%**	**0.048**

SOURCE	ACRONYM
American Community Survey	ACS
American College Testing	ACT
Annie E. Casey Foundation	AECF
U.S. Bureau of Justice Statistics	BJS
U.S. Bureau of Labor Statistics	BLS
College Board	CB
Centers for Disease Control and Prevention	CDC
CDC Youth Risk Behavior Survey	CDC YRBS
U.S. Census Bureau	Census
U.S. Census Bureau, Survey of Income & Program Participation	Census SIPP
Current Population Survey: Annual Social and Economic Supplement	CPS ASEC
Employee Benefit Research Institute	EBRI
U.S. Equal Employment Opportunity Commission	EEOC
The Education Trust	ET
Federal Bureau of Investigation	FBI
Home Mortgage Disclosure Act	HMDA
National Archive of Criminal Justice Data	NACJD
National Collegiate Athletic Association	NCAA
National Center for Education Statistics	NCES
National Center for Juvenile Justice	NCJJ
National Telecommunications and Information Administration	NTIA
Office of Personal Management	OPM
Education Law Center, Is School Funding Fair?	SFF
Substance Abuse & Mental Health Services Administration	SAMHSA
SRI International	SRI
U.S. Department of Defense	USDD
U.S. Department of Justice	USDJ

METRO AREA BLACK-WHITE
UNEMPLOYMENT EQUALITY

RANKING OF METRO AREAS FROM MOST TO LEAST EQUAL	Rank	Black Unemployment Rate	White Unemployment Rate	Black-White Index
Augusta–Richmond County, GA–SC	1	13.3	8.5	63.9%
Riverside–San Bernardino–Ontario, CA	2	19.2	12.2	63.5%
Palm Bay–Melbourne–Titusville, FL*	3	13.0	8.2	63.1%
Las Vegas–Paradise, NV	4	18.8	11.7	62.2%
Chattanooga, TN–GA	5	14.4	8.8	61.1%
San Diego–Carlsbad–San Marcos, CA	6	13.5	8.2	60.7%
Providence–New Bedford–Fall River, RI–MA	7	14.5	8.8	60.7%
Lakeland–Winter Haven, FL	8	20.7	12.1	58.5%
Seattle–Tacoma–Bellevue, WA	9	12.2	7.0	57.4%
Durham–Chapel Hill, NC	10	11.4	6.4	56.1%
Los Angeles–Long Beach–Santa Ana, CA	11	16.8	9.4	56.0%
Tampa–St. Petersburg–Clearwater, FL	12	17.2	9.6	55.8%
Deltona–Daytona Beach–Ormond Beach, FL*	13	12.6	7.0	55.6%
Nashville–Davidson–Murfreesboro–Franklin, TN	14	12.3	6.8	55.3%
Columbia, SC	15	14.8	8.1	54.7%
Knoxville, TN*	16	11.3	6.1	54.0%
Greenville–Mauldin–Easley, SC	17	15.2	8.2	53.9%
Oklahoma City, OK	18	9.0	4.7	52.2%
Orlando–Kissimmee–Sanford, FL	19	18.4	9.5	51.6%
San Antonio–New Braunfels, TX	20	11.5	5.9	51.3%
Phoenix–Mesa–Glendale, AZ	21	14.6	7.4	50.7%
Dallas–Fort Worth–Arlington, TX	22	12.7	6.4	50.4%
Boston–Cambridge–Quincy, MA–NH	23	13.3	6.7	50.4%
Virginia Beach–Norfolk–Newport News, VA–NC	24	13.1	6.5	49.6%
Austin–Round Rock–San Marcos, TX	25	11.9	5.9	49.6%
Jacksonville, FL	26	19.6	9.6	49.0%
Birmingham–Hoover, AL	27	13.7	6.7	48.9%
Dayton, OH	28	17.7	8.5	48.0%
Charleston–North Charleston–Summerville, SC	29	17.3	8.3	48.0%
Atlanta–Sandy Springs–Marietta, GA	30	17.0	8.1	47.6%
Charlotte–Gastonia–Rock Hill, NC–SC	31	16.8	8.0	47.6%
Louisville/Jefferson County, KY–IN	32	16.4	7.6	46.3%
Miami–Fort Lauderdale–Pompano Beach, FL	33	19.4	8.9	45.9%
New York–Northern New Jersey–Long Island, NY–NJ–PA	34	15.7	7.2	45.9%
Sacramento–Arden–Arcade–Roseville, CA	35	24.5	11.1	45.3%

★ 25 Areas With Largest Black Populations **Bold:** Higher than U.S. Black-White Index

RANKING OF METRO AREAS FROM MOST TO LEAST EQUAL	Rank	Black Unemployment Rate	White Unemployment Rate	Black-White Index
Denver-Aurora-Broomfield, CO	36	14.4	6.5	45.1%
Raleigh-Cary, NC	37	12.9	5.8	45.0%
New Haven-Milford, CT	38	20.4	9.1	44.6%
Houston-Sugar Land-Baytown, TX	39	14.8	6.5	43.9%
Greensboro-High Point, NC	40	18.5	8.1	43.8%
Philadelphia-Camden-Wilmington, PA-NJ-DE-MD	41	18.3	8.0	43.7%
Richmond, VA	42	13.3	5.8	43.6%
New Orleans-Metairie-Kenner, LA	43	15.3	6.6	43.1%
Syracuse, NY*	44	14.7	6.3	42.9%
Albany-Schenectady-Troy, NY**	45	12.9	5.4	41.9%
Tulsa, OK	46	15.1	6.3	41.7%
Cincinnati-Middletown, OH-KY-IN	47	17.1	7.1	41.5%
Hartford-West Hartford-East Hartford, CT	48	17.5	7.1	40.6%
Columbus, OH	49	14.6	5.9	40.4%
Baltimore-Towson, MD	50	15.1	6.1	40.4%
Kansas City, MO-KS	51	16.0	6.4	40.0%
Scranton-Wilkes-Barre, PA*	52	15.8	6.3	39.9%
Toledo, OH	53	23.7	9.4	39.7%
Memphis, TN-MS-AR	54	16.6	6.5	39.2%
Buffalo-Niagara Falls, NY	55	16.1	6.3	39.1%
Omaha-Council Bluffs, NE-IA	56	13.1	5.1	38.9%
Harrisburg-Carlisle, PA*	57	12.4	4.8	38.7%
Jackson, MS	58	15.6	6.0	38.5%
Rochester, NY	59	18.0	6.9	38.3%
Detroit-Warren-Livonia, MI	60	24.0	9.0	37.5%
Youngstown-Warren-Boardman, OH-PA*	61	21.4	8.0	37.4%
Little Rock-North Little Rock-Conway, AR	62	15.3	5.7	37.3%
Bridgeport-Stamford-Norwalk, CT	63	19.6	7.2	36.7%
Pittsburgh, PA	64	16.9	6.2	36.7%
Indianapolis-Carmel, IN	65	18.8	6.8	36.2%
San Francisco-Oakland-Fremont, CA	66	18.6	6.7	36.0%
Akron, OH	67	21.9	7.8	35.6%
St. Louis, MO-IL	68	19.6	6.9	35.2%
Washington-Arlington-Alexandria, D.C.-VA-MD-WV	69	12.0	4.2	35.0%
Chicago-Joliet-Naperville, IL-IN-WI	70	23.0	7.6	33.0%
Cleveland-Elyria-Mentor, OH	71	21.2	7.0	33.0%
Baton Rouge, LA	72	12.8	4.1	32.0%
Des Moines-West Des Moines, IA*	73	13.7	4.3	31.4%
Minneapolis-St. Paul-Bloomington, MN-WI	74	18.0	5.2	28.9%
Milwaukee-Waukesha-West Allis, WI	75	20.1	5.6	27.9%
Lancaster, PA*	76	16.9	4.7	27.8%
Madison, WI*	77	18.5	4.4	23.8%

Source: Census ACS 2012 1-year estimates (unless otherwise noted); Black is Black or African American alone, not Hispanic
*ACS 2010 5-year estimates, Black is Black or African American alone   **Black is Black or African American alone

METRO AREA BLACK-WHITE
INCOME EQUALITY

RANKING OF METRO AREAS FROM MOST TO LEAST EQUAL	Rank	Black Median Household Income, Dollars	White Median Household Income, Dollars	Black-White Index
Riverside–San Bernardino–Ontario, CA	1	44,572	57,252	77.9%
San Diego–Carlsbad–San Marcos, CA	2	48,161	66,416	72.5%
Palm Bay–Melbourne–Titusville, FL*	3	35,800	51,112	70.0%
Greensboro–High Point, NC	4	32,239	47,177	68.3%
Las Vegas–Paradise, NV	5	37,138	54,517	68.1%
Lakeland–Winter Haven, FL	6	29,262	44,014	66.5%
San Antonio–New Braunfels, TX	7	42,446	65,663	64.6%
Phoenix–Mesa–Glendale, AZ	8	37,286	57,760	64.6%
Providence–New Bedford–Fall River, RI–MA	9	38,068	59,004	64.5%
Tampa–St. Petersburg–Clearwater, FL	10	31,108	48,421	64.2%
Orlando–Kissimmee–Sanford, FL	11	34,394	53,763	64.0%
Virginia Beach–Norfolk–Newport News, VA–NC	12	40,897	65,141	62.8%
Nashville–Davidson–Murfreesboro–Franklin, TN	13	35,208	56,706	62.1%
Columbia, SC	14	35,252	56,794	62.1%
Atlanta–Sandy Springs–Marietta, GA	15	41,463	67,196	61.7%
Austin–Round Rock–San Marcos, TX	16	42,672	69,244	61.6%
Deltona–Daytona Beach–Ormond Beach, FL*	17	28,550	46,556	61.3%
Miami–Fort Lauderdale–Pompano Beach, FL	18	35,618	59,039	60.3%
Harrisburg–Carlisle, PA*	19	34,819	58,733	59.3%
Washington–Arlington–Alexandria, D.C.–VA–MD–WV	20	62,726	106,597	58.8%
Augusta–Richmond County, GA–SC	21	31,419	53,527	58.7%
Birmingham–Hoover, AL	22	32,086	55,000	58.3%
Columbus, OH	23	34,347	59,036	58.2%
Richmond, VA	24	39,012	67,277	58.0%
Raleigh–Cary, NC	25	40,017	69,730	57.4%
Charlotte–Gastonia–Rock Hill, NC–SC	26	36,007	62,877	57.3%
Chattanooga, TN–GA	27	27,276	47,963	56.9%
Seattle–Tacoma–Bellevue, WA	28	39,774	69,998	56.8%
Jacksonville, FL	29	30,622	54,196	56.5%
Lancaster, PA*	30	32,202	57,240	56.3%
Little Rock–North Little Rock–Conway, AR	31	31,267	55,611	56.2%
Dallas–Fort Worth–Arlington, TX	32	39,523	70,669	55.9%
Dayton, OH	33	27,452	49,109	55.9%
Oklahoma City, OK	34	30,217	54,683	55.3%
Boston–Cambridge–Quincy, MA–NH	35	43,230	78,551	55.0%

★ 25 Areas With Largest Black Populations   **Bold:** Higher than U.S. Black-White Index

RANKING OF METRO AREAS FROM MOST TO LEAST EQUAL	Rank	Black Median Household Income, Dollars	White Median Household Income, Dollars	Black-White Index
Durham-Chapel Hill, NC	36	34,069	62,268	54.7%
New York-Northern New Jersey-Long Island, NY-NJ-PA	37	44,474	81,865	54.3%
Sacramento-Arden-Arcade-Roseville, CA	38	35,225	64,847	54.3%
Baltimore-Towson, MD	39	43,663	80,487	54.2%
Denver-Aurora-Broomfield, CO	40	37,460	69,410	54.0%
Greenville-Mauldin-Easley, SC	41	26,482	49,112	53.9%
Pittsburgh, PA	42	28,193	52,370	53.8%
Memphis, TN-MS-AR	43	31,576	58,819	53.7%
Houston-Sugar Land-Baytown, TX	44	40,129	75,201	53.4%
Albany-Schenectady-Troy, NY**	45	33,619	63,039	53.3%
Baton Rouge, LA	46	33,226	62,441	53.2%
Los Angeles-Long Beach-Santa Ana, CA	47	39,088	73,865	52.9%
Knoxville, TN*	48	25,472	48,201	52.8%
Tulsa, OK	49	27,291	52,119	52.4%
New Haven-Milford, CT	50	36,291	69,617	52.1%
Charleston-North Charleston-Summerville, SC	51	31,136	59,883	52.0%
Louisville/Jefferson County, KY-IN	52	27,359	52,993	51.6%
Madison, WI*	53	32,270	62,585	51.6%
Hartford-West Hartford-East Hartford, CT	54	38,587	75,265	51.3%
Syracuse, NY*	55	27,040	52,963	51.1%
Indianapolis-Carmel, IN	56	30,639	60,286	50.8%
Kansas City, MO-KS	57	30,878	60,883	50.7%
Scranton-Wilkes-Barre, PA*	58	22,314	44,065	50.6%
Philadelphia-Camden-Wilmington, PA-NJ-DE-MD	59	35,989	71,122	50.6%
Detroit-Warren-Livonia, MI	60	28,988	57,533	50.4%
Jackson, MS	61	30,104	59,853	50.3%
New Orleans-Metairie-Kenner, LA	62	29,331	58,317	50.3%
Youngstown-Warren-Boardman, OH-PA*	63	21,959	44,334	49.5%
Rochester, NY	64	27,210	55,002	49.5%
St. Louis, MO-IL	65	28,500	59,607	47.8%
Chicago-Joliet-Naperville, IL-IN-WI	66	33,674	70,890	47.5%
Omaha-Council Bluffs, NE-IA	67	28,053	59,094	47.5%
San Francisco-Oakland-Fremont, CA	68	40,753	90,452	45.1%
Cleveland-Elyria-Mentor, OH	69	24,749	55,084	44.9%
Des Moines-West Des Moines, IA*	70	26,976	60,385	44.7%
Buffalo-Niagara Falls, NY	71	24,165	55,642	43.4%
Toledo, OH	72	21,053	48,753	43.2%
Cincinnati-Middletown, OH-KY-IN	73	24,272	57,481	42.2%
Milwaukee-Waukesha-West Allis, WI	74	26,132	62,100	42.1%
Bridgeport-Stamford-Norwalk, CT	75	39,643	97,654	40.6%
Akron, OH	76	21,772	53,984	40.3%
Minneapolis-St. Paul-Bloomington, MN-WI	77	28,784	71,376	40.3%

Source: Census ACS 2012 1-year estimates (unless otherwise noted); Black is Black or African American alone, not Hispanic
*ACS 2010 5-year estimates, Black is Black or African American alone   **Black is Black or African American alone

NATIONAL URBAN LEAGUE

2014 HISPANIC-WHITE

EQUALITY

INDEX

IHS GLOBAL INSIGHT

⚊ Updated   ★ History Revised   ⚊ Removed Weight in 2013   ⚊ New Series 2014   ★ No New Data

2014 EQUALITY INDEX OF HISPANIC AMERICA	Source	Year	Hispanic	White	Index	Diff ('14-'13)
Total Equality Weighted Index					**75.8%**	**0.012**
ECONOMICS (30%)						
MEDIAN INCOME (0.25)						
Median Household Income (Real), Dollars	ACS	2012	40,417	56,565	71%	(0.001)
Median Male Earnings, Dollars	ACS	2012	31,427	52,148	60%	0.00
Median Female Earnings, Dollars	ACS	2012	27,892	40,558	69%	(0.01)
POVERTY (0.15)						
Population Living Below Poverty Line, %	ACS	2012	25.4	11.0	43%	0.01
Population Living Below 50% of Poverty Line, %	ACS	2012	10.0	4.9	49%	0.01
Population Living Below 125% of Poverty Line, %	ACS	2012	33.4	14.6	44%	0.00
Population Living Below Poverty Line (Under 18), %	CPS ASEC	2012	33.8	12.3	36%	(0.00)
Population Living Below Poverty Line (18-64), %	CPS ASEC	2012	21.6	9.7	45%	(0.02)
Population Living Below Poverty Line (65 and Older), %	CPS ASEC	2012	20.6	6.8	33%	(0.03)
EMPLOYMENT ISSUES (0.20)						
Unemployment Rate, %	BLS	2013	9.1	6.5	71%	0.02
Unemployment Rate: Male, %	BLS	2013	8.8	6.8	77%	0.03
Unemployment Rate: Female, %	BLS	2013	9.5	6.2	65%	0.01
Unemployment Rate Persons Ages 16 to 19, %	BLS	2013	27.5	20.3	74%	(0.01)
Percent Not in Workforce: Ages 16 to 19, %	BLS	2013	69.0	63.1	92%	0.00
Percent Not in Workforce: Ages 16 and Older, %	BLS	2013	34	36.5	107%	0.00
Labor Force Participation Rate, %	BLS	2013	66.0	63.5	104%	0.00
LFPR 16 to 19, %	BLS	2013	31.0	36.9	84%	0.00
LFPR 20 to 24, %	BLS	2013	71.7	73.1	98%	0.01
LFPR Over 25: Less Than High School Grad, %	BLS	2013	60.6	46.3	131%	0.03
LFPR Over 25, High School Grad, No College, %	BLS	2013	69.8	58.3	120%	(0.01)
LFPR Over 25: Some College, No Degree, %	BLS	2013	74.4	64.0	116%	0.00
LFPR Over 25: Associate's Degree, %	BLS	2013	76.6	71.9	107%	(0.01)
LFPR Over 25: Some College or Associate Degree, %	BLS	2013	75.2	67.0	112%	(0.00)
LFPR Over 25: College Grad., %	BLS	2013	80.1	75.0	107%	0.00
Employment to Pop. Ratio, %	BLS	2013	60.0	59.4	101%	0.01
HOUSING & WEALTH (0.34)						
Home Ownership Rate, %	Census	2012	46.1	73.5	63%	(0.01)
Mortgage Application Denial Rate (Total), %	HMDA	2012	24.6	13.2	54%	(0.04)
Mortgage Application Denial Rate (Male), %	HMDA	2012	24.6	15.5	63%	(0.03)
Mortgage Application Denial Rate (Female), %	HMDA	2012	25.7	15.3	59%	(0.04)
Mortgage Application Denial Rate (Joint), %	HMDA	2012	23.4	10.8	46%	(0.04)
Home Improvement Loans Denials (Total), %	HMDA	2012	55.2	30.5	55%	(0.00)
Home Improvement Loans Denials (Male), %	HMDA	2012	57.1	37.2	65%	0.00
Home Improvement Loans Denials (Female), %	HMDA	2012	60.2	38.8	64%	0.01
Home Improvement Loans Denials (Joint), %	HMDA	2012	44.2	21.7	49%	(0.02)

48

2014 EQUALITY INDEX OF HISPANIC AMERICA	Source	Year	Hispanic	White	Index	Diff. ('14-'13)
Percent of High-Priced Loans (More Than 3% Above Treasury)	HMDA	2012	8.5	3.2	37%	(0.00)
Median Home Value, 2000 Dollars	Census	2000	105,600	123,400	86%	0.00
Median Wealth, 2010 Dollars	Census SIPP	2011	7,683	110,500	7%	0.00
Equity in Home, Dollars	Census SIPP	2011	47,000	85,000	55%	0.05
Percent Investing in 401(K), %	EBRI	2009	18.0	36.9	49%	0.00
Percent Investing in IRA, %	EBRI	2009	6.0	25.6	23%	0.00
DIGITAL DIVIDE (0.05)						
Households With Computer at Home, %	Census	2011	68.0	84.8	80%	(0.03)
Households With the Internet, %	Census	2011	58.3	76.2	77%	(0.02)
Adult Users With Broadband Access, %	Census	2011	55.5	72.9	76%	(0.03)
TRANSPORTATION (0.01)						
Car Ownership, %	Census	2011	77.3	88.3	88%	0.01
Means of Transportation to Work: Drive Alone, %	ACS	2012	68.4	79.7	86%	0.00
Means of Transportation to Work: Public Transportation, %	ACS	2012	7.8	3.0	38%	0.01
Economic Weighted Index					**60.6%**	**(0.002)**

HEALTH (25%)

DEATH RATES & LIFE EXPECTANCY (0.45)

	Source	Year	Hispanic	White	Index	Diff.
Life Expectancy at Birth	CDC	2010	81.2	78.8	103%	0.00
Male	CDC	2010	78.5	76.4	103%	0.00
Female	CDC	2010	83.8	81.1	103%	0.00
Life Expectancy at 65 (Additional Expected Years)	CDC	2010	20.6	19.1	108%	0.00
Male at 65	CDC	2010	18.8	17.7	106%	0.00
Female at 65	CDC	2010	22.0	20.3	108%	0.00
Age-Adjusted Death Rates (Per 100,000): All Causes	CDC	2010	558.6	755.0	135%	0.00
Age-Adjusted Death Rates (Per 100,000): Male	CDC	2010	677.7	892.5	132%	0.00
Age-Adjusted Death Rates (Per 100,000): Female	CDC	2010	463.4	643.3	139%	0.00
Age-Adjusted Death Rates (Per 100,000): Heart Disease	CDC	2010	132.8	179.9	135%	0.00
Ischemic Heart Disease	CDC	2010	92.3	115.0	125%	0.00
Age-Adjusted Death Rates (Per 100,000): Stroke (Cerebrovascular)	CDC	2010	32.1	37.8	118%	0.00
Age-Adjusted Death Rates (Per 100,000): Cancer	CDC	2010	119.7	176.5	147%	0.00
Trachea, Bronchus, and Lung	CDC	2010	20.4	50.8	249%	0.00
Colon, Rectum, and Anus	CDC	2010	12.3	15.5	126%	0.00
Prostate (Male)	CDC	2010	18.4	20.3	110%	0.00
Breast (Female)	CDC	2010	14.4	22.1	153%	0.00
Age-Adjusted Death Rates (Per 100,000): Chronic Lower Respiratory	CDC	2010	19.6	46.6	238%	0.00

☆ Updated   ★ History Revised   ☆ Removed Weight in 2013   ☆ New Series 2014   ★ No New Data

2014 EQUALITY INDEX OF HISPANIC AMERICA	Source	Year	Hispanic	White	Index	Diff. ('14–'13)
Age-Adjusted Death Rates (Per 100,000): Influenza and Pneumonia	CDC	2010	13.7	14.9	109%	0.00
Age-Adjusted Death Rates (Per 100,000): Chronic Liver Disease and Cirrhosis	CDC	2010	13.7	9.4	69%	0.00
Age-Adjusted Death Rates (Per 100,000): Diabetes	CDC	2010	27.1	18.2	67%	0.00
Age-Adjusted Death Rates (Per 100,000): HIV	CDC	2010	2.8	1.1	39%	0.00
Unintentional Injuries	CDC	2010	25.8	42.4	164%	0.00
Motor Vehicle-Related Injuries	CDC	2010	9.6	11.9	124%	0.00
Age-Adjusted Death Rates (Per 100,000): Suicide	CDC	2010	5.9	15.0	254%	0.00
Age-Adjusted Death Rates (Per 100,000): Suicide Males	CDC	2010	9.9	24.2	244%	0.00
Death Rates (Per 100,000): Suicide Males Ages 15–24	CDC	2010	10.7	20.4	191%	0.00
Age-Adjusted Death Rates (Per 100,000): Suicide Females	CDC	2010	2.1	6.2	295%	0.00
Death Rates (Per 100,000): Suicide Females Ages 15–24	CDC	2010	3.1	4.4	142%	0.00
Age-Adjusted Death Rates (Per 100,000): Homicide	CDC	2010	5.3	2.5	47%	0.00
Age-Adjusted Death Rates (Per 100,000): Homicide Male	CDC	2010	8.7	3.3	38%	0.00
Death Rates (Per 100,000): Homicide Males Ages 15–24	CDC	2010	19.7	4.1	21%	0.00
Age-Adjusted Death Rates (Per 100,000): Homicide female	CDC	2010	1.8	1.8	100%	0.00
Death Rates (Per 100,000): Homicide Females Ages 15–24	CDC	2010	2.6	1.8	69%	0.00
Death Rates (Per 100,000) By Age Cohort: <1 Male	CDC	2010	556.8	575.9	103%	0.00
Death Rates (Per 100,000) By Age Cohort: 1–4 Male	CDC	2010	25.0	27.5	110%	0.00
Death Rates (Per 100,000) By Age Cohort: 5–14 Male	CDC	2010	11.4	14.3	125%	0.00
Death Rates (Per 100,000) By Age Cohort: 15–24 Male	CDC	2010	79.4	93.4	118%	0.00
Death Rates (Per 100,000) By Age Cohort: 25–34 Male	CDC	2010	100.9	143.6	142%	0.00
Death Rates (Per 100,000) By Age Cohort: 35–44 Male	CDC	2010	146.2	219.1	150%	0.00
Death Rates (Per 100,000) By Age Cohort: 45–54 Male	CDC	2010	331.9	488.1	147%	0.00
Death Rates (Per 100,000) By Age Cohort: 55–64 Male	CDC	2010	815.1	1,046.2	128%	0.00
Death Rates (Per 100,000) By Age Cohort: 65–74 Male	CDC	2010	1,776.0	2,256.9	127%	0.00
Death Rates (Per 100,000) By Age Cohort: 75–84 Male	CDC	2010	4,461.9	5,770.3	129%	0.00
Death Rates (Per 100,000) By Age Cohort: 85+ Male	CDC	2010	11,779.8	15,816.6	134%	0.00
Death Rates (Per 100,000) By Age Cohort: <1 Female	CDC	2010	462.9	480.4	104%	0.00
Death Rates (Per 100,000) By Age Cohort: 1–4 Female	CDC	2010	20.2	21.8	108%	0.00
Death Rates (Per 100,000) By Age Cohort: 5–14 Female	CDC	2010	8.9	10.9	122%	0.00
Death Rates (Per 100,000) By Age Cohort: 15–24 Female	CDC	2010	26.3	38.4	146%	0.00
Death Rates (Per 100,000) By Age Cohort: 25–34 Female	CDC	2010	38.9	66.8	172%	0.00
Death Rates (Per 100,000) By Age Cohort: 35–44 Female	CDC	2010	75.2	133.1	177%	0.00
Death Rates (Per 100,000) By Age Cohort: 45–54 Female	CDC	2010	193.9	307.7	159%	0.00
Death Rates (Per 100,000) By Age Cohort: 55–64 Female	CDC	2010	450.1	631.5	140%	0.00
Death Rates (Per 100,000) By Age Cohort: 65–74 Female	CDC	2010	1,085.5	1,535.9	141%	0.00
Death Rates (Per 100,000) By Age Cohort: 75–84 Female	CDC	2010	3,067.4	4,232.6	138%	0.00
Death Rates (Per 100,000) By Age Cohort: 85+Female	CDC	2010	10,237.3	13,543.3	132%	0.00

✩ Updated   ★ History Revised   ✩ Removed Weight in 2013   ✩ New Series 2014   ★ No New Data

2014 EQUALITY INDEX OF HISPANIC AMERICA	Source	Year	Hispanic	White	Index	Diff. ('14–'13)
PHYSICAL CONDITION (0.10)						
Overweight: 18+ Years, % of Population	CDC	2011	38.8	35.7	92%	0.00
Overweight: Men 20 Years and Over, % of Population	CDC	2007–2010	44.7	39.5	88%	0.00
Overweight: Women 20 Years and Over, % of Population	CDC	2007–2010	33.5	27.8	83%	0.00
Obese, % of Population	CDC	2011	28.8	26.3	91%	0.00
Obese: Men 20 Years and Over, % of Population	CDC	2007–2010	35.3	33.8	96%	0.00
Obese: Women 20 Years and Over, % of Population	CDC	2007–2010	41.6	32.7	79%	0.00
Diabetes: Physician Diagnosed in Ages 20+, % of Population	CDC	2007–2010	11.1	6.7	60%	0.00
AIDS Cases Per 100,000 Males Ages 13+	CDC	2011	26.3	8.6	33%	0.01
AIDS Cases Per 100,000 Females Ages 13+	CDC	2011	5.9	1.4	24%	0.03
SUBSTANCE ABUSE (0.10)						
Binge Alcohol (5 Drinks in 1 Day, 1X a Year) Ages 18+, % of Population	CDC	2011	21.2	26.2	124%	0.00
Use of Illicit Drugs in the Past Month Ages 12+, % of Population	SAMHSA	2012	8.3	9.2	111%	(0.01)
Tobacco: Both Cigarette & Cigar Ages 12+, % of Population	SAMHSA	2012	19.2	29.2	152%	0.24
MENTAL HEALTH (0.02)						
Students Who Consider Suicide: Male, %	CDC YRBS	2011	12.6	12.8	102%	0.03
Students Who Carry Out Intent and Require Medical Attention: Male, %	CDC YRBS	2011	2.2	1.5	68%	0.18
Students That Act on Suicidal Feeling: Male, %	CDC YRBS	2011	6.9	4.6	67%	0.13
Students Who Consider Suicide: Female, %	CDC YRBS	2011	21.0	18.4	88%	0.08
Students Who Carry Out Intent and Require Medical Attention: Female, %	CDC YRBS	2011	4.1	2.2	54%	(0.00)
Students That Act on Suicidal Feeling: Female, %	CDC YRBS	2011	13.5	7.9	59%	0.04
ACCESS TO CARE (0.05)						
Private Insurance Payment for Health Care: Under 65 Years Old, % of Distribution	CPS ASEC	2012	43.4	74.6	58%	0.02
People Without Health Insurance, % of Population	CPS ASEC	2012	29.1	11.1	38%	0.01
People 18 to 64 Without a Usual Source of Health Insurance, % of Adults	CPS ASEC	2012	39.8	15.3	39%	0.01
People 18 to 64 and in Poverty Without a Usual Source of Health Insurance, % of Adults	CPS ASEC	2012	55.5	37.6	68%	(0.01)
Population Under 65 Covered By Medicaid, % of Population	CPS ASEC	2012	27.7	12.2	44%	0.01
ELDERLY HEALTH CARE (0.03)						
Population Over 65 Covered By Medicaid, % of Population	CPS ASEC	2012	23.6	5.6	24%	(0.04)
Medicare Expenditures Per Beneficiary, Dollars	CDC	2009	14,860	15,938	107%	0.00
PREGNANCY ISSUES (0.04)						
Prenatal Care Begins in 1st Trimester	CDC	2007	72.4	87.7	83%	0.00
Prenatal Care Begins in 3rd Trimester	CDC	2007	6.2	2.3	37%	0.00
Percent of Births to Mothers 18 and Under	CDC	2010	4.7	1.7	36%	0.00
Percent of Live Births to Unmarried Mothers	CDC	2010	53.4	29.0	54%	0.00
Infant Mortality Rates Among Mothers With Less Than 12 Years Education	CDC	2005	5.2	9.3	179%	0.00

✦ Updated   ★ History Revised   ✦ Removed Weight in 2013   ✦ New Series 2014   ✩ No New Data

2014 EQUALITY INDEX OF HISPANIC AMERICA	Source	Year	Hispanic	White	Index	Diff. ('14-'13)
Infant Mortality Rates Among Mothers With 12 Years Education	CDC	2005	5.4	7.1	131%	0.00
Infant Mortality Rates Among Mothers With 13 or More Years Education	CDC	2005	4.6	4.1	89%	0.00
Mothers Who Smoked Cigarettes During Pregnancy, %	CDC	2007	2.4	12.7	529%	0.00
Low Birth Weight, % of Live Births	CDC	2010	7.0	7.1	102%	0.00
Very Low Birth Weight, % of Live Births	CDC	2010	1.2	1.2	97%	0.00
REPRODUCTION ISSUES (0.01)						
Abortions, Per 1,000 Live Births	CDC	2007	193.0	159.0	82%	0.00
Women Using Contraception, % of Population	CDC	2006–2010	59.7	65.6	91%	0.01
DELIVERY ISSUES (0.10)						
All Infant Deaths: Neonatal and Post, Per 1,000 Live Births	CDC	2008	5.6	5.5	98%	0.00
Neonatal Deaths, Per 1,000 Live Births	CDC	2008	3.8	3.5	92%	0.00
Post Neonatal Deaths, Per 1,000 Live Births	CDC	2008	1.8	2.0	111%	0.00
Maternal Mortality, Per 100,000 Live Births	CDC	2007	7.2	8.1	113%	0.00
CHILDREN'S HEALTH (0.10)						
Babies Breastfed, %	CDC	2007	80.6	76.2	106%	0.00
Children Without a Health Care Visit in Past 12 Months (Up to 6 Years Old), %	CDC	2010-2011	6.7	3.5	52%	0.00
Vaccinations of Children Below Poverty: Combined Vacc. Series 4:3:1:5:1:4, % of Children 19-35 Months	CDC	2011	68.0	60.0	113%	0.11
Uninsured Children, %	CPS ASEC	2012	14.1	6.5	46%	0.01
Overweight Boys 6-11 Years Old, % of Population	CDC	2007-2010	24.3	18.6	77%	0.00
Overweight Girls 6-11 Years Old, % of Population	CDC	2007-2010	22.4	14.0	63%	0.00
AIDS Cases Per 100,000 All Children Under 13	CDC	2011	0.0	0.0	30%	0.00
Health Weighted Index					**102.3%**	**0.012**

EDUCATION (25%)						
QUALITY (0.25)						
TEACHER QUALITY (0.10)						
Middle Grades: Teacher Lacking at Least a College Minor in Subject Taught (High Vs. Low Minority Schools), %	ET	2000	49.0	40.0	85%	0.00
HS: Teacher Lacking an Undergraduate Major in Subject Taught (High Vs. Low Poverty Secondary Schools), %	ET	2007-2008	21.9	10.9	88%	0.00
Per Student Funding (High [30%] Vs. Low [0%] Poverty Districts), Dollars	SFF	2009	10,948	10,684	102%	0.00
Teachers With < 3 Years Experience (High Vs. Low Minority Schools), %	NCES	2007-2008	15.0	10.0	67%	0.00
Distribution of Underprepared Teachers (High Vs. Low Minority Schools), % (California Only)	SRI	2008-2009	5.0	1.0	20%	0.00
COURSE QUALITY (0.15)						
College Completion, % of All Entrants	NCES	2004	50.1	61.5	81%	0.00
% of ACT Test Takers With Strong HS Curriculum (Core Curriculum)	ACT	2013	72.0	76.0	95%	0.01

2014 EQUALITY INDEX OF HISPANIC AMERICA	Source	Year	Hispanic	White	Index	Diff. ('14–'13)
HS Students: Enrolled in Chemistry, %	NCES	2009	65.7	71.5	92%	0.04
HS Students: Enrolled in Algebra II, %	NCES	2009	71.1	77.1	92%	0.04
Students Taking: Precalculus, %	CB	2009	26.5	37.9	70%	0.06
Students Taking: Calculus, %	CB	2009	8.6	17.5	49%	0.07
Students Taking: Physics, %	CB	2009	28.6	37.6	76%	0.09
Students Taking: English Composition, %	CB	2009	35.0	43.0	81%	0.00
ATTAINMENT (0.20)						
Graduation Rates, 2-Year Institutions Where Students Started as Full Time, First Time Students, %	NCES	2006	32.8	32.0	103%	0.00
Graduation Rates, 4-Year Institutions Where Students Started as Full Time, First Time Students, %	NCES	2003	46.2	59.3	78%	0.00
NCAA Div. I College Freshmen Graduating Within 6 Years, %	NCAA	2005	42.0	52.0	81%	0.00
Degrees Earned: Associate, % of Population Aged 18–24 Yrs	NCES	2011–2012	2.4	3.6	65%	0.08
Degrees Earned: Bachelor's, % of Population Aged 18–29 Yrs	NCES	2011–2012	1.6	4.0	39%	0.02
Degrees Earned: Master's, % of Population Aged 18–34 Yrs	NCES	2011–2012	0.3	1.1	30%	0.02
Educational Attainment: at Least High School (25 Yrs. and Over), % of Population	Census	2012	65.0	92.5	70%	0.00
Educational Attainment: at Least Bachelor's (25 Yrs. and Over), % of Population	Census	2012	14.5	34.5	42%	0.00
Degrees Conferred, % Distribution, By Field						
Agriculture/Forestry	NCES	2012	0.8	1.7	48%	(0.02)
Art/Architecture	NCES	2012	0.8	0.7	119%	(0.07)
Business/Management	NCES	2012	20.6	18.9	108%	0.02
Communications	NCES	2012	3.7	3.9	97%	0.00
Computer and Information Sciences	NCES	2012	2.1	2.1	101%	0.03
Education	NCES	2012	9.2	12.6	73%	0.00
Engineering	NCES	2012	4.2	4.9	86%	(0.02)
English/Literature	NCES	2012	2.5	2.7	89%	0.02
Foreign Languages	NCES	2012	2.1	1.0	211%	0.04
Health Sciences	NCES	2012	8.7	11.9	73%	(0.01)
Liberal Arts/Humanities	NCES	2012	2.3	1.9	121%	(0.05)
Mathematics/Statistics	NCES	2012	0.7	0.9	76%	(0.02)
Natural Sciences	NCES	2012	4.8	5.4	88%	(0.01)
Philosophy/Religion/Theology	NCES	2012	0.5	0.6	80%	0.04
Psychology	NCES	2012	7.0	5.2	136%	(0.01)
Social Sciences/History	NCES	2012	9.3	7.5	123%	0.02
Other Fields	NCES	2012	20.9	18.1	115%	(0.00)
SCORES (0.25)						
PRESCHOOL 10% OF TOTAL SCORES (0.015)						
Children's School Readiness Skills (Ages 3–5), % With 3 or 4 Skills* *Recognizes all letters, counts to 20 or higher, writes name, reads or pretends to read	NCES	2005	26.0	46.8	55%	0.00

✶ Updated   ★ History Revised   ✶ Removed Weight in 2013   ✶ New Series 2014   ★ No New Data

2014 EQUALITY INDEX OF HISPANIC AMERICA	Source	Year	Hispanic	White	Index	Diff. ('14–'13)
ELEMENTARY 40% OF TOTAL SCORES (0.06)						
Average Scale Score in U.S. History, 8th Graders	NCES	2010	252	274	92%	0.00
Average Scale Score in U.S. History, 4th Graders	NCES	2010	198	224	88%	0.00
Average Scale Score in Math, 8th Graders	NCES	2013	272	294	93%	0.00
Average Scale Score in Math, 4th Graders	NCES	2013	231	250	92%	0.00
Average Scale Score in Reading, 8th Graders	NCES	2013	256	276	93%	0.01
Average Scale Score in Reading, 4th Graders	NCES	2013	207	232	89%	0.00
Average Scale Score in Science, 8th Graders	NCES	2011	137	163	84%	0.00
Average Scale Score in Science, 4th Graders	NCES	2009	131	163	80%	0.00
Average Scale Score (out of 300) in Writing, 8th Graders	NCES	2011	136	158	86%	0.00
Science Proficiency at or Above Proficient, 8th Graders, % of Students	NCES	2011	16	43	37%	0.08
Science Proficiency at or Above Proficient, 4th Graders, % of Students	NCES	2009	14	47	29%	0.00
Reading Proficiency at or Above Proficient, 8th Graders, % of Students	NCES	2013	22	48	46%	0.02
Reading Proficiency at or Above Proficient, 4th Graders, % of Students	NCES	2013	19	45	42%	(0.01)
Math Proficiency at or Above Proficient, 8th Graders, % of Students	NCES	2013	21	44	48%	0.01
Math Proficiency at or Above Proficient, 4th Graders, % of Students	NCES	2013	26	54	48%	0.02
Writing Proficiency at or Above Proficient, 8th Graders, % of Students	NCES	2011	14	34	41%	(0.03)
Writing Proficiency at or Above Proficient, 4th Graders, % of Students	NCES	2013	19	45	42%	(0.01)
HIGH SCHOOL 50% OF TOTAL SCORES (0.075)						
Writing Proficiency at or Above Basic, 12th Graders, % of Students	NCES	2011	66	86	77%	0.00
Average Scale Score (out of 300) in Science, 12th Graders	NCES	2005	128	156	82%	0.00
Average Scale Score (out of 500) in U.S. History, 12th Graders	NCES	2010	275	296	93%	0.00
Average Scale Score (out of 500) in Reading, 12th Graders	NCES	2009	274	296	93%	0.00
High School GPAs for Those Taking The SAT	CB	2009	3.17	3.40	93%	0.00
SAT Reasoning Test: Mean Scores	CB	2013	1,354	1,576	86%	0.00
Mathematics, Joint	CB	2013	461	534	86%	0.00
Mathematics, Male	CB	2013	479	552	87%	0.00
Mathematics, Female	CB	2013	447	519	86%	0.00
Critical Reading, Joint	CB	2013	450	527	85%	0.00
Critical Reading, Male	CB	2013	455	530	86%	0.00
Critical Reading, Female	CB	2013	447	525	85%	0.01
Writing, Joint	CB	2013	443	515	86%	0.00
Writing, Male	CB	2013	439	508	86%	(0.00)
Writing, Female	CB	2013	445	521	85%	0.00
ACT: Average Composite Score	ACT	2013	18.9	22.2	85%	0.01

☆ Updated　★ History Revised　★ Removed Weight in 2013　★ New Series 2014　★ No New Data

2014 EQUALITY INDEX OF HISPANIC AMERICA	Source	Year	Hispanic	White	Index	Diff. ('14–'13)
ENROLLMENT (0.10)						
School Enrollment: ages 3–34, % of Population	Census	2012	56.4	55.6	101%	0.03
Preprimary School Enrollment	Census	2012	57.6	66.7	86%	0.03
3 and 4 Years Old	Census	2012	46.3	56.5	82%	0.08
5 and 6 Years Old	Census	2012	92.1	93.8	98%	(0.02)
7 to 13 Years Old	Census	2012	98.3	97.8	101%	0.01
14 and 15 Years Old	Census	2012	98.5	98.2	100%	0.01
16 and 17 Years Old	Census	2012	94.8	96.4	98%	(0.00)
18 and 19 Years Old	Census	2012	68.1	68.8	99%	0.09
20 and 21 Years Old	Census	2012	49.5	55.9	89%	0.07
22 to 24 Years Old	Census	2012	27.1	30.2	90%	0.18
25 to 29 Years Old	Census	2012	9.4	14.6	64%	(0.05)
30 to 34 Years Old	Census	2012	6.2	6.6	94%	0.36
35 and Over	Census	2012	1.8	1.6	113%	0.20
College Enrollment (Graduate or Undergraduate): Ages 14 and Over, % of Population	Census	2012	8.8	7.1	124%	0.46
14 to 17 Years Old	Census	2012	1.7	1.6	105%	0.09
18 to 19 Years Old	Census	2012	44.2	49.8	89%	0.06
20 to 21 Years Old	Census	2012	46.7	54.4	86%	0.06
22 to 24 Years Old	Census	2012	25.6	29.4	87%	0.17
25 to 29 Years Old	Census	2012	8.5	14.4	59%	(0.08)
30 to 34 Years Old	Census	2012	6.0	6.6	91%	0.35
35 Years Old and Over	Census	2012	1.5	1.6	99%	0.17
College Enrollment Rate As a Percent of All 18- to 24-Year-Old High School Completers, %	NCES	2011	34.8	44.7	78%	0.00
Adult Education Participation, % of Adult Population	NCES	2004–2005	38.0	46.0	83%	0.00
STUDENT STATUS & RISK FACTORS (0.10)						
High School Dropouts: Status Dropouts, % (Not Completed HS and Not Enrolled, Regardless of When Dropped Out)	Census	2009	20.8	9.1	44%	0.00
Children in Poverty, %	Census	2012	33.8	12.3	36%	(0.00)
Children in All Families Below Poverty Level, %	Census	2012	33.3	11.8	35%	0.00
Children in Families Below Poverty Level (Female Householder, No Spouse Present), %	Census	2012	54.5	36.5	67%	0.04
Children With No Parent in the Labor Force, %	AECF	2012	38.0	24.0	63%	0.00
Children (Under 18) With a Disability, %	Census	2012	3.8	4.1	108%	0.02
Public School Students (K-12): Repeated Grade, %	NCES	2007	11.8	8.7	74%	0.00
Public School Students (K-12): Suspended, %	NCES	2003	10.4	8.8	85%	0.00
Public School Students (K-12): Expelled, %	NCES	2003	1.4	1.4	100%	0.00
Center-Based Child Care of Preschool Children, %	NCES	2005	43.4	59.1	136%	0.00
Parental Care Only of Preschool Children, %	NCES	2005	38.0	24.1	158%	0.00
Teacher Stability: Remained in Public School, High Vs. Low Minority Schools, %	NCES	2009	83.4	85.6	97%	0.05
Teacher Stability: Remained in Private School, High Vs. Low Minority Schools, %	NCES	2009	77.0	78.9	98%	0.10

⚹ Updated   ★ History Revised   ⚹ Removed Weight in 2013   ⚹ New Series 2014   ☆ No New Data

2014 EQUALITY INDEX OF HISPANIC AMERICA	Source	Year	Hispanic	White	Index	Diff. ('14–'13)
Zero Days Missed in School Year, % of 10th Graders	NCES	2002	16.5	12.1	137%	0.00
3+ Days Late to School, % of 10th Graders	NCES	2002	46.1	44.4	96%	0.00
Never Cut Classes, % of 10th Graders	NCES	2002	64.6	70.3	92%	0.00
Home Literacy Activities (Age 3 to 5)						
Read to 3 or More Times a Week	NCES	2007	67.6	90.6	75%	0.00
Told a Story at Least Once a Month	NCES	2005	49.8	53.3	93%	0.00
Taught Words or Numbers Three or More Times a Week	NCES	2005	74.3	75.7	98%	0.00
Visited a Library at Least Once in Last Month	NCES	2007	27.0	40.8	66%	0.00
Education Weighted Index					**73.2%**	**0.015**

SOCIAL JUSTICE (10%)

EQUALITY BEFORE THE LAW (0.70)

	Source	Year	Hispanic	White	Index	Diff.
Stopped While Driving, %	BJS	2008	9.1	8.4	92%	0.00
Speeding	BJS	2002	44.4	57.0	128%	0.00
Vehicle Defect	BJS	2002	14.0	8.7	62%	0.00
Roadside Check for Drinking Drivers	BJS	2002	1.6	1.3	81%	0.00
Record Check	BJS	2002	7.8	11.3	145%	0.00
Seatbelt Violation	BJS	2002	5.5	4.4	80%	0.00
Illegal Turn/Lane Change	BJS	2002	5.7	4.5	79%	0.00
Stop Sign/Light Violation	BJS	2002	11.2	6.5	58%	0.00
Other	BJS	2002	6.2	4.0	65%	0.00
Incarceration Rate: Prisoners Per 100,000	BJS	2012	626	253	40%	0.02
Incarceration Rate: Prisoners Per 100,000 People: Male	BJS	2012	1,158	463	40%	0.01
Incarceration Rate: Prisoners Per 100,000 People: Female	BJS	2012	64	49	77%	0.05

VICTIMIZATION & MENTAL ANGUISH (0.20)

	Source	Year	Hispanic	White	Index	Diff.
Homicide Rate Per 100,000: Male	CDC	2010	9.5	3.3	35%	0.02
Homicide Rate Per 100,000: Female	CDC	2010	1.8	1.7	94%	0.13
Hate Crimes Victims, Rate Per 100,000	USDJ	2012	1.0	0.3	33%	0.09
Victims of Violent Crimes, Rate Per 1,000, Persons Age 12 or Older	BJS	2012	24.5	25.2	103%	0.12
Prisoners Under Sentence of Death, rate per 100,000	BJS	2011	1.1	0.9	80%	0.00
High School Students Carrying Weapons on School Property	CDC	2011	5.8	5.1	88%	0.00
High School Students Carrying Weapons Anywhere	CDC	2011	16.2	17.0	105%	0.00
Firearm-Related Death Rates Per 100,000: Males, All Ages	CDC	2007	13.4	16.1	120%	0.00
Ages 1–14	CDC	2007	0.8	0.7	86%	0.00
Ages 15–24	CDC	2007	30.7	13.4	44%	0.00
Ages 25–44	CDC	2007	17.7	18.3	104%	0.00
Ages 25–34	CDC	2007	21.8	18.0	82%	0.00
Ages 35–44	CDC	2007	12.6	18.7	148%	0.00

2014 EQUALITY INDEX OF HISPANIC AMERICA	Source	Year	Hispanic	White	Index	Diff. ('14-'13)
Ages 45–64	CDC	2007	9.7	19.5	202%	0.00
Age 65 and Older	CDC	2007	10.8	27.3	253%	0.00
Firearm-Related Death Rates Per 100,000: Females, All Ages	CDC	2007	1.5	2.9	187%	0.00
Ages 1–14	CDC	2007	0.28	0.31	111%	0.00
Ages 15–24	CDC	2007	2.8	2.5	87%	0.00
Ages 25–44	CDC	2007	2.3	4.1	176%	0.00
Ages 25–34	CDC	2007	2.5	3.4	136%	0.00
Ages 35–44	CDC	2007	2.1	4.6	222%	0.00
Ages 45–64	CDC	2007	1.5	3.9	262%	0.00
Age 65 and Older	CDC	2007	0.6	2.2	393%	0.00
Social Justice Weighted Index					**66.1%**	**0.027**

CIVIC ENGAGEMENT (10%)						
DEMOCRATIC PROCESS (0.4)						
Registered Voters, % of Citizen Population	Census	2012	58.7	73.7	80%	0.04
Actually Voted, % of Citizen Population	Census	2012	48.0	64.1	75%	0.11
COMMUNITY PARTICIPATION (0.3)						
Percent of Population Volunteering for Military Reserves, %	USDD	2010	0.4	1.0	40%	0.00
Volunteerism, %	BLS	2012	15.2	27.8	55%	0.02
Civic and Political	BLS	2012	3.7	5.7	65%	(0.02)
Educational or Youth Service	BLS	2012	31.2	25.1	124%	(0.18)
Environmental or Animal Care	BLS	2012	1.9	2.8	68%	0.22
Hospital or Other Health	BLS	2012	6.5	8.2	79%	0.04
Public Safety	BLS	2012	0.8	1.3	62%	0.26
Religious	BLS	2012	35.0	32.3	108%	0.05
Social or Community Service	BLS	2012	12.3	14.3	86%	0.14
Unpaid Volunteering of Young Adults	NCES	2000	30.7	32.2	95%	0.00
COLLECTIVE BARGAINING (0.2)						
Members of Unions, % of Employed	BLS	2012	9.8	11.1	88%	0.00
Represented By Unions, % of Employed	BLS	2012	10.9	12.3	89%	0.00
GOVERNMENTAL EMPLOYMENT (0.1)						
Federal Executive Branch (Nonpostal) Employment, % of Adult Population	OPM	2008	0.4	0.8	52%	0.00
State and Local Government Employment, %	EEOC	2009	1.8	2.5	73%	0.00
Civic Engagement Weighted Index					**71.2%**	**0.032**

Note: Weights were adjusted proportionally within the five categories to account for missing Hispanic data.

SOURCE	ACRONYM
American Community Survey	ACS
American College Testing	ACT
Annie E. Casey Foundation	AECF
U.S. Bureau of Justice Statistics	BJS
U.S. Bureau of Labor Statistics	BLS
College Board	CB
Centers for Disease Control and Prevention	CDC
CDC Youth Risk Behavior Survey	CDC YRBS
U.S. Census Bureau	Census
U.S. Census Bureau, Survey of Income & Program Participation	Census SIPP
Current Population Survey: Annual Social and Economic Supplement	CPS ASEC
Employee Benefit Research Institute	EBRI
U.S. Equal Employment Opportunity Commission	EEOC
The Education Trust	ET
Home Mortgage Disclosure Act	HMDA
National Archive of Criminal Justice Data	NACJD
National Collegiate Athletic Association	NCAA
National Center for Education Statistics	NCES
National Center for Juvenile Justice	NCJJ
National Telecommunications and Information Administration	NTIA
Office of Personal Management	OPM
Education Law Center, Is School Funding Fair?	SFF
Substance Abuse & Mental Health Services Administration	SAMHSA
SRI International	SRI
U.S. Department of Defense	USDD
U.S. Department of Justice	USDJ

METRO AREA HISPANIC-WHITE
UNEMPLOYMENT EQUALITY

RANKING OF METRO AREAS FROM MOST TO LEAST EQUAL	Rank	Hispanic Unemployment Rate	White Unemployment Rate	Hispanic-White Index
Memphis, TN–MS–AR	1	3.8	6.5	171.1%
Jacksonville, FL	2	8.5	9.6	112.9%
Indianapolis–Carmel, IN	3	6.1	6.8	111.5%
Nashville–Davidson–Murfreesboro–Franklin, TN	4	6.3	6.8	107.9%
Madison, WI*	5	4.5	4.4	97.8%
North Port–Bradenton–Sarasota, FL	6	10.7	10.3	96.3%
Oxnard–Thousand Oaks–Ventura, CA	7	10.3	9.9	96.1%
Poughkeepsie–Newburgh–Middletown, NY	8	8.9	8.4	94.4%
Las Vegas–Paradise, NV	9	12.7	11.7	92.1%
Tulsa, OK	10	6.9	6.3	91.3%
Lakeland–Winter Haven, FL	11	13.5	12.1	89.6%
Knoxville, TN*	12	7.0	6.1	87.1%
Miami–Fort Lauderdale–Pompano Beach, FL	13	10.4	8.9	85.6%
Dallas–Fort Worth–Arlington, TX	14	7.5	6.4	85.3%
Atlanta–Sandy Springs–Marietta, GA	15	9.6	8.1	84.4%
Portland–Vancouver–Hillsboro, OR–WA	16	10.9	9.1	83.5%
Columbus, OH	17	7.2	5.9	81.9%
Stockton, CA	18	16.7	13.5	80.8%
El Paso, TX	19	10.6	8.5	80.2%
Orlando–Kissimmee–Sanford, FL	20	11.9	9.5	79.8%
Riverside–San Bernardino–Ontario, CA	21	15.3	12.2	79.7%
Fresno, CA	22	16.6	13.2	79.5%
Houston–Sugar Land–Baytown, TX	23	8.2	6.5	79.3%
Los Angeles–Long Beach–Santa Ana, CA	24	12.2	9.4	77.0%
Modesto, CA	25	19.6	15.0	76.5%
St. Louis, MO–IL	26	9.1	6.9	75.8%
Tampa–St. Petersburg–Clearwater, FL	27	12.7	9.6	75.6%
Palm Bay–Melbourne–Titusville, FL*	28	10.9	8.2	75.2%
Deltona–Daytona Beach–Ormond Beach, FL*	29	9.4	7.0	74.5%
Sacramento–Arden–Arcade–Roseville, CA	30	15.1	11.1	73.5%
Raleigh–Cary, NC	31	7.9	5.8	73.4%
Cape Coral–Fort Myers, FL	32	15.0	10.9	72.7%
Provo–Orem, UT*	33	7.3	5.3	72.6%
Charlotte–Gastonia–Rock Hill, NC–SC	34	11.2	8.0	71.4%
Seattle–Tacoma–Bellevue, WA	35	9.9	7.0	70.7%
Denver–Aurora–Broomfield, CO	36	9.2	6.5	70.7%
Phoenix–Mesa–Glendale, AZ	37	10.5	7.4	70.5%
Austin–Round Rock–San Marcos, TX	38	8.4	5.9	70.2%
Youngstown–Warren–Boardman, OH–PA*	39	11.5	8.0	69.6%

★ 25 Areas With Largest Hispanic Populations   **Bold:** Higher than U.S. Hispanic-White Index

RANKING OF METRO AREAS FROM MOST TO LEAST EQUAL	Rank	Hispanic Unemployment Rate	White Unemployment Rate	Hispanic–White Index
Colorado Springs, CO	40	11.9	8.2	68.9%
Baltimore-Towson, MD	41	8.9	6.1	68.5%
Oklahoma City, OK	42	6.9	4.7	68.1%
San Diego-Carlsbad-San Marcos, CA	43	12.2	8.2	67.2%
Wichita, KS	44	9.4	6.1	64.9%
Tucson, AZ	45	13.1	8.5	64.9%
San Antonio-New Braunfels, TX	46	9.1	5.9	64.8%
Washington-Arlington-Alexandria, D.C.-VA-MD-WV	47	6.6	4.2	63.6%
Chicago-Joliet-Naperville, IL-IN-WI	48	12.0	7.6	63.3%
New York-Northern New Jersey-Long Island, NY-NJ-PA	49	11.4	7.2	63.2%
Omaha-Council Bluffs, NE-IA	50	8.1	5.1	63.0%
Detroit-Warren-Livonia, MI	51	14.3	9.0	62.9%
Kansas City, MO-KS	52	10.2	6.4	62.7%
San Francisco-Oakland-Fremont, CA	53	10.9	6.7	61.5%
New Orleans-Metairie-Kenner, LA	54	11.0	6.6	60.0%
Albuquerque, NM	55	10.9	6.5	59.6%
Allentown-Bethlehem-Easton, PA-NJ	56	13.3	7.9	59.4%
San Jose-Sunnyvale-Santa Clara, CA	57	12.3	7.2	58.5%
New Haven-Milford, CT	58	15.7	9.1	58.0%
Bakersfield-Delano, CA	59	16.9	9.7	57.4%
Bridgeport-Stamford-Norwalk, CT	60	12.7	7.2	56.7%
Salt Lake City, UT	61	11.3	6.3	55.8%
Providence-New Bedford-Fall River, RI-MA	62	16.0	8.8	55.0%
Boise City-Nampa, ID	63	13.1	7.2	55.0%
Philadelphia-Camden-Wilmington, PA-NJ-DE-MD	64	14.6	8.0	54.8%
McAllen-Edinburg-Mission, TX*	65	10.3	5.6	54.4%
Worcester, MA	66	14.4	7.7	53.5%
Milwaukee-Waukesha-West Allis, WI	67	10.5	5.6	53.3%
Ogden-Clearfield, UT	68	7.9	4.2	53.2%
Honolulu, HI	69	11.9	6.3	52.9%
Harrisburg-Carlisle, PA*	70	9.3	4.8	51.6%
Des Moines-West Des Moines, IA*	71	8.4	4.3	51.2%
Scranton-Wilkes-Barre, PA*	72	12.5	6.3	50.4%
Grand Rapids-Wyoming, MI	73	15.2	7.6	50.0%
Minneapolis-St. Paul-Bloomington, MN-WI	74	10.5	5.2	49.5%
Virginia Beach-Norfolk-Newport News, VA-NC	75	13.2	6.5	49.2%
Syracuse, NY*	76	13.1	6.3	48.1%
Rochester, NY	77	14.5	6.9	47.6%
Boston-Cambridge-Quincy, MA-NH	78	14.2	6.7	47.2%
Richmond, VA	79	12.9	5.8	45.0%
Hartford-West Hartford-East Hartford, CT	80	16.2	7.1	43.8%
Cleveland-Elyria-Mentor, OH	81	16.7	7.0	41.9%
Springfield, MA	82	19.3	7.7	39.9%
Lancaster, PA*	83	12.5	4.7	37.6%

Source: Census ACS 2012 1-year estimates (unless otherwise noted); Black is Black or African American alone, not Hispanic
*ACS 2010 5-year estimates

METRO AREA HISPANIC-WHITE
INCOME EQUALITY

RANKING OF METRO AREAS FROM MOST TO LEAST EQUAL	Rank	Hispanic Median Household Income, Dollars	White Median Household Income, Dollars	Hispanic-White Index
Lakeland–Winter Haven, FL	1	39,434	44,014	89.6%
Palm Bay–Melbourne–Titusville, FL*	2	45,445	51,112	88.9%
Jacksonville, FL	3	45,894	54,196	84.7%
Deltona–Daytona Beach–Ormond Beach, FL*	4	37,934	46,556	81.5%
Riverside–San Bernardino–Ontario, CA	5	45,912	57,252	80.2%
Honolulu, HI	6	58,161	73,519	79.1%
Modesto, CA	7	40,167	52,907	75.9%
Las Vegas–Paradise, NV	8	41,247	54,517	75.7%
North Port–Bradenton–Sarasota, FL	9	37,514	50,262	74.6%
Stockton, CA	10	43,185	58,281	74.1%
Tampa–St. Petersburg–Clearwater, FL	11	35,662	48,421	73.6%
Youngstown–Warren–Boardman, OH–PA*	12	32,381	44,334	73.0%
Madison, WI*	13	45,514	62,585	72.7%
Detroit–Warren–Livonia, MI	14	41,046	57,533	71.3%
Tulsa, OK	15	36,809	52,119	70.6%
Knoxville, TN*	16	33,820	48,201	70.2%
Virginia Beach–Norfolk–Newport News, VA–NC	17	45,590	65,141	70.0%
Oxnard–Thousand Oaks–Ventura, CA	18	54,751	78,457	69.8%
Wichita, KS	19	36,457	52,324	69.7%
Baltimore–Towson, MD	20	55,983	80,487	69.6%
Provo–Orem, UT*	21	40,923	59,151	69.2%
Miami–Fort Lauderdale–Pompano Beach, FL	22	40,482	59,039	68.6%
Colorado Springs, CO	23	40,556	59,355	68.3%
Omaha–Council Bluffs, NE–IA	24	40,038	59,094	67.8%
Richmond, VA	25	45,509	67,277	67.6%
Albuquerque, NM	26	37,931	56,231	67.5%
San Diego–Carlsbad–San Marcos, CA	27	44,746	66,416	67.4%
Kansas City, MO–KS	28	41,000	60,883	67.3%
Phoenix–Mesa–Glendale, AZ	29	38,743	57,760	67.1%
Poughkeepsie–Newburgh–Middletown, NY	30	47,502	71,218	66.7%
Orlando–Kissimmee–Sanford, FL	31	35,830	53,763	66.6%
Portland–Vancouver–Hillsboro, OR–WA	32	39,795	59,725	66.6%
St. Louis, MO–IL	33	39,026	59,607	65.5%
Seattle–Tacoma–Bellevue, WA	34	45,799	69,998	65.4%
Tucson, AZ	35	33,643	51,546	65.3%
Grand Rapids–Wyoming, MI	36	35,302	54,106	65.2%
Bakersfield–Delano, CA	37	37,135	57,186	64.9%
Chicago–Joliet–Naperville, IL–IN–WI	38	45,884	70,890	64.7%
El Paso, TX	39	35,673	55,239	64.6%

★ 25 Areas With Largest Hispanic Populations **Bold:** Higher than U.S. Hispanic-White Index

RANKING OF METRO AREAS FROM MOST TO LEAST EQUAL	Rank	Hispanic Median Household Income, Dollars	White Median Household Income, Dollars	Hispanic-White Index
San Antonio-New Braunfels, TX	40	42,045	65,663	64.0%
Des Moines-West Des Moines, IA*	41	38,639	60,385	64.0%
New Orleans-Metairie-Kenner, LA	42	37,291	58,317	63.9%
Sacramento-Arden-Arcade-Roseville, CA	43	41,251	64,847	63.6%
Nashville-Davidson-Murfreesboro-Franklin, TN	44	35,960	56,706	63.4%
Indianapolis-Carmel, IN	45	38,215	60,286	63.4%
McAllen-Edinburg-Mission, TX*	46	29,579	46,737	63.3%
Syracuse, NY*	47	33,420	52,963	63.1%
Charlotte-Gastonia-Rock Hill, NC-SC	48	39,348	62,877	62.6%
Boise City-Nampa, ID	49	31,681	50,710	62.5%
Cape Coral-Fort Myers, FL	50	32,047	51,340	62.4%
Fresno, CA	51	34,157	54,974	62.1%
Allentown-Bethlehem-Easton, PA-NJ	52	36,034	58,603	61.5%
Salt Lake City, UT	53	38,796	63,609	61.0%
Austin-Round Rock-San Marcos, TX	54	42,175	69,244	60.9%
Los Angeles-Long Beach-Santa Ana, CA	55	44,868	73,865	60.7%
Oklahoma City, OK	56	33,075	54,683	60.5%
Columbus, OH	57	35,682	59,036	60.4%
Memphis, TN-MS-AR	58	35,541	58,819	60.4%
Denver-Aurora-Broomfield, CO	59	41,916	69,410	60.4%
Washington-Arlington-Alexandria, D.C.-VA-MD-WV	60	63,779	106,597	59.8%
Minneapolis-St. Paul-Bloomington, MN-WI	61	41,776	71,376	58.5%
Scranton-Wilkes-Barre, PA*	62	25,368	44,065	57.6%
Dallas-Fort Worth-Arlington, TX	63	40,278	70,669	57.0%
San Francisco-Oakland-Fremont, CA	64	51,420	90,452	56.8%
Atlanta-Sandy Springs-Marietta, GA	65	38,064	67,196	56.6%
Ogden-Clearfield, UT	66	36,463	64,753	56.3%
Milwaukee-Waukesha-West Allis, WI	67	34,894	62,100	56.2%
Houston-Sugar Land-Baytown, TX	68	42,160	75,201	56.1%
Harrisburg-Carlisle, PA*	69	32,800	58,733	55.8%
Cleveland-Elyria-Mentor, OH	70	30,559	55,084	55.5%
Rochester, NY	71	30,486	55,002	55.4%
San Jose-Sunnyvale-Santa Clara, CA	72	55,302	99,899	55.4%
Lancaster, PA*	73	30,975	57,240	54.1%
Raleigh-Cary, NC	74	35,592	69,730	51.0%
Philadelphia-Camden-Wilmington, PA-NJ-DE-MD	75	36,175	71,122	50.9%
New York-Northern New Jersey-Long Island, NY-NJ-PA	76	41,101	81,865	50.2%
Bridgeport-Stamford-Norwalk, CT	77	48,968	97,654	50.1%
Providence-New Bedford-Fall River, RI-MA	78	29,165	59,004	49.4%
Boston-Cambridge-Quincy, MA-NH	79	38,505	78,551	49.0%
New Haven-Milford, CT	80	33,979	69,617	48.8%
Worcester, MA	81	31,506	67,078	47.0%
Hartford-West Hartford-East Hartford, CT	82	32,113	75,265	42.7%
Springfield, MA	83	20,762	58,549	35.5%

Source: Census ACS 2012 1-year estimates (unless otherwise noted); Black is Black or African American alone, not Hispanic
ACS 2010 5-year estimates

BALTIMORE

**MAYOR STEPHANIE
RAWLINGS-BLAKE**

BALTIMORE, MD

IN BALTIMORE CITY, MORE THAN 1 IN 5 (21.7%) AFRICAN AMERICAN RESIDENTS LIVE IN POVERTY. THE NUMBERS ARE EVEN WORSE WHEN WE LOOK AT JUST OUR KIDS, WITH THE NUMBERS SHOWING THAT ALMOST 1 IN EVERY 3 (29.1%) AFRICAN AMERICAN CHILDREN AND TEENS ARE LIVING IN POVERTY. THOUGH BALTIMORE'S POVERTY NUMBERS ARE LOWER THAN THE NATIONAL AVERAGE, THE OPPORTUNITY GAP IS WIDENING. AS A NATION, WE NEED TO DO MORE TO ERADICATE POVERTY AND TO REDUCE ECONOMIC INEQUALITY.

The need for persistence and audacity was more than apparent in our efforts to rehabilitate Baltimore's schools—some of the oldest in Maryland, serving many of our state's poorest citizens. It was not easy, but I could not give up. I insisted on an education system that could give our children opportunity and the hope to achieve their dreams. Through perseverance, innovative partnerships, and outside-the-box thinking, Baltimore City has been able to secure $1.1 billion for school construction and renovation over the next 10 years. It is a revolutionary victory. But a quality education system is just the beginning.

To conquer poverty, America's urban centers must develop comprehensive workforce pipelines to equip all of our citizens for the jobs of the future. Many sectors—even blue-collar sectors that once provided jobs for a relatively unskilled workforce—now require complicated and specific training in science, technology, engineering, and math. Tragically, our communities of color are often left behind.

That is why we are putting resources directly into the communities that need them most. Through the Mayor's Office of Employment Development (MOED), Baltimore City has partnered with local grassroots organizations to provide Community Job Hubs—centers of learning and resource. They are "just around the corner"—easily accessible, even for residents who do not own a vehicle, which includes 26 percent of Baltimore's African American residents—and offer professional training, job search and resume assistance, and digital resources often unavailable to job seekers living in poverty.

I am proud of these accomplishments, but I recognize that a well-trained workforce only gets us halfway there. As mayor, I'm also working to ensure that when Baltimore's residents are ready to join the workforce, jobs are there for them. Eradicating poverty requires creating economic opportunity. Accordingly, I have worked to bring major construction and development to Baltimore, and I have made local hiring a priority.

When planning was underway for the Horseshoe Casino Baltimore, we developed a memorandum of understanding to require the casino to work collaboratively with the city to promote local hiring for the 1,700 new jobs created by the project. The MOU outlines a plan that will generate significant community benefit—complete with a community recruitment coordinator, priority hiring for city residents, and training and outreach around MOED's Community Job Hubs. When the casino opens, the biggest winners will be the city residents who receive the opportunity to lift themselves out of poverty. Similar plans are underway for other major projects in Baltimore, like the $1 billion Harbor Point development, which is expected to generate roughly 7,175 construction jobs and 9,158 additional, permanent jobs.

Baltimore will continue to invest in efforts like our Food Policy Initiative that eliminate food deserts and ensure the availability of proper nutrition for our residents; efforts like Vacants to Value that eliminate urban blight citywide and increase property values in our poorest communities, and efforts like our new recreation center model, a direct result of the City's commitment to expanding programming like camps and after-school programs.

Poverty is a deep-rooted ill, permeated with inequity, and it will take a focused, concerted assault on all fronts to excise it. We must think outside the box, and be bold as we confront the challenges that lie in our path. I am committed to the fight. ★

BALTIMORE

	Black	Hispanic	White	BALTIMORE-TOWSON, MD Black-White Index	Hispanic-White Index	UNITED STATES Black-White Index	Hispanic-White Index
ECONOMICS							
Median Household Income (Real), Dollars	43,663	55,983	80,487	54%	70%	60%	71%
POVERTY							
Population Living Below Poverty Line, %	21.7	14.5	6.2	29%	43%	39%	43%
Population Living Below Poverty Line (Under 18), %	29.1	17.8	5.9	20%	33%	32%	36%
Population Living Below Poverty Line (18–64), %	19.2	13.2	6.5	34%	49%	41%	45%
Population Living Below Poverty Line (65 and Older), %	18.4	6.1	5.2	28%	85%	37%	33%
EMPLOYMENT ISSUES							
Unemployment Rate, %	15.1	8.9	6.1	40%	69%	50%	71%
Labor Force Participation Rate, %	64.5	74.0	67.4	96%	110%	96%	104%
HOUSING & WEALTH							
Home Ownership Rate, %	45.2	47.7	76.5	59%	62%	60%	63%
Median Home Value, Dollars	178,600	251,400	293,800	61%	86%	65%	86%
TRANSPORTATION							
Car Ownership, %	74.0	87.4	94.0	79%	93%	80%	88%
Means of Transportation to Work: Drive Alone, %	68.5	62.2	81.0	85%	77%	90%	86%
Means of Transportation to Work: Public Transportation, %	16.0	10.1	2.6	16%	26%	26%	38%
EDUCATION							
ATTAINMENT							
Educational Attainment: at Least High School (25 Yrs. and Over), % of Population	84.2	71.0	92.6	91%	77%	92%	70%
Educational Attainment: at Least Bachelor's (25 Yrs. and Over), % of Population	21.4	25.7	41.4	52%	62%	62%	42%
Educational Attainment: Graduate or Professional Degree (25 Yrs. and Over), % of Population	9.3	9.2	17.9	52%	51%	60%	34%
STUDENT STATUS AND RISK FACTORS							
Children in All Families Below Poverty Level, %	23.4	14.7	5.8	25%	40%	31%	35%
Children in Families Below Poverty Level (Female Householder, No Spouse Present), %	35.3	29.3	19.8	56%	68%	68%	67%
Children (Under 18) With a Disability, %	5.0	3.5	3.3	66%	94%	80%	93%
HEALTH							
People Without Health Insurance, %	10.8	29.2	5.7	53%	20%	58%	38%
People With Private Health Insurance, %	57.3	48.7	83.9	68%	58%	68%	58%
SOCIAL JUSTICE							
Incarceration Rate: Prisoners in Jail Per 100,000 People	707.7	84.3	105.6	15%	125%	18%	40%

Source: Census ACS 2012 1 year estimates (unless otherwise noted); Black is Black or African American alone, not Hispanic. Incarceration rates are IHS calculations, using Bureau of Justice Statistics, Annual Survey of Jails, 2011 and Census population estimates

BALTIMORE POPULATION DEMOGRAPHICS

★ Black **28%** ★ Hispanic **5%**
★ White **59%** ★ Other **8%**

J. HOWARD HENDERSON
PRESIDENT, GREATER BALTIMORE URBAN LEAGUE

Black-White Equality Index: Baltimore vs. United States

★ *Baltimore* ★ *United States*

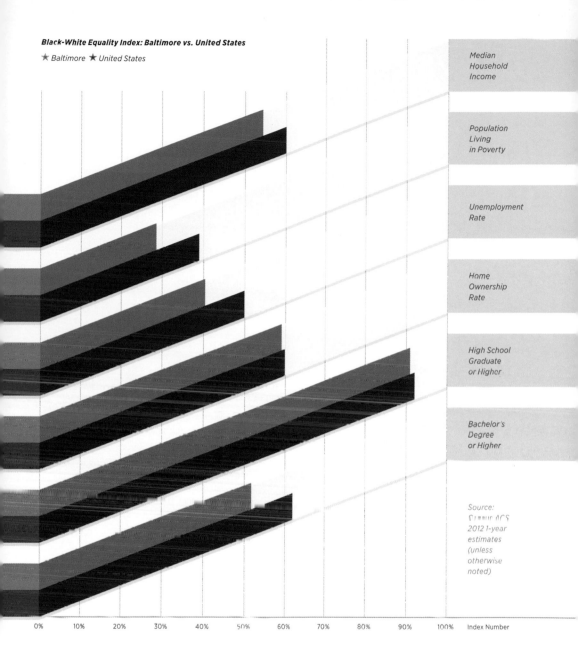

Median Household Income

Population Living in Poverty

Unemployment Rate

Home Ownership Rate

High School Graduate or Higher

Bachelor's Degree or Higher

Source: Census ACS 2012 1-year estimates (unless otherwise noted)

0% 10% 20% 30% 40% 50% 60% 70% 80% 90% 100%   Index Number

THE MEDIAN HOUSEHOLD INCOME FOR BLACKS IN BALTIMORE IS $43,633

THE MEDIAN HOUSEHOLD INCOME FOR HISPANICS IN BALTIMORE IS $55,983

THE MEDIAN HOUSEHOLD INCOME FOR WHITES IN BALTIMORE IS $80,487

⊚ NATIONAL URBAN LEAGUE

DENVER

MAYOR MICHAEL B. HANCOCK

DENVER, CO

IN 1963, THIS NATION'S OVERLOOKED AND UNDERSERVED COMMUNITIES MARCHED ON WASHINGTON TO DEMAND EQUAL ACCESS TO GOOD PAYING JOBS, HEALTHY FOODS AND ACTIVITIES, AFFORDABLE HOUSING

Our country has come a long way since then, but poverty continues to plague our communities of color. We must create more opportunity by addressing low wages and low workforce participation.

President Obama is right; we are still leaving far too many people behind, particularly our minority and immigrant populations. We must do everything we can to inspire hope in our young people and break the cycle of poverty.

In Denver, more than 100,000 residents live below the poverty line, and 65 percent of families live paycheck to paycheck. One of the ways to address this is to invest in our young people by preparing them for success from cradle to career.

Beginning with our youngest and most vulnerable, Denver launched a program to prepare students for the critical transition between preschool and kindergarten so they start school ready to learn and ready to read. The goal is to close the achievement gap before it begins by improving high quality early childhood education in some of our most economically challenged neighborhoods.

The value of healthy and positive after-school activities grows as a child does. Our MYDenver card offers Denver's 90,000 school-age children free access to all of the city's 26 recreation centers and 29 swimming pools. The card already acts as a library card, and we're planning to expand it to include access to museums and other cultural institutions, perhaps even the city's public transportation system. The city also offers free, healthy snacks and suppers at rec centers in low-income areas.

To prepare young people to compete and succeed in the 21st century, Denver's Youth Services has expanded its reach to offer at-risk youth training for middle skill jobs. These kids are learning a trade that will help them make a liveable wage in growth industries such as healthcare, manufacturing and information technology—each of which offers plenty of upward career mobility.

Denver is also reconfiguring its ordinance around certified minority and women-owned businesses to increase capacity and sophistication in areas such as construction and professional services. Research shows that ethnic businesses are more likely to hire the same ethnicity. By helping such businesses succeed, we work to address low workforce participation among minorities.

By preparing our kids to succeed, supporting our businesses and bringing opportunity back to our communities, Denver is working to break the cycle and prepare our kids to compete in the 21st century. ★

DENVER

	DENVER-AURORA-BROOMFIELD, CO					UNITED STATES	
	Black	Hispanic	White	Black-White Index	Hispanic-White Index	Black-White Index	Hispanic-White Index
ECONOMICS							
Median Household Income (Real), Dollars	37,460	41,916	69,410	54%	60%	60%	71%
POVERTY							
Population Living Below Poverty Line, %	31.2	23.1	7.5	24%	33%	39%	43%
Population Living Below Poverty Line (Under 18), %	46.0	29.2	7.1	15%	24%	32%	36%
Population Living Below Poverty Line (18–64), %	26.5	19.8	8.1	31%	41%	41%	45%
Population Living Below Poverty Line (65 and Older), %	16.0	19.5	4.8	30%	25%	37%	33%
EMPLOYMENT ISSUES							
Unemployment Rate, %	14.4	9.2	6.5	45%	71%	50%	71%
Labor Force Participation Rate, %	68.2	70.0	71.3	96%	98%	96%	104%
HOUSING & WEALTH							
Home Ownership Rate, %	39.4	43.7	68.4	58%	64%	60%	63%
Median Home Value, Dollars	188,600	182,000	261,500	72%	70%	65%	86%
TRANSPORTATION							
Car Ownership, %	84.9	90.7	95.0	89%	96%	80%	88%
Means of Transportation to Work: Drive Alone, %	67.2	70.6	77.8	86%	91%	90%	86%
Means of Transportation to Work: Public Transportation, %	15.0	6.1	3.2	21%	53%	26%	38%
EDUCATION							
ATTAINMENT							
Educational Attainment: at Least High School (25 Yrs. and Over), % of Population	89.6	66.3	96.2	93%	69%	92%	70%
Educational Attainment: at Least Bachelor's (25 Yrs. and Over), % of Population	25.8	12.7	47.3	55%	27%	62%	42%
Educational Attainment: Graduate or Professional Degree (25 Yrs. and Over), % of Population	10.1	4.0	16.8	60%	24%	60%	34%
STUDENT STATUS AND RISK FACTORS							
Children in All Families Below Poverty Level, %	32.8	27.5	6.9	21%	25%	31%	35%
Children in Families Below Poverty Level (Female Householder, No Spouse Present), %	44.5	38.6	20.2	45%	52%	68%	67%
Children (Under 18) With a Disability, %	2.7	4.0	2.9	107%	73%	80%	93%
HEALTH							
People Without Health Insurance, %	17.5	28.6	9.9	57%	35%	58%	38%
People With Private Health Insurance, %	45.8	43.2	79.5	58%	54%	68%	58%
SOCIAL JUSTICE							
Incarceration Rate: Prisoners in Jail Per 100,000 People	NA	NA	NA	NA	NA	18%	40%

Source: Census ACS 2012 1 year estimates (unless otherwise noted); Black is Black or African American alone, not Hispanic.
NA: Not Available

DENVER POPULATION DEMOGRAPHICS

★ Black **6%** ★ Hispanic **23%**
★ White **65%** ★ Other **6%**

URBAN LEAGUE OF METROPOLITAN DENVER

Hispanic-White Equality Index: Denver vs. United States

★ Denver ★ United States

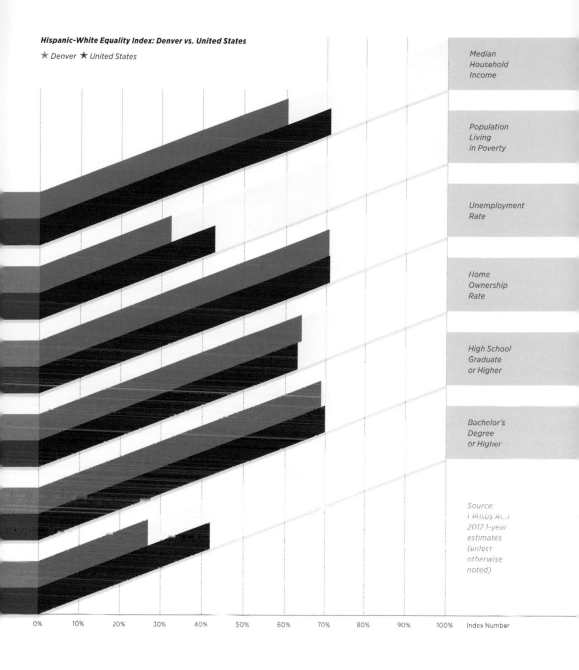

Median Household Income	
Population Living in Poverty	
Unemployment Rate	
Home Ownership Rate	
High School Graduate or Higher	
Bachelor's Degree or Higher	

Source: Census ACS 2012 1-year estimates (unless otherwise noted)

0%   10%   20%   30%   40%   50%   60%   70%   80%   90%   100%   Index Number

---

15.0% OF BLACKS IN DENVER TAKE PUBLIC TRANSPORTATION TO WORK

6.1% OF HISPANICS IN DENVER TAKE PUBLIC TRANSPORTATION TO WORK

3.2% OF WHITES IN DENVER TAKE PUBLIC TRANSPORTATION TO WORK

JACKSONVILLE

MAYOR ALVIN BROWN

JACKSONVILLE, FL

AS MAYOR, I BELIEVE THAT CREATING POSITIVE OPPORTUNITIES AND SUPPORT FOR THE NEXT GENERATION IS ESSENTIAL TO MAKING JACKSONVILLE A SAFER, MORE PROSPEROUS AND VIBRANT COMMUNITY FOR EVERYONE.

That is why a comprehensive initiative to promote youth opportunity and empowerment is central to my administration. We created the city's first-ever education commissioner position to partner and advocate on youth development and education. Supported by public-private partnerships at no cost to taxpayers, the position is staffed by an education leader through an executive-on-loan agreement.

Specific elements of our youth opportunity/ empowerment initiative, which I announced at our annual Martin Luther King, Jr. Day Breakfast, include:

// SUMMER JOBS
Involving employers from the private, public and nonprofit sectors, this program offers part-time and full-time work experiences to promising young people who otherwise might not have the opportunity. In 2013, nearly 700 youth received job readiness training, coaching and real-world work experience. As mayor, I have seen what a difference it can make when teens spend their summer on the job instead of on the street.

// YOUNG LEADERS ADVISORY COUNCIL
We created this Council, composed of diverse high school juniors and seniors, to help develop the future leaders of our community. These young people learn about city government and effective citizenship so they can make a positive difference as young leaders. They also share ideas with me and other city officials on youth issues.

// LEARN2EARN
This program offers high school students the chance to experience life on local college campuses with the goal of inspiring them to pursue higher education. It is designed for rising sophomores and juniors who would be the first in their families to go to college. At no cost to their families, the students have a week-long immersion experience to learn what it takes to be a college student. They live on campus, take part in classes, work on-campus jobs and receive college application counseling.

// MAYOR'S MENTORS
Working with businesses, community organizations and the school district, this program recruits, trains and places adults as in-school mentors. More than 600 adults have committed to at least one hour per week to serve as role models. They work one-on-one in the classroom with students and serve as a positive, encouraging influence.

// JUVENILE JUSTICE
The city provides support to increase the number of participants in the Teen Court, a restorative justice program which is a constructive alternative to arrest and detention for nonviolent misdemeanor offenses. Teen Court holds teens accountable for nonviolent misdemeanor offenses without the need for incarceration. We also improved the mental health and substance abuse response for juvenile offenders, so they receive immediate referrals and access to services before their first court dates.

There is no single solution for youth opportunity and empowerment, and government cannot do it alone. That is why our youth initiative takes a comprehensive approach with public-private partnerships as part of a broader commitment to job creation and economic opportunity for all residents of Jacksonville. ★

JACKSONVILLE

	JACKSONVILLE, FL					UNITED STATES	
	Black	Hispanic	White	Black-White Index	Hispanic-White Index	Black-White Index	Hispanic-White Index
ECONOMICS							
Median Household Income (Real), Dollars	30,622	45,894	54,196	57%	85%	60%	71%
POVERTY							
Population Living Below Poverty Line, %	28.8	17.8	11.3	39%	64%	39%	43%
Population Living Below Poverty Line (Under 18), %	38.5	25.3	13.9	36%	55%	32%	36%
Population Living Below Poverty Line (18–64), %	26.1	15.4	11.7	45%	76%	41%	45%
Population Living Below Poverty Line (65 and Older), %	17.0	6.2	6.7	39%	108%	37%	33%
EMPLOYMENT ISSUES							
Unemployment Rate, %	19.6	8.5	9.6	49%	113%	50%	71%
Labor Force Participation Rate, %	63.7	65.8	62.3	102%	106%	96%	104%
HOUSING & WEALTH							
Home Ownership Rate, %	47.6	54.4	71.6	67%	76%	60%	63%
Median Home Value, Dollars	104,700	150,300	155,700	67%	97%	65%	86%
TRANSPORTATION							
Car Ownership, %	84.0	96.5	95.2	88%	101%	80%	88%
Means of Transportation to Work: Drive Alone, %	79.3	77.0	82.1	97%	94%	90%	86%
Means of Transportation to Work: Public Transportation, %	4.3	1.3	0.5	12%	39%	26%	38%
EDUCATION							
ATTAINMENT							
Educational Attainment: at Least High School (25 Yrs. and Over), % of Population	84.5	86.0	90.1	94%	95%	92%	70%
Educational Attainment: at Least Bachelor's (25 Yrs. and Over), % of Population	16.3	26.6	30.0	54%	89%	62%	42%
Educational Attainment: Graduate or Professional Degree (25 Yrs. and Over), % of Population	4.7	8.8	9.4	50%	94%	60%	34%
STUDENT STATUS AND RISK FACTORS							
Children in All Families Below Poverty Level, %	31.8	19.1	12.4	39%	65%	31%	35%
Children in Families Below Poverty Level (Female Householder, No Spouse Present), %	47.8	48.2	31.5	66%	65%	68%	67%
Children (Under 18) With a Disability, %	3.6	4.7	4.7	131%	100%	80%	93%
HEALTH							
People Without Health Insurance, %	19.5	22.8	13.9	71%	61%	58%	38%
People With Private Health Insurance, %	48.8	54.7	70.3	69%	78%	68%	58%
SOCIAL JUSTICE							
Incarceration Rate: Prisoners in Jail Per 100,000 People	1,286.4	11.8	329.6	26%	2,782%	18%	40%

Source: Census ACS 2012 1 year estimates (unless otherwise noted); Black is Black or African American alone, not Hispanic. Incarceration rates are IHS calculations, using Bureau of Justice Statistics, Annual Survey of Jails, 2011 and Census population estimates

JACKSONVILLE POPULATION DEMOGRAPHICS

★ Black **21%** ★ Hispanic **7%**
☆ White **65%** ★ Other **7%**

RICHARD D. DANFORD, JR., PH.D.
PRESIDENT, JACKSONVILLE
URBAN LEAGUE

Black-White Equality Index: Jacksonville vs. United States

★ _Jacksonville_ ★ _United States_

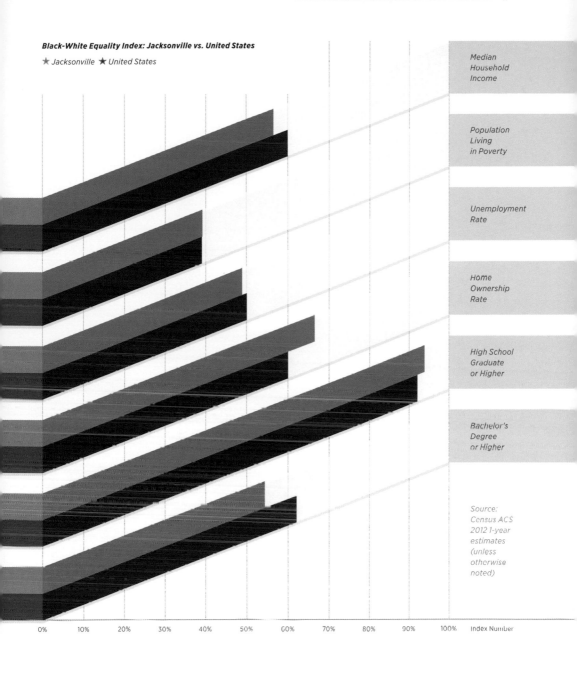

Median Household Income

Population Living in Poverty

Unemployment Rate

Home Ownership Rate

High School Graduate or Higher

Bachelor's Degree or Higher

Source: Census ACS 2012 1-year estimates (unless otherwise noted)

0% 10% 20% 30% 40% 50% 60% 70% 80% 90% 100% Index Number

19.5% OF BLACKS IN JACKSONVILLE LACK HEALTH INSURANCE

22.8% OF HISPANICS IN JACKSONVILLE LACK HEALTH INSURANCE

13.9% OF WHITES IN JACKSONVILLE LACK HEALTH INSURANCE

⊕ NATIONAL URBAN LEAGUE

MEMPHIS

MAYOR AC WHARTON

MEMPHIS, TN

THE LINK BETWEEN RACE AND POVERTY REMAINS ONE OF OUR NATION'S MOST PERSISTENT CHALLENGES. IN THE WAKE OF THE GREAT RECESSION, A POVERTY RATE IN MEMPHIS GREW FROM 20.6 PERCENT IN 2000 TO 27 PERCENT, AND THE RATE FOR AFRICAN AMERICANS WAS THREE AND A HALF TIMES LARGER THAN FOR WHITES.

It is obvious that we must align social services, job training, and affordable housing to support low-income families; but it's even more obvious that there is nothing more effective than jobs to rebuild our cities and America.

To this end, my administration has launched an innovative program—the Memphis Blueprint for Prosperity—to reduce our poverty rate from 27 percent to 17 percent in 10 years and free 64,000 Memphians from the grip of poverty. Working with the Lumina Foundation, we also created a coalition of university presidents who are pursuing an equally bold goal for 55 percent of our people to obtain postsecondary success by 2025.

Based on the number of families living below the poverty line, we calculate that $200 million in annual aggregate income is necessary to achieve our poverty reduction goal. This is in addition to dynamic partnerships, existing federal funds and resources, and regional growth opportunities that will also play an important role.

Our Blueprint for Prosperity identifies ways to drive opportunity and shared prosperity in Memphis. These include cost of living reductions in transportation, housing, and energy. Of the $200 million goal, the Center for Neighborhood Technology estimates that reducing these costs can account for 16 percent, or $32 million.

My administration recognizes that without reliable and complete transit options, many low-income Memphians struggle to secure and maintain jobs. Improved jobs access can account for 35 percent, or $73 million, of our poverty reduction needs, and because of it, we are working with federal officials to find ways to ensure that Memphis Area Transit Authority (MATA) effectively connects people in the urban core to regional job centers. We estimate that

capturing these regional growth opportunities can account for 41 percent, or $81 million.

Memphis also has developed a rich array of local partnerships to create new economic engines, improve equity through transit access and neighborhood building, and maintain federal-state-local partnerships that play a crucial role in expanding this work, particularly with transportation management associations and public-private partnerships that can influence and align policies that create jobs.

Poor households become poor and remain poor for many reasons. Low educational attainment, lack of marketable skills, social capital gaps, and regulatory barriers to acquiring necessary resources all conspire to produce and maintain a condition of poverty that's difficult to escape.

Narrow, piecemeal efforts to decrease poverty will not have the impact that we need or desire. Instead, we are working comprehensively to address the multiple systemic factors that confine 27 percent of our citizens to poverty. We have laid a strong foundation, and working with our federal partners and with the leadership of our Strong Cities Strong Communities team, we are confident that our Blueprint for Prosperity will set a national standard in creating prosperity and reducing poverty. ★

MEMPHIS

	MEMPHIS, TN–MS–AR					UNITED STATES	
	Black	Hispanic	White	Black-White Index	Hispanic-White Index	Black-White Index	Hispanic-White Index
ECONOMICS							
Median Household Income (Real), Dollars	31,576	35,541	58,819	54%	60%	60%	71%
POVERTY							
Population Living Below Poverty Line, %	29.6	33.3	8.7	29%	26%	39%	43%
Population Living Below Poverty Line (Under 18), %	41.6	44.9	10.8	26%	24%	32%	36%
Population Living Below Poverty Line (18–64), %	24.7	26.0	8.9	36%	34%	41%	45%
Population Living Below Poverty Line (65 and Older), %	24.1	20.0	5.1	21%	26%	37%	33%
EMPLOYMENT ISSUES							
Unemployment Rate, %	16.6	3.8	6.5	39%	171%	50%	71%
Labor Force Participation Rate, %	64.0	69.8	64.8	99%	108%	96%	104%
HOUSING & WEALTH							
Home Ownership Rate, %	48.3	40.7	76.0	64%	54%	60%	63%
Median Home Value, Dollars	87,200	100,200	158,700	55%	63%	65%	86%
TRANSPORTATION							
Car Ownership, %	85.3	95.9	96.5	88%	99%	80%	88%
Means of Transportation to Work: Drive Alone, %	80.2	70.2	86.8	92%	81%	90%	86%
Means of Transportation to Work: Public Transportation, %	2.4	0.0	0.4	17%	NA	26%	38%
EDUCATION							
ATTAINMENT							
Educational Attainment: at Least High School (25 Yrs. and Over), % of Population	81.6	58.8	92.5	88%	64%	92%	70%
Educational Attainment: at Least Bachelor's (25 Yrs. and Over), % of Population	16.7	13.9	34.2	48%	41%	62%	42%
Educational Attainment: Graduate or Professional Degree (25 Yrs. and Over), % of Population	5.7	4.4	11.9	48%	37%	60%	34%
STUDENT STATUS AND RISK FACTORS							
Children in All Families Below Poverty Level, %	34.0	39.0	8.7	26%	22%	31%	35%
Children in Families Below Poverty Level (Female Householder, No Spouse Present), %	49.2	66.5	21.1	43%	32%	68%	67%
Children (Under 18) With a Disability, %	4.4	2.7	3.2	73%	119%	80%	93%
HEALTH							
People Without Health Insurance, %	16.9	40.9	10.7	63%	26%	58%	38%
People With Private Health Insurance, %	50.8	31.0	76.6	66%	41%	68%	58%
SOCIAL JUSTICE							
Incarceration Rate: Prisoners in Jail Per 100,000 People	1,176.2	406.6	253.2	22%	62%	18%	40%

Source: Census ACS 2012 1-year estimates (unless otherwise noted). Black is Black or African American alone, not Hispanic. Incarceration rates are IHS calculations, using Bureau of Justice Statistics, Annual Survey of Jails, 2011 and Census population estimates.

MEMPHIS POPULATION DEMOGRAPHICS

★ Black **46%** ★ Hispanic **5%**
★ White **45%** ★ Other **4%**

TONJA SESLEY-BAYMON
PRESIDENT,
MEMPHIS URBAN LEAGUE

Black–White Equality Index: Memphis vs. United States

★ Memphis ★ United States

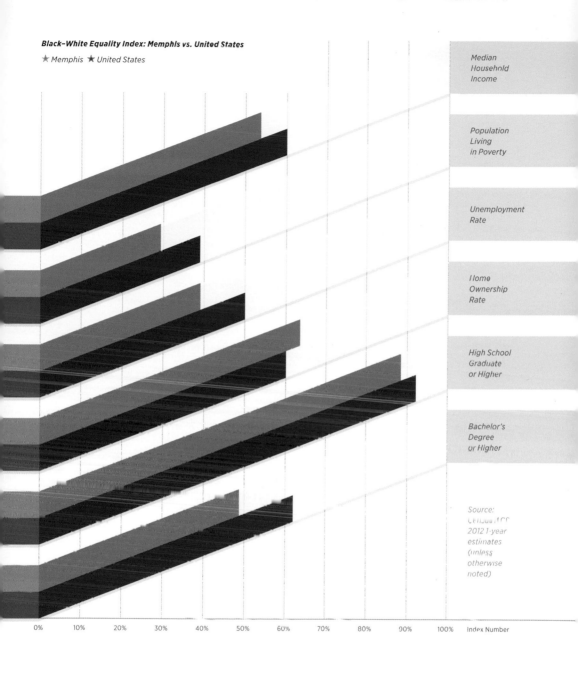

0%	10%	20%	30%	40%	50%	60%	70%	80%	90%	100%	Index Number

Median Household Income

Population Living in Poverty

Unemployment Rate

Home Ownership Rate

High School Graduate or Higher

Bachelor's Degree or Higher

Source: Census ACS 2012 1-year estimates (unless otherwise noted)

THE HISPANIC-WHITE UNEMPLOYMENT INDEX IN MEMPHIS IS 171.1%

THE BLACK-WHITE UNEMPLOYMENT INDEX IN MEMPHIS IS 39.2%

ATLANTA

	ATLANTA-SANDY SPRINGS-MARIETTA, GA					UNITED STATES	
	Black	Hispanic	White	Black-White Index	Hispanic-White Index	Black-White Index	Hispanic-White Index
ECONOMICS							
Median Household Income (Real), Dollars	41,463	38,064	67,196	62%	57%	60%	71%
POVERTY							
Population Living Below Poverty Line, %	23.5	29.8	9.3	40%	31%	39%	43%
Population Living Below Poverty Line (Under 18), %	33.0	41.7	10.1	31%	24%	32%	36%
Population Living Below Poverty Line (18–64), %	20.2	23.6	9.4	47%	40%	41%	45%
Population Living Below Poverty Line (65 and Older), %	16.8	8.8	7.4	44%	84%	37%	33%
EMPLOYMENT ISSUES							
Unemployment Rate, %	17.0	9.6	8.1	48%	84%	50%	71%
Labor Force Participation Rate, %	68.5	71.7	65.8	104%	109%	96%	104%
HOUSING & WEALTH							
Home Ownership Rate, %	48.5	43.5	76.0	64%	57%	60%	63%
Median Home Value, Dollars	117,400	125,900	180,000	65%	70%	65%	86%
TRANSPORTATION							
Car Ownership, %	89.1	91.0	96.9	92%	94%	80%	88%
Means of Transportation to Work: Drive Alone, %	77.1	61.0	82.0	94%	74%	90%	86%
Means of Transportation to Work: Public Transportation, %	5.8	4.4	1.1	19%	25%	26%	38%
EDUCATION							
ATTAINMENT							
Educational Attainment: at Least High School (25 Yrs. and Over), % of Population	88.6	61.6	91.5	97%	67%	92%	70%
Educational Attainment: at Least Bachelor's (25 Yrs. and Over), % of Population	27.0	15.6	41.1	66%	38%	62%	42%
Educational Attainment: Graduate or Professional Degree (25 Yrs. and Over), % of Population	9.2	4.7	14.5	63%	32%	60%	34%
STUDENT STATUS AND RISK FACTORS							
Children in All Families Below Poverty Level, %	27.2	34.6	10.0	37%	29%	31%	35%
Children in Families Below Poverty Level (Female Householder, No Spouse Present), %	41.2	56.8	34.5	84%	61%	68%	67%
Children (Under 18) With a Disability, %	3.7	2.5	3.6	97%	144%	80%	93%
HEALTH							
People Without Health Insurance, %	20.2	42.6	11.6	57%	27%	58%	38%
People With Private Health Insurance, %	57.1	35.5	76.8	74%	46%	68%	58%
SOCIAL JUSTICE							
Incarceration Rate: Prisoners in Jail Per 100,000 People	614.0	206.4	195.4	32%	95%	18%	40%

Source: Census ACS 2012 1-year estimates (unless otherwise noted). Black is Black or African American alone, not Hispanic. Incarceration rates are IHS calculations, using Bureau of Justice Statistics, Annual Survey of Jails, 2011 and Census population estimates.

ATLANTA POPULATION DEMOGRAPHICS

★ Black **32%** ★ Hispanic **11%**
★ White **50%** ★ Other **7%**

NANCY FLAKE JOHNSON
PRESIDENT, URBAN LEAGUE OF GREATER ATLANTA

BIRMINGHAM

	BIRMINGHAM–HOOVER, AL			UNITED STATES
	Black	White	Black-White Index	Black-White Index
ECONOMICS				
Median Household Income (Real), Dollars	32,086	55,000	58%	60%
POVERTY				
Population Living Below Poverty Line, %	27.8	10.9	39%	39%
Population Living Below Poverty Line (Under 18), %	41.6	12.2	29%	32%
Population Living Below Poverty Line (18–64), %	23.2	11.4	49%	41%
Population Living Below Poverty Line (65 and Older), %	19.2	7.4	39%	37%
EMPLOYMENT ISSUES				
Unemployment Rate, %	13.7	6.7	49%	50%
Labor Force Participation Rate, %	59.3	60.2	99%	96%
HOUSING & WEALTH				
Home Ownership Rate, %	51.3	78.3	66%	60%
Median Home Value, Dollars	93,700	158,300	59%	65%
TRANSPORTATION				
Car Ownership, %	86.0	95.8	90%	80%
Means of Transportation to Work: Drive Alone, %	86.2	86.9	99%	90%
Means of Transportation to Work: Public Transportation, %	1.3	0.2	15%	26%
EDUCATION				
ATTAINMENT				
Educational Attainment: at Least High School (25 Yrs. and Over), % of Population	85.6	88.1	97%	92%
Educational Attainment: at Least Bachelor's (25 Yrs. and Over), % of Population	18.6	31.8	59%	62%
Educational Attainment: Graduate or Professional Degree (25 Yrs. and Over), % of Population	6.4	12.3	52%	60%
STUDENT STATUS AND RISK FACTORS				
Children in All Families Below Poverty Level, %	34.8	12.9	37%	31%
Children in Families Below Poverty Level (Female Householder, No Spouse Present), %	49.2	42.5	86%	68%
Children (Under 18) With a Disability, %	3.0	4.0	133%	80%
HEALTH				
People Without Health Insurance, %	15.3	8.7	57%	58%
People With Private Health Insurance, %	53.4	77.2	69%	68%
SOCIAL JUSTICE				
Incarceration Rate: Prisoners in Jail Per 100,000 People	394.2	105.7	27%	18%

Source: Census ACS 2012 1-year estimates (unless otherwise noted). Black is Black or African American alone, not Hispanic. Incarceration rates are IHS calculations, using Bureau of Justice Statistics, Annual Survey of Jails, 2011 and Census population estimates.

The Hispanic population of Birmingham was not large enough to calculate an index.

BIRMINGHAM POPULATION DEMOGRAPHICS

★ Black **28%**   ★ White **65%**
★ Other **7%**

ELAINE S. JACKSON
PRESIDENT, BIRMINGHAM URBAN LEAGUE

© NATIONAL URBAN LEAGUE

BOSTON

	BOSTON–CAMBRIDGE–QUINCY, MA–NH					UNITED STATES	
	Black	Hispanic	White	Black-White Index	Hispanic-White Index	Black-White Index	Hispanic-White Index
ECONOMICS							
Median Household Income (Real), Dollars	43,230	38,505	78,551	55%	4%	60%	71%
POVERTY							
Population Living Below Poverty Line, %	20.5	25.7	7.1	35%	28%	39%	43%
Population Living Below Poverty Line (Under 18), %	28.2	31.5	6.8	24%	22%	32%	36%
Population Living Below Poverty Line (18–64), %	17.4	22.0	7.3	42%	33%	41%	45%
Population Living Below Poverty Line (65 and Older), %	19.0	36.2	6.8	36%	19%	37%	33%
EMPLOYMENT ISSUES							
Unemployment Rate, %	13.3	14.2	6.7	50%	47%	50%	71%
Labor Force Participation Rate, %	69.4	69.5	69.1	100%	101%	96%	104%
HOUSING & WEALTH							
Home Ownership Rate, %	32.5	25.2	68.5	4%	37%	60%	63%
Median Home Value, Dollars	289,600	303,900	361,400	80%	84%	65%	86%
TRANSPORTATION							
Car Ownership, %	71.7	71.6	90.1	80%	80%	80%	88%
Means of Transportation to Work: Drive Alone, %	55.1	53.6	72.8	76%	74%	90%	86%
Means of Transportation to Work: Public Transportation, %	26.2	20.8	9.5	36%	46%	26%	38%
EDUCATION							
ATTAINMENT							
Educational Attainment: at Least High School (25 Yrs. and Over), % of Population	82.2	68.9	94.3	87.2%	73%	92%	70%
Educational Attainment: at Least Bachelor's (25 Yrs. and Over), % of Population	21.5	18.8	46.1	46.6%	41%	62%	42%
Educational Attainment: Graduate or Professional Degree (25 Yrs. and Over), % of Population	8.0	7.2	20.1	39.8%	36%	60%	34%
STUDENT STATUS AND RISK FACTORS							
Children in All Families Below Poverty Level, %	24.7	29.3	6.8	27.5%	23%	31%	35%
Children in Families Below Poverty Level (Female Householder, No Spouse Present), %	37.7	47.5	25.8	68.4%	54%	68%	67%
Children (Under 18) With a Disability, %	5.2	5.8	3.8	73.1%	66%	80%	93%
HEALTH							
People Without Health Insurance, %	7.1	8.4	3.4	47.9%	41%	58%	38%
People With Private Health Insurance, %	54.4	46.7	83.2	65.4%	56%	68%	58%
SOCIAL JUSTICE							
Incarceration Rate: Prisoners in Jail Per 100,000 People	882.4	558.2	120.6	13.7%	22%	18%	40%

Source: Census ACS 2012 1-year estimates (unless otherwise noted). Black is Black or African American alone, not Hispanic. Incarceration rates are IHS calculations, using Bureau of Justice Statistics, Annual Survey of Jails, 2011 and Census population estimates.

BOSTON POPULATION DEMOGRAPHICS

★ Black **7%**   ★ Hispanic **10%**
★ White **74%**   ★ Other **9%**

DARNELL L. WILLIAMS
PRESIDENT, URBAN LEAGUE OF EASTERN MASSACHUSETTS

CHARLOTTE

	CHARLOTTE–GASTONIA–ROCK HILL, NC–SC					UNITED STATES	
	Black	Hispanic	White	Black-White Index	Hispanic-White Index	Black-White Index	Hispanic-White Index
ECONOMICS							
Median Household Income (Real), Dollars	36,007	39,348	62,877	57%	63%	60%	71%
POVERTY							
Population Living Below Poverty Line, %	24.7	29.1	8.9	36%	31%	39%	43%
Population Living Below Poverty Line (Under 18), %	35.5	39.6	8.9	25%	23%	32%	36%
Population Living Below Poverty Line (18–64), %	20.8	23.4	9.5	46%	41%	41%	45%
Population Living Below Poverty Line (65 and Older), %	18.8	13.0	6.2	33%	48%	37%	33%
EMPLOYMENT ISSUES							
Unemployment Rate, %	16.8	11.2	8.0	48%	71%	50%	71%
Labor Force Participation Rate, %	69.1	75.0	67.6	102%	111%	96%	104%
HOUSING & WEALTH							
Home Ownership Rate, %	45.6	42.2	73.8	62%	57%	60%	63%
Median Home Value, Dollars	120,600	138,600	177,600	68%	78%	65%	86%
TRANSPORTATION							
Car Ownership, %	87.1	95.6	96.3	90%	99%	80%	88%
Means of Transportation to Work: Drive Alone, %	78.5	59.8	82.0	96%	73%	90%	86%
Means of Transportation to Work: Public Transportation, %	4.7	3.8	0.9	19%	24%	26%	38%
EDUCATION							
ATTAINMENT							
Educational Attainment: at Least High School (25 Yrs. and Over), % of Population	86.4	59.4	91.7	94%	65%	92%	70%
Educational Attainment: at Least Bachelor's (25 Yrs. and Over), % of Population	21.7	14.8	38.7	56%	38%	62%	42%
Educational Attainment: Graduate or Professional Degree (25 Yrs. and Over), % of Population	6.7	3.6	11.9	56%	30%	60%	34%
STUDENT STATUS AND RISK FACTORS							
Children in All Families Below Poverty Level, %	29.5	36.3	8.1	28%	22%	31%	35%
Children in Families Below Poverty Level (Female Householder, No Spouse Present), %	45.0	60.8	27.8	62%	40%	68%	67%
Children (Under 18) With a Disability, %	4.1	2.8	3.0	73%	107%	80%	93%
HEALTH							
People Without Health Insurance, %	18.7	42.5	10.7	57%	25%	58%	38%
People With Private Health Insurance, %	53.4	31.7	77.2	69%	41%	68%	58%
SOCIAL JUSTICE							
Incarceration Rate: Prisoners in Jail Per 100,000 People	566.1	301.5	89.5	16%	30%	18%	40%

Source: Census ACS 2012 1-year estimates (unless otherwise noted). Black is Black or African American alone, not Hispanic. Incarceration rates are IHS calculations, using Bureau of Justice Statistics, Annual Survey of Jails, 2011 and Census population estimates.

CHARLOTTE POPULATION DEMOGRAPHICS

★ Black **24%** ★ Hispanic **10%**
★ White **60%** ★ Other **6%**

DR. PATRICK GRAHAM
PRESIDENT, URBAN LEAGUE OF CENTRAL CAROLINAS, INC.

◎ NATIONAL URBAN LEAGUE

CHICAGO

	CHICAGO–JOLIET–NAPERVILLE, IL					UNITED STATES	
	Black	Hispanic	White	Black-White Index	Hispanic-White Index	Black-White Index	Hispanic-White Index
ECONOMICS							
Median Household Income (Real), Dollars	33,674	45,884	70,890	48%	65%	60%	71%
POVERTY							
Population Living Below Poverty Line, %	30.5	21.0	7.3	24%	35%	39%	43%
Population Living Below Poverty Line (Under 18), %	43.7	27.7	7.9	18%	29%	32%	36%
Population Living Below Poverty Line (18–64), %	27.0	17.6	7.4	27%	42%	41%	45%
Population Living Below Poverty Line (65 and Older), %	18.7	16.9	6.5	35%	39%	37%	33%
EMPLOYMENT ISSUES							
Unemployment Rate, %	23.0	12.0	7.6	33%	63%	50%	71%
Labor Force Participation Rate, %	61.3	71.1	68.1	90%	104%	96%	104%
HOUSING & WEALTH							
Home Ownership Rate, %	40.2	52.1	75.5	53%	69%	60%	63%
Median Home Value, Dollars	134,200	159,000	228,400	59%	70%	65%	86%
TRANSPORTATION							
Car Ownership, %	72.8	89.2	91.3	80%	98%	80%	88%
Means of Transportation to Work: Drive Alone, %	62.9	66.6	74.9	84%	89%	90%	86%
Means of Transportation to Work: Public Transportation, %	21.0	10.4	9.0	43%	87%	26%	38%
EDUCATION							
ATTAINMENT							
Educational Attainment: at Least High School (25 Yrs. and Over), % of Population	85.4	61.6	94.1	91%	66%	92%	70%
Educational Attainment: at Least Bachelor's (25 Yrs. and Over), % of Population	20.1	12.9	42.0	48%	31%	62%	42%
Educational Attainment: Graduate or Professional Degree (25 Yrs. and Over), % of Population	7.5	3.8	16.3	46%	23%	60%	34%
STUDENT STATUS AND RISK FACTORS							
Children in All Families Below Poverty Level, %	36.1	23.5	7.4	21%	32%	31%	35%
Children in Families Below Poverty Level (Female Householder, No Spouse Present), %	49.3	41.2	26.2	53%	64%	68%	67%
Children (Under 18) With a Disability, %	4.4	3.1	3.2	73%	103%	80%	93%
HEALTH							
People Without Health Insurance, %	17.2	26.1	8.1	47%	31%	58%	38%
People With Private Health Insurance, %	46.8	43.6	80.9	58%	54%	68%	58%
SOCIAL JUSTICE							
Incarceration Rate: Prisoners in Jail Per 100,000 People	697.5	184.4	56.4	8%	31%	18%	40%

Source: Census ACS 2012 1-year estimates (unless otherwise noted). Black is Black or African American alone, not Hispanic. Incarceration rates are IHS calculations, using Bureau of Justice Statistics, Annual Survey of Jails, 2011 and Census population estimates.

CHICAGO POPULATION DEMOGRAPHICS

★ Black **17%**   ★ Hispanic **21%**
★ White **54%**   ★ Other **8%**

ANDREA ZOPP
PRESIDENT, CHICAGO URBAN LEAGUE

CLEVELAND

	CLEVELAND-ELYRIA-MENTOR, OH					UNITED STATES	
	Black	Hispanic	White	Black-White Index	Hispanic-White Index	Black-White Index	Hispanic-White Index
ECONOMICS							
Median Household Income (Real), Dollars	24,749	30,559	55,084	45%	56%	60%	71%
POVERTY							
Population Living Below Poverty Line, %	33.9	29.9	9.4	28%	31%	39%	43%
Population Living Below Poverty Line (Under 18), %	45.1	39.9	11.5	26%	29%	32%	36%
Population Living Below Poverty Line (18–64), %	31.2	24.9	9.3	30%	37%	41%	45%
Population Living Below Poverty Line (65 and Older), %	21.5	18.0	7.3	34%	41%	37%	33%
EMPLOYMENT ISSUES							
Unemployment Rate, %	21.2	16.7	7.0	33%	42%	50%	71%
Labor Force Participation Rate, %	57.9	65.6	65.1	89%	101%	96%	104%
HOUSING & WEALTH							
Home Ownership Rate, %	37.6	41.5	74.0	51%	56%	60%	63%
Median Home Value, Dollars	82,400	84,800	150,200	55%	57%	65%	86%
TRANSPORTATION							
Car Ownership, %	73.8	88.0	92.7	80%	95%	80%	88%
Means of Transportation to Work: Drive Alone, %	71.9	74.6	85.0	85%	88%	90%	86%
Means of Transportation to Work: Public Transportation, %	11.6	6.6	1.4	12%	21%	26%	38%
EDUCATION							
ATTAINMENT							
Educational Attainment: at Least High School (25 Yrs. and Over), % of Population	81.1	69.4	91.2	89%	76%	92%	70%
Educational Attainment: at Least Bachelor's (25 Yrs. and Over), % of Population	14.2	14.9	31.6	45%	47%	62%	42%
Educational Attainment: Graduate or Professional Degree (25 Yrs. and Over), % of Population	5.3	6.6	12.0	44%	55%	60%	34%
STUDENT STATUS AND RISK FACTORS							
Children in All Families Below Poverty Level, %	40.8	38.4	10.8	27%	28%	31%	35%
Children in Families Below Poverty Level (Female Householder, No Spouse Present), %	48.1	58.1	34.6	72%	60%	68%	67%
Children (Under 18) With a Disability, %	5.5	6.2	4.1	75%	66%	80%	93%
HEALTH							
People Without Health Insurance, %	15.9	18.8	8.6	54%	45%	58%	38%
People With Private Health Insurance, %	47.5	44.7	76.9	62%	58%	68%	58%
SOCIAL JUSTICE							
Incarceration Rate: Prisoners in Jail Per 100,000 People	NA	NA	NA	NA	NA	18%	40%

Source: Census ACS 2012 1-year estimates (unless otherwise noted). Black is Black or African American alone, not Hispanic. Incarceration rates are IHS calculations, using Bureau of Justice Statistics, Annual Survey of Jails, 2011 and Census population estimates.
NA: Not Available

CLEVELAND POPULATION DEMOGRAPHICS

★ Black **20%** ★ Hispanic **5%**
★ White **71%** ★ Other **4%**

MARSHA MOCKABEE
PRESIDENT, URBAN LEAGUE OF GREATER CLEVELAND

DALLAS

	DALLAS–FORT WORTH–ARLINGTON, TX					UNITED STATES	
	Black	*Hispanic*	*White*	*Black-White Index*	*Hispanic-White Index*	*Black-White Index*	*Hispanic-White Index*
ECONOMICS							
Median Household Income (Real), Dollars	39,523	40,278	70,669	56%	57%	60%	71%
POVERTY							
Population Living Below Poverty Line, %	23.1	24.1	7.7	33%	32%	39%	43%
Population Living Below Poverty Line (Under 18), %	31.8	32.4	8.5	27%	26%	32%	36%
Population Living Below Poverty Line (18–64), %	19.3	19.0	7.8	40%	41%	41%	45%
Population Living Below Poverty Line (65 and Older), %	21.8	22.1	6.5	30%	29%	37%	33%
EMPLOYMENT ISSUES							
Unemployment Rate, %	12.7	7.5	6.4	50%	85%	50%	71%
Labor Force Participation Rate, %	68.4	71.8	68.0	101%	106%	96%	104%
HOUSING & WEALTH							
Home Ownership Rate, %	38.4	51.1	68.8	56%	74%	60%	63%
Median Home Value, Dollars	120,500	100,900	166,900	72%	61%	65%	86%
TRANSPORTATION							
Car Ownership, %	88.3	95.8	96.4	92%	99%	80%	88%
Means of Transportation to Work: Drive Alone, %	80.0	76.8	83.3	96%	92%	90%	86%
Means of Transportation to Work: Public Transportation, %	4.2	1.3	0.8	19%	62%	26%	38%
EDUCATION							
ATTAINMENT							
Educational Attainment: at Least High School (25 Yrs. and Over), % of Population	88.8	55.5	93.8	95%	59%	92%	70%
Educational Attainment: at Least Bachelor's (25 Yrs. and Over), % of Population	23.2	10.9	39.9	58%	27%	62%	42%
Educational Attainment: Graduate or Professional Degree (25 Yrs. and Over), % of Population	6.7	3.2	13.1	51%	24%	60%	34%
STUDENT STATUS AND RISK FACTORS							
Children in All Families Below Poverty Level, %	26.7	27.8	7.0	26%	25%	31%	35%
Children in Families Below Poverty Level (Female Householder, No Spouse Present), %	40.7	48.8	23.0	57%	47%	68%	67%
Children (Under 18) With a Disability, %	4.0	2.8	3.3	83%	118%	80%	93%
HEALTH							
People Without Health Insurance, %	21.4	39.7	12.9	60%	33%	58%	38%
People With Private Health Insurance, %	51.5	35.4	75.7	68%	47%	68%	58%
SOCIAL JUSTICE							
Incarceration Rate: Prisoners in Jail Per 100,000 People	822.4	263.0	186.2	23%	71%	18%	40%

Source: Census ACS 2012 1-year estimates (unless otherwise noted). Black is Black or African American alone, not Hispanic. Incarceration rates are IHS calculations, using Bureau of Justice Statistics, Annual Survey of Jails, 2011 and Census population estimates.

DALLAS POPULATION DEMOGRAPHICS

★ *Black* **15%** ★ *Hispanic* **28%**
★ *White* **49%** ★ *Other* **8%**

BEVERLY K. MITCHELL-BROOKS, PH.D.
PRESIDENT, URBAN LEAGUE OF GREATER DALLAS AND NORTH CENTRAL TEXAS

DETROIT

	DETROIT-WARREN-LIVONIA, MI					UNITED STATES	
	Black	Hispanic	White	Black-White Index	Hispanic-White Index	Black-White Index	Hispanic-White Index
ECONOMICS							
Median Household Income (Real), Dollars	28,988	41,046	57,533	50%	71%	60%	71%
POVERTY							
Population Living Below Poverty Line, %	50.6	33.3	15.3	30%	46%	39%	43%
Population Living Below Poverty Line (Under 18), %	32.0	24.2	10.6	33%	44%	32%	36%
Population Living Below Poverty Line (18–64), %	18.8	16.7	6.9	37%	41%	41%	45%
Population Living Below Poverty Line (65 and Older), %	24.0	14.3	9.0	38%	63%	37%	33%
EMPLOYMENT ISSUES							
Unemployment Rate, %	42.7	34.7	36.4	85%	105%	50%	71%
Labor Force Participation Rate, %	57.3	65.2	63.6	90%	103%	96%	104%
HOUSING & WEALTH							
Home Ownership Rate, %	44.2	55.7	77.9	57%	72%	60%	63%
Median Home Value, Dollars	53,000	82,900	129,700	41%	64%	65%	86%
TRANSPORTATION							
Car Ownership, %	77.5	92.2	94.0	82%	98%	80%	88%
Means of Transportation to Work: Drive Alone, %	76.5	75.2	86.2	89%	87%	90%	86%
Means of Transportation to Work: Public Transportation, %	6.7	2.4	0.3	5%	13%	26%	38%
EDUCATION							
ATTAINMENT							
Educational Attainment: at Least High School (25 Yrs. and Over), % of Population	84.1	69.0	90.4	93%	76%	92%	70%
Educational Attainment: at Least Bachelor's (25 Yrs. and Over), % of Population	16.7	20.3	30.4	55%	67%	62%	42%
Educational Attainment: Graduate or Professional Degree (25 Yrs. and Over), % of Population	6.6	7.1	11.5	57%	62%	60%	34%
STUDENT STATUS AND RISK FACTORS							
Children in All Families Below Poverty Level, %	43.0	29.5	13.3	31%	45%	31%	35%
Children in Families Below Poverty Level (Female Householder, No Spouse Present), %	56.0	49.7	36.1	65%	73%	68%	67%
Children (Under 18) With a Disability, %	7.0	4.0	4.4	63%	110%	80%	93%
HEALTH							
People Without Health Insurance, %	16.5	19.6	10.1	61%	52%	58%	38%
People With Private Health Insurance, %	46.3	50.5	76.3	61%	66%	68%	58%
SOCIAL JUSTICE							
Incarceration Rate: Prisoners in Jail Per 100,000 People	364.3	2.8	100.0	27%	3,593%	18%	40%

Source: Census ACS 2012 1-year estimates (unless otherwise noted). Black is Black or African American alone, not Hispanic. Incarceration rates are IHS calculations, using Bureau of Justice Statistics, Annual Survey of Jails, 2011 and Census population estimates.

DETROIT POPULATION DEMOGRAPHICS

★ Black **23%** ★ Hispanic **4%**
★ White **67%** ★ Other **6%**

N. CHARLES ANDERSON
PRESIDENT, URBAN LEAGUE OF DETROIT AND SOUTHEASTERN MICHIGAN

HOUSTON

	HOUSTON-SUGAR LAND-BAYTOWN, TX					UNITED STATES	
	Black	Hispanic	White	Black-White Index	Hispanic-White Index	Black-White Index	Hispanic-White Index
ECONOMICS							
Median Household Income (Real), Dollars	40,129	42,160	75,201	53%	56%	60%	71%
POVERTY							
Population Living Below Poverty Line, %	22.6	24.6	7.2	32%	29%	39%	43%
Population Living Below Poverty Line (Under 18), %	32.3	33.5	7.3	23%	22%	32%	36%
Population Living Below Poverty Line (18–64), %	19.0	19.9	7.4	39%	37%	41%	45%
Population Living Below Poverty Line (65 and Older), %	18.6	19.1	6.2	33%	33%	37%	33%
EMPLOYMENT ISSUES							
Unemployment Rate, %	14.8	8.2	6.5	44%	79%	50%	71%
Labor Force Participation Rate, %	66.2	70.5	65.1	102%	108%	96%	104%
HOUSING & WEALTH							
Home Ownership Rate, %	42.4	53.4	73.1	58%	73%	60%	63%
Median Home Value, Dollars	111,000	101,700	165,400	67%	62%	65%	86%
TRANSPORTATION							
Car Ownership, %	86.8	94.0	96.6	90%	97%	80%	88%
Means of Transportation to Work: Drive Alone, %	79.3	75.6	83.3	95%	91%	90%	86%
Means of Transportation to Work: Public Transportation, %	5.7	2.3	1.6	28%	70%	26%	38%
EDUCATION							
ATTAINMENT							
Educational Attainment: at Least High School (25 Yrs. and Over), % of Population	87.8	58.1	93.6	94%	62%	92%	70%
Educational Attainment: at Least Bachelor's (25 Yrs. and Over), % of Population	24.3	11.6	40.2	60%	29%	62%	42%
Educational Attainment: Graduate or Professional Degree (25 Yrs. and Over), % of Population	8.5	3.2	13.8	62%	23%	60%	34%
STUDENT STATUS AND RISK FACTORS							
Children in All Families Below Poverty Level, %	26.5	27.9	6.5	25%	23%	31%	35%
Children in Families Below Poverty Level (Female Householder, No Spouse Present), %	41.6	50.2	22.5	54%	45%	68%	67%
Children (Under 18) With a Disability, %	5.6	3.6	3.1	55%	86%	80%	93%
HEALTH							
People Without Health Insurance, %	20.1	38.0	11.8	59%	31%	58%	38%
People With Private Health Insurance, %	53.2	35.6	76.7	69%	46%	68%	58%
SOCIAL JUSTICE							
Incarceration Rate: Prisoners in Jail Per 100,000 People	803.2	49.4	318.3	40%	644%	18%	40%

Source: Census ACS 2012 1 year estimates (unless otherwise noted). Black is Black or African American alone, not Hispanic. Incarceration rates are IHS calculations, using Bureau of Justice Statistics, Annual Survey of Jails, 2011 and Census population estimates.

HOUSTON POPULATION DEMOGRAPHICS

★ *Black* **17%**   ★ *Hispanic* **36%**
★ *White* **39%**   ★ *Other* **9%**

JUDSON W. ROBINSON III
PRESIDENT, HOUSTON AREA URBAN LEAGUE

LOS ANGELES

	LOS ANGELES–LONG BEACH–SANTA ANA, CA					UNITED STATES	
	Black	Hispanic	White	Black-White Index	Hispanic-White Index	Black-White Index	Hispanic-White Index
ECONOMICS							
Median Household Income (Real), Dollars	39,088	44,868	73,865	53%	61%	60%	71%
POVERTY							
Population Living Below Poverty Line, %	24.9	24.0	9.6	39%	40%	39%	43%
Population Living Below Poverty Line (Under 18), %	34.4	32.8	8.7	25%	27%	32%	36%
Population Living Below Poverty Line (18–64), %	23.5	20.4	10.0	43%	49%	41%	45%
Population Living Below Poverty Line (65 and Older), %	16.0	16.8	8.6	54%	51%	37%	33%
EMPLOYMENT ISSUES							
Unemployment Rate, %	16.8	12.2	9.4	56%	77%	50%	71%
Labor Force Participation Rate, %	59.5	67.3	64.3	93%	105%	96%	104%
HOUSING & WEALTH							
Home Ownership Rate, %	34.2	37.6	58.7	58%	64%	60%	63%
Median Home Value, Dollars	324,300	321,200	518,300	63%	62%	65%	86%
TRANSPORTATION							
Car Ownership, %	82.1	90.1	93.4	88%	97%	80%	80%
Means of Transportation to Work: Drive Alone, %	73.5	69.8	78.4	94%	89%	90%	86%
Means of Transportation to Work: Public Transportation, %	10.4	9.4	2.3	22%	25%	26%	38%
EDUCATION							
ATTAINMENT							
Educational Attainment: at Least High School (25 Yrs. and Over), % of Population	89.4	57.8	94.7	94%	61%	92%	70%
Educational Attainment: at Least Bachelor's (25 Yrs. and Over), % of Population	24.7	11.1	46.4	53%	24%	62%	42%
Educational Attainment: Graduate or Professional Degree (25 Yrs. and Over), % of Population	8.7	3.3	17.7	49%	19%	60%	34%
STUDENT STATUS AND RISK FACTORS							
Children in All Families Below Poverty Level, %	28.7	28.4	7.9	28%	28%	31%	35%
Children in Families Below Poverty Level (Female Householder, No Spouse Present), %	41.4	45.5	21.1	51%	46%	68%	67%
Children (Under 18) With a Disability, %	5.2	2.6	2.5	48%	96%	80%	93%
HEALTH							
People Without Health Insurance, %	17.3	29.9	10.5	61%	35%	58%	38%
People With Private Health Insurance, %	54.0	39.9	75.1	72%	53%	68%	58%
SOCIAL JUSTICE							
Incarceration Rate: Prisoners in Jail Per 100,000 People	759.7	253.2	118.8	16%	47%	18%	40%

Source: Census ACS 2012 1-year estimates (unless otherwise noted). Black is Black or African American alone, not Hispanic. Incarceration rates are IHS calculations, using Bureau of Justice Statistics, Annual Survey of Jails, 2011 and Census population estimates.

LOS ANGELES POPULATION DEMOGRAPHICS

★ Black **7%** ★ Hispanic **45%**
★ White **31%** ★ Other **18%**

NOLAN ROLLINS
PRESIDENT, LOS ANGELES URBAN LEAGUE

MIAMI

	MIAMI–FT. LAUDERDALE–POMPANO BEACH, FL					UNITED STATES	
	Black	Hispanic	White	Black-White Index	Hispanic-White Index	Black-White Index	Hispanic-White Index
ECONOMICS							
Median Household Income (Real), Dollars	35,618	40,482	59,039	60%	69%	60%	71%
POVERTY							
Population Living Below Poverty Line, %	27.7	19.3	9.6	35%	50%	39%	43%
Population Living Below Poverty Line (Under 18), %	39.2	26.7	9.9	25%	37%	32%	36%
Population Living Below Poverty Line (18–64), %	23.3	16.2	10.1	43%	62%	41%	45%
Population Living Below Poverty Line (65 and Older), %	23.1	22.5	8.0	35%	37%	37%	33%
EMPLOYMENT ISSUES							
Unemployment Rate, %	19.4	10.4	8.9	46%	86%	50%	71%
Labor Force Participation Rate, %	66.4	66.3	58.2	114%	114%	96%	104%
HOUSING & WEALTH							
Home Ownership Rate, %	46.5	54.6	74.3	63%	74%	60%	63%
Median Home Value, Dollars	127,000	168,300	206,000	62%	82%	65%	86%
TRANSPORTATION							
Car Ownership, %	86.1	89.9	93.2	92%	96%	80%	88%
Means of Transportation to Work: Drive Alone, %	76.3	76.7	80.2	95%	96%	90%	86%
Means of Transportation to Work: Public Transportation, %	9.5	4.1	1.5	16%	37%	26%	38%
EDUCATION							
ATTAINMENT							
Educational Attainment: at Least High School (25 Yrs. and Over), % of Population	79.8	77.8	93.8	85%	83%	92%	70%
Educational Attainment: at Least Bachelor's (25 Yrs. and Over), % of Population	17.3	24.2	39.5	44%	61%	62%	42%
Educational Attainment: Graduate or Professional Degree (25 Yrs. and Over), % of Population	6.1	7.5	15.6	39%	48%	60%	34%
STUDENT STATUS AND RISK FACTORS							
Children in All Families Below Poverty Level, %	31.6	22.3	9.3	29%	42%	31%	35%
Children in Families Below Poverty Level (Female Householder, No Spouse Present), %	44.1	39.0	22.1	50%	57%	68%	67%
Children (Under 18) With a Disability, %	2.7	2.6	2.0	74%	77%	80%	93%
HEALTH							
People Without Health Insurance, %	29.1	32.8	12.7	44%	39%	58%	38%
People With Private Health Insurance, %	40.5	40.9	69.7	58%	59%	68%	58%
SOCIAL JUSTICE							
Incarceration Rate: Prisoners in Jail Per 100,000 People	NA	NA	NA	NA	NA	18%	40%

Source: Census ACS 2012 1-year estimates (unless otherwise noted). Black is Black or African American alone, not Hispanic. Incarceration rates are IHS calculations, using Bureau of Justice Statistics, Annual Survey of Jails, 2011 and Census population estimates.
NA: Not Available

MIAMI POPULATION DEMOGRAPHICS

★ *Black* **20%**   ★ *Hispanic* **42%**
★ *White* **34%**   ★ *Other* **4%**

T. WILLARD FAIR
PRESIDENT, URBAN LEAGUE OF GREATER MIAMI

NEW ORLEANS

	NEW ORLEANS-METAIRIE-KENNER, LA					UNITED STATES	
	Black	Hispanic	White	Black-White Index	Hispanic-White Index	Black-White Index	Hispanic-White Index
ECONOMICS							
Median Household Income (Real), Dollars	29,331	37,291	58,317	50%	64%	60%	71%
POVERTY							
Population Living Below Poverty Line, %	31.1	22.8	11.4	37%	50%	39%	43%
Population Living Below Poverty Line (Under 18), %	42.9	29.2	14.6	34%	50%	32%	36%
Population Living Below Poverty Line (18–64), %	27.2	20.5	11.2	41%	55%	41%	45%
Population Living Below Poverty Line (65 and Older), %	21.8	21.5	8.1	37%	38%	37%	33%
EMPLOYMENT ISSUES							
Unemployment Rate, %	15.3	11.0	6.6	43%	60%	50%	71%
Labor Force Participation Rate, %	59.6	69.5	63.7	94%	109%	96%	104%
HOUSING & WEALTH							
Home Ownership Rate, %	46.1	40.7	71.4	65%	57%	60%	63%
Median Home Value, Dollars	142,400	178,700	193,300	74%	92%	65%	86%
TRANSPORTATION							
Car Ownership, %	81.9	88.4	94.4	87%	94%	80%	88%
Means of Transportation to Work: Drive Alone, %	76.5	70.4	82.2	93%	86%	90%	86%
Means of Transportation to Work: Public Transportation, %	6.3	3.3	0.9	14%	27%	26%	38%
EDUCATION							
ATTAINMENT							
Educational Attainment: at Least High School (25 Yrs. and Over), % of Population	79.5	68.9	90.4	88%	76%	92%	70%
Educational Attainment: at Least Bachelor's (25 Yrs. and Over), % of Population	15.8	19.8	33.0	48%	60%	62%	42%
Educational Attainment: Graduate or Professional Degree (25 Yrs. and Over), % of Population	4.8	6.6	12.0	40%	55%	60%	34%
STUDENT STATUS AND RISK FACTORS							
Children in All Families Below Poverty Level, %	37.6	26.2	11.8	31%	45%	31%	35%
Children in Families Below Poverty Level (Female Householder, No Spouse Present), %	53.3	16.3	71.1	58%	69%	68%	67%
Children (Under 18) With a Disability, %	4.8	7.9	5.0	104%	63%	80%	93%
HEALTH							
People Without Health Insurance, %	17.8	34.4	12.1	68%	35%	58%	38%
People With Private Health Insurance, %	44.5	42.9	70.7	63%	61%	68%	58%
SOCIAL JUSTICE							
Incarceration Rate: Prisoners in Jail Per 100,000 People	NA	NA	NA	NA	NA	18%	40%

Source: Census ACS 2012 1-year estimates (unless otherwise noted). Black is Black or African American alone, not Hispanic. Incarceration rates are IHS calculations, using Bureau of Justice Statistics, Annual Survey of Jails, 2011 and Census population estimates.
NA: Not Available

NEW ORLEANS POPULATION DEMOGRAPHICS

★ Black **34%** ★ Hispanic **8%**
★ White **53%** ★ Other **5%**

ERIKA MCCONDUIT-DIGGS, ESQ.
PRESIDENT, URBAN LEAGUE OF GREATER NEW ORLEANS

NEW YORK

	NEW YORK–NORTHERN NEW JERSEY–LONG ISLAND, NY–NJ–PA					UNITED STATES	
	Black	Hispanic	White	Black-White Index	Hispanic-White Index	Black-White Index	Hispanic-White Index
ECONOMICS							
Median Household Income (Real), Dollars	44,474	41,101	81,865	54%	50%	60%	71%
POVERTY							
Population Living Below Poverty Line, %	20.9	24.4	7.9	38%	32%	39%	43%
Population Living Below Poverty Line (Under 18), %	30.2	32.7	10.5	35%	32%	32%	36%
Population Living Below Poverty Line (18–64), %	18.3	20.8	7.2	39%	35%	41%	45%
Population Living Below Poverty Line (65 and Older), %	16.3	24.3	7.6	47%	31%	37%	33%
EMPLOYMENT ISSUES							
Unemployment Rate, %	15.7	11.4	7.2	46%	63%	50%	71%
Labor Force Participation Rate, %	63.7	66.6	64.4	99%	103%	96%	104%
HOUSING & WEALTH							
Home Ownership Rate, %	32.8	25.3	66.7	49%	38%	60%	63%
Median Home Value, Dollars	351,100	346,600	413,100	85%	84%	65%	86%
TRANSPORTATION							
Car Ownership, %	55.6	53.6	78.1	71%	69%	80%	88%
Means of Transportation to Work: Drive Alone, %	41.8	36.9	60.2	69%	61%	90%	86%
Means of Transportation to Work: Public Transportation, %	44.7	38.8	21.9	49%	56%	26%	38%
EDUCATION							
ATTAINMENT							
Educational Attainment: at Least High School (25 Yrs. and Over), % of Population	83.8	66.6	93.3	90%	71%	92%	70%
Educational Attainment: at Least Bachelor's (25 Yrs. and Over), % of Population	23.0	16.3	46.6	49%	35%	62%	42%
Educational Attainment: Graduate or Professional Degree (25 Yrs. and Over), % of Population	7.9	5.4	20.3	39%	27%	60%	34%
STUDENT STATUS AND RISK FACTORS							
Children in All Families Below Poverty Level, %	24.8	28.9	7.8	32%	27%	31%	35%
Children in Families Below Poverty Level (Female Householder, No Spouse Present), %	36.6	47.5	20.4	56%	43%	68%	67%
Children (Under 18) With a Disability, %	3.5	4.0	2.5	71%	63%	80%	93%
HEALTH							
People Without Health Insurance, %	13.3	23.8	6.5	49%	27%	58%	38%
People With Private Health Insurance, %	55.2	41.6	80.0	69%	52%	68%	58%
SOCIAL JUSTICE							
Incarceration Rate: Prisoners in Jail Per 100,000 People	561.7	241.2	56.7	10%	24%	18%	40%

Source: Census ACS 2012 1-year estimates (unless otherwise noted). Black is Black or African American alone, not Hispanic. Incarceration rates are IHS calculations, using Bureau of Justice Statistics, Annual Survey of Jails, 2011 and Census population estimates.

NEW YORK POPULATION DEMOGRAPHICS

★ Black **16%** ★ Hispanic **24%**
★ White **48%** ★ Other **13%**

ARVA RICE
PRESIDENT, NEW YORK URBAN LEAGUE

ORLANDO

	ORLANDO–KISSIMMEE–SANFORD, FL					UNITED STATES	
	Black	Hispanic	White	Black-White Index	Hispanic-White Index	Black-White Index	Hispanic-White Index
ECONOMICS							
Median Household Income (Real), Dollars	34,394	35,830	53,763	64%	67%	60%	71%
POVERTY							
Population Living Below Poverty Line, %	25.7	23.5	11.1	43%	47%	39%	43%
Population Living Below Poverty Line (Under 18), %	38.1	30.9	14.4	38%	47%	32%	36%
Population Living Below Poverty Line (18–64), %	21.0	20.4	11.5	55%	56%	41%	45%
Population Living Below Poverty Line (65 and Older), %	18.3	21.8	6.1	33%	28%	37%	33%
EMPLOYMENT ISSUES							
Unemployment Rate, %	18.4	11.9	9.5	52%	80%	50%	71%
Labor Force Participation Rate, %	69.3	66.5	63.6	109%	105%	96%	104%
HOUSING & WEALTH							
Home Ownership Rate, %	40.5	48.6	70.6	57%	69%	60%	63%
Median Home Value, Dollars	113,500	118,000	153,400	74%	77%	65%	86%
TRANSPORTATION							
Car Ownership, %	87.2	92.7	96.3	91%	96%	80%	88%
Means of Transportation to Work: Drive Alone, %	77.1	76.8	83.6	92%	92%	90%	86%
Means of Transportation to Work: Public Transportation, %	6.5	1.8	0.6	9%	33%	26%	38%
EDUCATION							
ATTAINMENT							
Educational Attainment: at Least High School (25 Yrs. and Over), % of Population	85.3	79.2	92.3	90%	86%	92%	70%
Educational Attainment: at Least Bachelor's (25 Yrs. and Over), % of Population	18.6	18.0	33.0	56%	55%	62%	42%
Educational Attainment: Graduate or Professional Degree (25 Yrs. and Over), % of Population	7.1	5.1	11.1	64%	46%	60%	34%
STUDENT STATUS AND RISK FACTORS							
Children in All Families Below Poverty Level, %	29.3	29.7	12.5	43%	42%	31%	35%
Children in Families Below Poverty Level (Female Householder, No Spouse Present), %	41.5	54.2	32.0	70%	60%	68%	67%
Children (Under 18) With a Disability, %	7.1	5.6	3.2	45%	57%	80%	93%
HEALTH							
People Without Health Insurance, %	25.1	30.4	13.8	55%	45%	58%	38%
People With Private Health Insurance, %	46.7	43.2	72.0	65%	60%	68%	58%
SOCIAL JUSTICE							
Incarceration Rate: Prisoners in Jail Per 100,000 People	908.8	20.2	238.0	26%	1,177%	18%	40%

Source: Census ACS 2012 1-year estimates (unless otherwise noted). Black is Black or African American alone, not Hispanic. Incarceration rates are IHS calculations, using Bureau of Justice Statistics, Annual Survey of Jails, 2011 and Census population estimates.

ORLANDO POPULATION DEMOGRAPHICS

★ Black **15%** ★ Hispanic **27%**
★ White **52%** ★ Other **6%**

CENTRAL FLORIDA URBAN LEAGUE

PHILADELPHIA

	PHILADELPHIA–CAMDEN–WILMINGTON, PA–NJ–DE– MD					UNITED STATES	
	Black	Hispanic	White	Black-White Index	Hispanic-White Index	Black-White Index	Hispanic-White Index
ECONOMICS							
Median Household Income (Real), Dollars	35,989	36,175	71,122	51%	51%	60%	71%
POVERTY							
Population Living Below Poverty Line, %	25.3	29.6	7.4	29%	25%	39%	43%
Population Living Below Poverty Line (Under 18), %	34.2	37.5	6.9	20%	18%	32%	36%
Population Living Below Poverty Line (18–64), %	23.0	25.5	7.6	33%	30%	41%	45%
Population Living Below Poverty Line (65 and Older), %	17.1	24.8	7.0	41%	28%	37%	33%
EMPLOYMENT ISSUES							
Unemployment Rate, %	18.3	14.6	8.0	44%	55%	50%	71%
Labor Force Participation Rate, %	60.2	64.8	66.2	91%	98%	96%	104%
HOUSING & WEALTH							
Home Ownership Rate, %	48.3	44.2	75.9	64%	58%	60%	63%
Median Home Value, Dollars	126,600	152,700	254,500	50%	60%	65%	86%
TRANSPORTATION							
Car Ownership, %	69.2	77.7	91.7	76%	85%	80%	88%
Means of Transportation to Work: Drive Alone, %	59.8	59.6	78.7	76%	76%	90%	86%
Means of Transportation to Work: Public Transportation, %	24.4	13.5	5.4	22%	40%	26%	38%
EDUCATION							
ATTAINMENT							
Educational Attainment: at Least High School (25 Yrs. and Over), % of Population	84.8	67.7	92.8	91%	73%	92%	70%
Educational Attainment: at Least Bachelor's (25 Yrs. and Over), % of Population	18.0	14.9	38.8	46%	38%	62%	42%
Educational Attainment: Graduate or Professional Degree (25 Yrs. and Over), % of Population	6.5	5.2	15.1	43%	34%	60%	34%
STUDENT STATUS AND RISK FACTORS							
Children in All Families Below Poverty Level, %	28.0	35.3	6.4	23%	18%	31%	35%
Children in Families Below Poverty Level (Female Householder, No Spouse Present), %	38.6	54.7	20.2	52%	37%	68%	67%
Children (Under 18) With a Disability, %	5.4	7.0	3.9	72%	56%	80%	93%
HEALTH							
People Without Health Insurance, %	13.4	22.7	6.5	49%	29%	58%	38%
People With Private Health Insurance, %	51.4	40.8	82.3	63%	50%	68%	58%
SOCIAL JUSTICE							
Incarceration Rate: Prisoners in Jail Per 100,000 People	1027.5	521.3	144.4	14%	28%	18%	40%

Source: Census ACS 2012 1-year estimates (unless otherwise noted). Black is Black or African American alone, not Hispanic. Incarceration rates are IHS calculations, using Bureau of Justice Statistics, Annual Survey of Jails, 2011 and Census population estimates.

PHILADELPHIA POPULATION DEMOGRAPHICS

★ *Black* **20%**   ★ *Hispanic* **8%**
★ *White* **64%**   ★ *Other* **8%**

PATRICIA A. COULTER
PRESIDENT, URBAN LEAGUE OF PHILADELPHIA

RICHMOND

	Black	Hispanic	White	Black-White Index	Hispanic-White Index	Black-White Index	Hispanic-White Index
		RICHMOND, VA				**UNITED STATES**	
ECONOMICS							
Median Household Income (Real), Dollars	39,012	45,509	67,277	58%	68%	60%	71%
POVERTY							
Population Living Below Poverty Line, %	19.7	22.5	7.3	37%	32%	39%	43%
Population Living Below Poverty Line (Under 18), %	28.5	26.5	6.5	23%	25%	32%	36%
Population Living Below Poverty Line (18–64), %	17.3	21.2	8.0	46%	38%	41%	45%
Population Living Below Poverty Line (65 and Older), %	13.6	6.5	5.6	41%	86%	37%	33%
EMPLOYMENT ISSUES							
Unemployment Rate, %	13.3	12.9	5.8	44%	45%	50%	71%
Labor Force Participation Rate, %	63.0	76.3	66.2	95%	115%	96%	104%
HOUSING & WEALTH							
Home Ownership Rate, %	51.3	48.4	76.2	67%	64%	60%	63%
Median Home Value, Dollars	157,100	200,700	225,500	70%	89%	65%	86%
TRANSPORTATION							
Car Ownership, %	86.4	91.7	96.2	90%	95%	80%	88%
Means of Transportation to Work: Drive Alone, %	77.8	67.7	84.2	92%	80%	90%	86%
Means of Transportation to Work: Public Transportation, %	3.6	4.8	0.6	17%	13%	26%	30%
EDUCATION							
ATTAINMENT							
Educational Attainment: at Least High School (25 Yrs. and Over), % of Population	80.1	65.2	92.1	87%	71%	92%	70%
Educational Attainment: at Least Bachelor's (25 Yrs. and Over), % of Population	17.6	20.6	38.9	45%	53%	62%	42%
Educational Attainment: Graduate or Professional Degree (25 Yrs. and Over), % of Population	6.6	6.7	14.1	47%	48%	60%	34%
STUDENT STATUS AND RISK FACTORS							
Children in All Families Below Poverty Level, %	24.6	17.6	7.0	29%	40%	31%	35%
Children in Families Below Poverty Level (Female Householder, No Spouse Present), %	38.5	35.1	25.0	65%	71%	68%	67%
Children (Under 18) With a Disability, %	6.0	5.1	3.3	55%	65%	80%	93%
HEALTH							
People Without Health Insurance, %	16.4	35.0	8.9	54%	25%	58%	38%
People With Private Health Insurance, %	59.5	44.3	81.8	73%	54%	68%	58%
SOCIAL JUSTICE							
Incarceration Rate: Prisoners in Jail Per 100,000 People	1,103.8	NA	212.0	19%	NA	18%	40%

Source: Census ACS 2012 1-year estimates (unless otherwise noted). Black is Black or African American alone, not Hispanic. Incarceration rates are IHS calculations, using Bureau of Justice Statistics, Annual Survey of Jails, 2011 and Census population estimates.
NA: Not Available

RICHMOND POPULATION DEMOGRAPHICS

★ Black **30%** ★ Hispanic **5%**
★ White **59%** ★ Other **6%**

TIFFANY FORTUNE
BOARD CHAIR,
URBAN LEAGUE OF
GREATER RICHMOND, INC.

RIVERSIDE

	RIVERSIDE–SAN BERNADINO–ONTARIO, CA					UNITED STATES	
	Black	Hispanic	White	Black-White Index	Hispanic-White Index	Black-White Index	Hispanic-White Index
ECONOMICS							
Median Household Income (Real), Dollars	44,572	45,912	57,252	78%	80%	60%	71%
POVERTY							
Population Living Below Poverty Line, %	27.5	23.9	12.1	44%	51%	39%	43%
Population Living Below Poverty Line (Under 18), %	39.1	31.7	13.5	35%	43%	32%	36%
Population Living Below Poverty Line (18–64), %	24.1	20.0	12.9	54%	65%	41%	45%
Population Living Below Poverty Line (65 and Older), %	16.7	15.1	8.3	40%	55%	37%	33%
EMPLOYMENT ISSUES							
Unemployment Rate, %	19.2	15.3	12.2	64%	80%	50%	71%
Labor Force Participation Rate, %	55.6	63.3	56.4	99%	112%	96%	104%
HOUSING & WEALTH							
Home Ownership Rate, %	45.5	53.8	71.1	64%	76%	60%	63%
Median Home Value, Dollars	215,600	182,400	223,500	97%	82%	65%	86%
TRANSPORTATION							
Car Ownership, %	90.4	94.7	94.8	95%	100%	80%	88%
Means of Transportation to Work: Drive Alone, %	79.0	76.7	79.4	100%	97%	90%	86%
Means of Transportation to Work: Public Transportation, %	3.5	1.6	1.1	31%	69%	26%	38%
EDUCATION							
ATTAINMENT							
Educational Attainment: at Least High School (25 Yrs. and Over), % of Population	88.8	61.1	92.0	97%	66%	92%	70%
Educational Attainment: at Least Bachelor's (25 Yrs. and Over), % of Population	19.2	8.2	25.7	75%	32%	62%	42%
Educational Attainment: Graduate or Professional Degree (25 Yrs. and Over), % of Population	7.0	2.1	9.8	71%	21%	60%	34%
STUDENT STATUS AND RISK FACTORS							
Children in All Families Below Poverty Level, %	30.9	26.7	12.8	41%	48%	31%	35%
Children in Families Below Poverty Level (Female Householder, No Spouse Present), %	49.1	47.7	29.5	60%	62%	68%	67%
Children (Under 18) With a Disability, %	5.1	2.6	2.9	57%	112%	80%	93%
HEALTH							
People Without Health Insurance, %	15.3	27.1	13.6	90%	50%	58%	38%
People With Private Health Insurance, %	52.0	43.0	67.1	78%	64%	68%	58%
SOCIAL JUSTICE							
Incarceration Rate: Prisoners in Jail Per 100,000 People	850.9	313.9	205.7	24%	66%	18%	40%

Source: Census ACS 2012 1-year estimates (unless otherwise noted). Black is Black or African American alone, not Hispanic. Incarceration rates are IHS calculations, using Bureau of Justice Statistics, Annual Survey of Jails, 2011 and Census population estimates.

RIVERSIDE POPULATION DEMOGRAPHICS

★ Black **7%**   ★ Hispanic **48%**
★ White **35%**   ★ Other **9%**

THE MEDIAN HOUSEHOLD INCOME FOR HISPANICS IN RIVERSIDE IS $45,912

SAN FRANCISCO

	SAN FRANCISCO-OAKLAND-FREMONT, CA					UNITED STATES	
	Black	Hispanic	White	Black-White Index	Hispanic-White Index	Black-White Index	Hispanic-White Index
ECONOMICS							
Median Household Income (Real), Dollars	40,753	51,420	90,452	45%	57%	60%	71%
POVERTY							
Population Living Below Poverty Line, %	25.4	17.5	7.3	29%	42%	39%	43%
Population Living Below Poverty Line (Under 18), %	36.5	23.2	6.1	17%	26%	32%	36%
Population Living Below Poverty Line (18–64), %	23.9	15.3	7.9	33%	52%	41%	45%
Population Living Below Poverty Line (65 and Older), %	14.0	11.9	5.8	41%	49%	37%	33%
EMPLOYMENT ISSUES							
Unemployment Rate, %	18.6	10.9	6.7	36%	62%	50%	71%
Labor Force Participation Rate, %	59.9	70.0	66.7	90%	105%	96%	104%
HOUSING & WEALTH							
Home Ownership Rate, %	32.5	37.3	59.8	54%	62%	60%	63%
Median Home Value, Dollars	327,700	370,500	621,200	53%	60%	65%	86%
TRANSPORTATION							
Car Ownership, %	76.6	88.9	88.9	86%	100%	80%	88%
Means of Transportation to Work: Drive Alone, %	60.6	60.5	61.9	98%	98%	90%	86%
Means of Transportation to Work: Public Transportation, %	20.7	14.6	14.0	68%	96%	26%	38%
EDUCATION							
ATTAINMENT							
Educational Attainment: at Least High School (25 Yrs. and Over), % of Population	89.2	67.4	96.6	92%	70%	92%	70%
Educational Attainment: at Least Bachelor's (25 Yrs. and Over), % of Population	23.3	18.2	56.6	41%	32%	62%	42%
Educational Attainment: Graduate or Professional Degree (25 Yrs. and Over), % of Population	8.0	5.7	23.6	34%	24%	60%	34%
STUDENT STATUS AND RISK FACTORS							
Children in All Families Below Poverty Level, %	31.4	20.5	4.6	15%	22%	31%	35%
Children in Families Below Poverty Level (Female Householder, No Spouse Present), %	44.4	42.6	15.3	35%	36%	68%	67%
Children (Under 18) With a Disability, %	5.7	3.6	2.5	44%	69%	80%	93%
HEALTH							
People Without Health Insurance, %	12.2	22.8	6.4	53%	28%	58%	38%
People With Private Health Insurance, %	56.2	51.9	84.0	67%	62%	68%	58%
SOCIAL JUSTICE							
Incarceration Rate: Prisoners in Jail Per 100,000 People	1,190.3	261.5	103.9	9%	40%	18%	40%

Source: Census ACS 2012 1-year estimates (unless otherwise noted). Black is Black or African American alone, not Hispanic. Incarceration rates are IHS calculations, using Bureau of Justice Statistics, Annual Survey of Jails, 2011 and Census population estimates.

SAN FRANCISCO POPULATION DEMOGRAPHICS

★ Black **8%**   ★ Hispanic **22%**
★ White **42%**   ★ Other **29%**

THE MEDIAN HOME VALUE OF BLACKS IN SAN FRANCISCO IS $327,700 COMPARED TO $621,200 FOR WHITES

ST. LOUIS

	ST. LOUIS, MO–IL					UNITED STATES	
	Black	Hispanic	White	Black-White Index	Hispanic-White Index	Black-White Index	Hispanic-White Index
ECONOMICS							
Median Household Income (Real), Dollars	28,500	39,026	59,607	48%	66%	60%	71%
POVERTY							
Population Living Below Poverty Line, %	32.9	25.2	9.1	28%	36%	39%	43%
Population Living Below Poverty Line (Under 18), %	47.7	29.3	11.2	24%	38%	32%	36%
Population Living Below Poverty Line (18–64), %	29.1	23.8	9.3	32%	39%	41%	45%
Population Living Below Poverty Line (65 and Older), %	16.6	15.2	5.7	34%	38%	37%	33%
EMPLOYMENT ISSUES							
Unemployment Rate, %	19.6	9.1	6.9	35%	76%	50%	71%
Labor Force Participation Rate, %	61.2	70.1	66.7	92%	105%	96%	104%
HOUSING & WEALTH							
Home Ownership Rate, %	41.1	47.4	77.3	53%	61%	60%	63%
Median Home Value, Dollars	88,500	139,600	161,200	55%	87%	65%	86%
TRANSPORTATION							
Car Ownership, %	76.5	91.2	94.8	81%	96%	80%	88%
Means of Transportation to Work: Drive Alone, %	74.8	72.2	84.4	89%	86%	90%	86%
Means of Transportation to Work: Public Transportation, %	10.0	0.8	0.9	9%	113%	26%	38%
EDUCATION							
ATTAINMENT							
Educational Attainment: at Least High School (25 Yrs. and Over), % of Population	82.0	73.6	92.0	89%	80%	92%	70%
Educational Attainment: at Least Bachelor's (25 Yrs. and Over), % of Population	16.8	20.9	33.0	51%	63%	62%	42%
Educational Attainment: Graduate or Professional Degree (25 Yrs. and Over), % of Population	6.8	8.7	12.2	56%	71%	60%	34%
STUDENT STATUS AND RISK FACTORS							
Children in All Families Below Poverty Level, %	40.4	27.3	11.1	28%	41%	31%	35%
Children in Families Below Poverty Level (Female Householder, No Spouse Present), %	51.6	48.8	30.2	59%	62%	68%	67%
Children (Under 18) With a Disability, %	4.7	11.0	4.2	89%	38%	80%	93%
HEALTH							
People Without Health Insurance, %	19.6	23.5	8.6	44%	37%	58%	38%
People With Private Health Insurance, %	43.5	55.3	78.3	56%	71%	68%	58%
SOCIAL JUSTICE							
Incarceration Rate: Prisoners in Jail Per 100,000 People	720.7	27.0	47.4	7%	176%	18%	40%

Source: Census ACS 2012 1-year estimates (unless otherwise noted). Black is Black or African American alone, not Hispanic. Incarceration rates are IHS calculations, using Bureau of Justice Statistics, Annual Survey of Jails, 2011 and Census population estimates.

ST. LOUIS POPULATION DEMOGRAPHICS

★ Black **18%** ★ Hispanic **3%**
★ White **75%** ★ Other **5%**

MICHAEL P. MCMILLAN
PRESIDENT, URBAN LEAGUE METROPOLITAN ST. LOUIS

TAMPA

	TAMPA-ST. PETERSBURG-CLEARWATER, FL					UNITED STATES	
	Black	Hispanic	White	Black-White Index	Hispanic-White Index	Black-White Index	Hispanic-White Index
ECONOMICS							
Median Household Income (Real), Dollars	31,108	35,662	48,421	64%	74%	60%	71%
POVERTY							
Population Living Below Poverty Line, %	31.4	25.1	11.7	37%	47%	39%	43%
Population Living Below Poverty Line (Under 18), %	42.8	32.5	15.0	35%	46%	32%	36%
Population Living Below Poverty Line (18-64), %	27.4	22.0	12.6	46%	57%	41%	45%
Population Living Below Poverty Line (65 and Older), %	23.1	22.7	6.9	30%	30%	37%	33%
EMPLOYMENT ISSUES							
Unemployment Rate, %	17.2	12.7	9.6	56%	76%	50%	71%
Labor Force Participation Rate, %	63.2	66.4	57.3	110%	116%	96%	104%
HOUSING & WEALTH							
Home Ownership Rate, %	40.1	49.1	70.7	57%	69%	60%	63%
Median Home Value, Dollars	112,600	120,800	135,300	83%	89%	65%	86%
TRANSPORTATION							
Car Ownership, %	85.5	91.2	93.3	92%	98%	80%	88%
Means of Transportation to Work: Drive Alone, %	81.4	74.3	81.6	100%	91%	90%	86%
Means of Transportation to Work: Public Transportation, %	4.6	1.6	0.6	13%	38%	26%	38%
EDUCATION							
ATTAINMENT							
Educational Attainment: at Least High School (25 Yrs. and Over), % of Population	83.9	77.8	91.2	92%	85%	92%	70%
Educational Attainment: at Least Bachelor's (25 Yrs. and Over), % of Population	19.0	18.9	28.8	66%	66%	62%	42%
Educational Attainment: Graduate or Professional Degree (25 Yrs. and Over), % of Population	7.1	6.3	9.9	72%	64%	60%	34%
STUDENT STATUS AND RISK FACTORS							
Children in All Families Below Poverty Level, %	34.5	29.4	12.6	37%	43%	31%	35%
Children in Families Below Poverty Level (Female Householder, No Spouse Present), %	40.3	44.7	26.3	57%	59%	68%	67%
Children (Under 18) With a Disability, %	5.0	4.6	4.4	88%	96%	80%	93%
HEALTH							
People Without Health Insurance, %	19.8	29.3	14.2	72%	49%	58%	38%
People With Private Health Insurance, %	45.8	41.1	65.5	70%	63%	68%	58%
SOCIAL JUSTICE							
Incarceration Rate: Prisoners in Jail Per 100,000 People	1,123.5	281.5	291.0	26%	103%	18%	40%

Source: Census ACS 2012 1-year estimates (unless otherwise noted). Black is Black or African American alone, not Hispanic. Incarceration rates are IHS calculations, using Bureau of Justice Statistics, Annual Survey of Jails, 2011 and Census population estimates.

TAMPA POPULATION DEMOGRAPHICS

★ *Black* **11%** ★ *Hispanic* **17%**
★ *White* **66%** ★ *Other* **5%**

18.9% OF HISPANICS OVER 25 IN TAMPA HAVE EARNED A BACHELOR'S DEGREE

VIRGINIA BEACH

	VIRGINIA BEACH–NORFOLK–NEWPORT NEWS, VA					UNITED STATES	
	Black	Hispanic	White	Black-White Index	Hispanic-White Index	Black-White Index	Hispanic-White Index
ECONOMICS							
Median Household Income (Real), Dollars	40,897	45,590	65,141	63%	70%	60%	71%
POVERTY							
Population Living Below Poverty Line, %	21.7	21.0	7.9	36%	38%	39%	43%
Population Living Below Poverty Line (Under 18), %	33.0	26.4	9.9	30%	38%	32%	36%
Population Living Below Poverty Line (18–64), %	18.1	18.9	8.0	44%	42%	41%	45%
Population Living Below Poverty Line (65 and Older), %	14.8	5.1	4.8	32%	94%	37%	33%
EMPLOYMENT ISSUES							
Unemployment Rate, %	13.1	13.2	6.5	50%	49%	50%	71%
Labor Force Participation Rate, %	63.7	63.3	61.4	104%	103%	96%	104%
HOUSING & WEALTH							
Home Ownership Rate, %	43.2	40.0	70.9	61%	56%	60%	63%
Median Home Value, Dollars	190,300	241,000	247,100	77%	98%	65%	86%
TRANSPORTATION							
Car Ownership, %	86.8	95.7	96.7	90%	99%	80%	88%
Means of Transportation to Work: Drive Alone, %	78.5	71.7	83.2	94%	86%	90%	86%
Means of Transportation to Work: Public Transportation, %	4.9	1.3	0.6	12%	46%	26%	38%
EDUCATION							
ATTAINMENT							
Educational Attainment: at Least High School (25 Yrs. and Over), % of Population	85.0	79.7	92.8	92%	86%	92%	70%
Educational Attainment: at Least Bachelor's (25 Yrs. and Over), % of Population	18.7	19.7	33.4	56%	59%	62%	42%
Educational Attainment: Graduate or Professional Degree (25 Yrs. and Over), % of Population	6.6	6.2	12.5	53%	50%	60%	34%
STUDENT STATUS AND RISK FACTORS							
Children in All Families Below Poverty Level, %	27.0	30.2	9.4	35%	31%	31%	35%
Children in Families Below Poverty Level (Female Householder, No Spouse Present), %	41.5	59.3	28.8	69%	49%	68%	67%
Children (Under 18) With a Disability, %	4.3	3.6	3.7	86%	103%	80%	93%
HEALTH							
People Without Health Insurance, %	14.9	21.2	8.7	58%	41%	58%	38%
People With Private Health Insurance, %	60.5	64.6	82.8	73%	78%	68%	58%
SOCIAL JUSTICE							
Incarceration Rate: Prisoners in Jail Per 100,000 People	1,289.6	418.8	233.0	18%	56%	18%	40%

Source: Census ACS 2012 1-year estimates (unless otherwise noted). Black is Black or African American alone, not Hispanic. Incarceration rates are IHS calculations, using Bureau of Justice Statistics, Annual Survey of Jails, 2011 and Census population estimates.

VIRGINIA BEACH POPULATION DEMOGRAPHICS

★ Black **30%**   ★ Hispanic **6%**
★ White **57%**   ★ Other **7%**

EDITH G. WHITE
PRESIDENT, URBAN LEAGUE OF HAMPTON ROADS

WASHINGTON, D.C.

	WASHINGTON–ARLINGTON–ALEXANDRIA, D.C.–VA–MD–WV					UNITED STATES	
	Black	Hispanic	White	Black-White Index	Hispanic-White Index	Black-White Index	Hispanic-White Index
ECONOMICS							
Median Household Income (Real), Dollars	62,726	63,779	106,597	59%	60%	60%	71%
POVERTY							
Population Living Below Poverty Line, %	13.6	12.8	4.6	34%	36%	39%	43%
Population Living Below Poverty Line (Under 18), %	19.1	15.5	4.5	24%	29%	32%	36%
Population Living Below Poverty Line (18–64), %	11.9	11.6	4.8	40%	41%	41%	45%
Population Living Below Poverty Line (65 and Older), %	11.3	11.4	3.8	34%	33%	37%	33%
EMPLOYMENT ISSUES							
Unemployment Rate, %	12.0	6.6	4.2	35%	64%	50%	71%
Labor Force Participation Rate, %	70.6	78.4	70.9	100%	111%	96%	104%
HOUSING & WEALTH							
Home Ownership Rate, %	50.2	46.2	71.6	70%	65%	60%	65%
Median Home Value, Dollars	278,700	302,600	406,200	69%	75%	65%	86%
TRANSPORTATION							
Car Ownership, %	82.0	88.4	93.0	88%	95%	80%	88%
Means of Transportation to Work: Drive Alone, %	64.7	56.4	68.7	94%	82%	90%	86%
Means of Transportation to Work: Public Transportation, %	20.1	16.4	11.4	57%	70%	26%	38%
EDUCATION							
ATTAINMENT							
Educational Attainment: at Least High School (25 Yrs. and Over), % of Population	89.9	65.3	96.2	94%	68%	92%	70%
Educational Attainment: at Least Bachelor's (25 Yrs. and Over), % of Population	30.9	24.7	59.7	52%	41%	62%	42%
Educational Attainment: Graduate or Professional Degree (25 Yrs. and Over), % of Population	13.7	9.7	29.7	46%	33%	60%	34%
STUDENT STATUS AND RISK FACTORS							
Children in All Families Below Poverty Level, %	14.5	13.9	3.5	24%	25%	31%	35%
Children in Families Below Poverty Level (Female Householder, No Spouse Present), %	25.4	31.1	16.0	63%	51%	68%	67%
Children (Under 18) With a Disability, %	4.1	1.7	2.7	66%	159%	80%	93%
HEALTH							
People Without Health Insurance, %	10.9	31.7	5.4	50%	17%	58%	38%
People With Private Health Insurance, %	68.0	49.9	89.1	76%	56%	68%	58%
SOCIAL JUSTICE							
Incarceration Rate: Prisoners in Jail Per 100,000 People	607.6	163.6	129.7	21%	79%	18%	40%

Source: Census ACS 2012 1-year estimates (unless otherwise noted). Black is Black or African American alone, not Hispanic. Incarceration rates are IHS calculations, using Bureau of Justice Statistics, Annual Survey of Jails, 2011 and Census population estimates.

WASHINGTON, D.C. POPULATION DEMOGRAPHICS

★ Black **25%** ★ Hispanic **15%**
★ White **48%** ★ Other **13%**

GEORGE H. LAMBERT, JR.
PRESIDENT, GREATER WASHINGTON URBAN LEAGUE

21ST CENTURY AGENDA FOR JOBS AND FREEDOM

A SPECIAL COLLECTION OF ARTICLES & OP-EDS

OPEN

VOTER REGISTRATION

© NATIONAL URBAN LEAGUE

INTRODUCTION TO THE SPECIAL SECTION

CHANELLE P. HARDY, ESQ.,
NATIONAL URBAN LEAGUE WASHINGTON BUREAU

Recent reports indicate that nearly 1 in 5 African Americans were unemployed in 2013. Even as our *State of Black America* 2013 Equality Index indicated tremendous gains in educational achievement by African Americans over the course of the last 50 years, we continue to see that African Americans at all levels of education are twice as likely as whites to be unemployed. Even as our nation as a whole is encouraged by signs of a modest economic recovery, African Americans—and communities of color— remain challenged by a complex set of interconnected barriers to equality.

On one hand, there is reason to rejoice:

- *The Department of Education issued much-needed guidance on discriminatory school discipline practices.*
- *The initial rollout of a set of Common Core State Standards promises to promote educational equity.*
- *More than 3 million Americans have enrolled in health insurance coverage through the ACA.*
- *Thousands who have languished in prison could be freed thanks to proposals to reduce sentencing disparities in some drug crimes.*
- *Legislation introduced this year to resuscitate Section 5 of the Voting Rights Act has become one of the few examples of bipartisan cooperation.*

- *Investments in job training and placement could help put millions of long-term unemployed back-to-work.*

On the other hand, we are reminded of the heavy civil rights and social justice losses we have recently experienced:

- *Devastating set-backs in affirmative action and voting rights threaten a 50-year legacy of progress.*
- *Crippling budget cuts literally take food from the mouths of hungry children.*
- *Insulated leaders are seemingly unable to empathize with the regular people they were elected to represent.*
- *A wealthy few enjoy excellent returns on the stock market even as the masses face foreclosure and dwindling bank accounts.*

It is against this backdrop that we present this year's *State of Black America, One Nation Underemployed: Jobs Rebuild America*, a title that captures both our hope for a united nation and our commitment to addressing the root cause of economic inequality. It's also a title that speaks to the legacy and mission of the National Urban League which, for more than a century, has worked to level the economic playing field and ensure that we all have an equal opportunity to succeed.

This year's special section features commentary on the *21st Century Agenda for Jobs and Freedom*, a blueprint created to achieve this mission.

Last year the African American Leaders Convening, a coalition that comprises civil rights, social justice, business and community leaders, put forth this policy agenda that lays out the steps needed to pave the way to job growth, recovery and empowerment for African American and urban communities and all low-income and working-class Americans. This year's special section is informed by that agenda and features insights, perspectives and, most important, solutions from elected officials including Congressmen Rubén Hinojosa and Representative Mike Honda; civil rights leaders like Leadership Conference on Civil and Human Rights head, Wade Henderson; and scholars such as Thomas M. Shapiro from Brandeis University, who weigh in on its five underlying principles for achieving empowerment:

1. ACHIEVING ECONOMIC PARITY FOR AFRICAN AMERICANS

2. PROMOTING EQUITY IN EDUCATIONAL OPPORTUNITY

3. PROTECTING AND DEFENDING VOTING RIGHTS

4. PROMOTING A HEALTHIER NATION BY ELIMINATING HEALTHCARE DISPARITIES

5. ACHIEVING COMPREHENSIVE CRIMINAL JUSTICE SYSTEM REFORM

As a network of direct service providers and public policy advocates, the National Urban League and our affiliates have been at the forefront in tackling issues that impact the poor, vulnerable and underserved—overwhelmingly people of color. We are heartened by the ways in which proven solutions such as investments in job training and early childhood education have been elevated in the national policy dialogue. We are encouraged that income inequality; high and equitable education standards, discriminatory school discipline practices that exacerbate the school-to-prison pipeline; sentencing reform; the re-employment of ex-offenders; and the right to vote are now being addressed through bipartisan legislation and executive action.

This is a pivotal moment for our country; if men and women of good will continue to force our way through partisanship, greed and apathy, we can deliver on the promise of these proposed reforms. But the heavy civil rights and social justice losses of 2013 are a painful reminder that we must remain vigilant to protect the gains of yesterday even as we labor onwards to a future that is bright, prosperous and has room enough for all. ★

EQUITY & EXCELLENCE
LEAD TO OPPORTUNITY

THE HONORABLE MIKE HONDA

The Civil Rights Act of 1964 continues to have a powerful impact on our nation. It brought the struggle for equality into every living room, helping to create a national call for change. Through civil disobedience and the affirmation that separate is inherently unequal, that change eventually came.

The *Brown v. Board of Education* decision led the struggle for equity in education, declaring separate but equal as unconstitutional.

Sadly, 50 years later, our nation's children continue to face extreme inequities in their schools. White students are nearly three times more likely than Black students to be at or above proficient in reading and 3.4 times[1] more likely to be at or above proficient in math. The high school graduation rate for white students is twenty points higher than African Americans at 85 percent compared to 67 percent.[2]

In addition, in 2011, more than one-third of higher-poverty schools had lower funding levels per pupil than the wealthier schools in their districts.[3] This gap denies equal, let alone equitable, resources for the students most in need and forces high-poverty neighborhoods to make do with resources that would never be acceptable in wealthier areas.

In order to solve this crisis we need to ensure that each and every child is given a real opportunity to succeed.

Today, average daily attendance determines the funding in most educational systems. This model is based on the idea that an equal amount of support per child is necessary for students to be educated. Since each child is different, simply providing equal resources per child is inherently unequal. Each and every child must be supported by fiscal and human resources according to their individually assessed needs. Until we embrace the principle that full funding of our schools leads to equity we will not achieve true equality.

Every child can learn regardless of their station in life, their zip code, or their physical, psychological and linguistic skills. Equity in fiscal and human resources applied to each and every child based on their individual assessed needs is the next civil rights struggle.

As a former teacher, principal, and school board member, I have made parity in education the driving force of my career. Through legislation, I am advocating the expansion of access to technology in the classroom, promoting science programs for minorities and women, and funding universal preschool. I believe all avenues must be explored to generate the prosperity our children deserve.

As a member of Congress representing California's Silicon Valley—widely regarded as the birthplace of digital innovation—we must continue to look for new ways to help each student reach his or her potential. There exists a strong need to foster innovation in education policy, not limit it.

To meaningfully close the opportunity gap, we must eliminate blind adherence to existing school funding formulas. The future of our children—and our nation—depends on it. Parents, lawmakers, community organizers, and educators must coalesce to assert that each and every child receives the support and opportunities necessary to be successful.

Equity and excellence are the demands of our times. ★

NOTES

[1] U.S. Department of Education, Institute of Education Sciences, National Center for Education Statistics, National Assessment of Educational Progress (NAEP), various years, 1990–2013 Mathematics and Reading Assessments. Retrieved from: *http://nationsreportcard.gov/reading_math_2013/#/student-groups.*

[2] Stillwell,R., Sable,J. (2013). Public School Graduates and Dropouts from the Common Core of Data: School Year 2009–10. National Center for Education Statistics. Retrieved from: *http://nces.ed.gov/pubs2013/2013309rev.pdf.*

[3] Heuer, R., Stullich, S. (2011) Comparability of State and Local Expenditures Among Schools Within Districts: A Report from the Study of School-Level Expenditures. U.S. Department of Education. Retrieved from: *http://www2.ed.gov/rschstat/eval/title-i/school-level-expenditures/school-level-expenditures.pdf.*

POLICIES OF EXCLUSION PERPETUATE
THE RACIAL WEALTH GAP

THOMAS M. SHAPIRO, PH.D.

"The gap in wealth between races has not lessened, it's grown."—President Barack Obama at the Lincoln Memorial at the 50th Anniversary of the March on Washington for Jobs and Justice

The dramatic and widening gap in household wealth along racial lines in the United States reflects policies and institutional practices that create different opportunities for whites and African Americans. Personal ambition and behavioral choices are but a small part of the equation.

Last year, my colleagues at the Institute on Assets and Social Policy at Brandeis University and I published research based on a sample of 1,700 working-age households that were followed over a 25-year period—from 1984 to 2009. This approach offers a unique opportunity to understand what happens to the wealth gap over the course of a generation and the effect of policy and institutional decision-making on how average families accumulate wealth.

In gross terms, the difference in median wealth between America's white and African American households has grown stunningly large. The wealth gap almost tripled from 1984 to 2009, increasing from $85,000 to $236,500.[1] The median net worth of white households in the study grew to $265,000 over the 25-year period compared with just $28,500 for the Black households.[2]

The dramatic increase in the racial wealth gap materialized and accelerated despite the country's movement beyond the Civil Rights era into a period of legal equality. We statistically validated five "fundamental factors" that together account for two-thirds of the proportional increase in the racial wealth gap.[3] These include the number of years of home ownership; average family income; employment stability, particularly through the Great Recession; college education, and family financial support and inheritance.

These particular factors provide compelling evidence that various government and institutional policies that shape where we live, where we learn and where we work propel the large majority of the widening racial wealth gap. For example, homeownership alone accounts for 27 percent of the growth in the racial wealth gap. Some of the reasons why home equity rises dramatically faster for whites than for African Americans include:

- *White families buy homes and start acquiring equity eight years earlier than Black families because they are far more likely to receive family assistance or an inheritance for down payments.*
- *A larger up-front payment by white homeowners lowers interest rates.*
- *Residential segregation places an artificial ceiling on home equity in non-white neighborhoods.*
- *The home ownership rate for white families is 28 percent higher.*

Hard evidence shows in stark terms that it is not just the last recession and implosion of the housing market that contributed to widening racial wealth disparities. Past policies of exclusion, such as discriminatory mortgage lending, which continues today, ensure that certain groups reap a greater share of what America has to offer while others are left out.

All families need a financial cushion to be economically secure and create opportunities for the next generation. Wealth—what we own minus what we owe—allows families to move forward by moving to better and safer neighborhoods, investing in businesses, saving for retirement and supporting their children's college aspirations.

Our economy cannot sustain its growth in the face of extreme wealth and racial inequality; thus the road ahead is clear. Policymakers must take such steps as strengthening and enforcing

fair housing, mortgage and lending policies; raising the minimum wage and enforcing equal pay provisions; investing in high-quality childcare and early childhood development; and overhauling preferential tax treatments for dividend and interest income and the home mortgage deduction. ★

NOTES

[1] Shapiro, T., Meschede, T. & Osoro, S. (2013, Feb). *The Roots of the Widening Racial Wealth Gap: Explaining the Black-White Economic Divide.* Waltham, MA: Institute on Assets and Social Policy. All figures are in 2009 constant dollars.

[2] Ibid.

[3] Ibid.

FINANCIAL LITERACY

THE HONORABLE RUBÉN HINOJOSA

"It is not enough to teach our young people to be successful...so they can realize their ambitions, so they can earn good livings, so they can accumulate the material things that this society bestows. Those are worthwhile goals. But it is not enough to progress as individuals while our friends and neighbors are left behind."

—*Cesar E. Chavez*

Hispanic Americans and African Americans face similar barriers to prosperity, and so it is fitting for the National Urban League to explore the conditions faced by both groups. Our fates are intertwined as we all fight the same foes of poverty, inequality, and injustice. I am honored to share my perspective as Chairman of the Congressional Hispanic Caucus.

In the 20 years since the passing of Cesar Chavez, the wealth gap between Hispanics and whites has grown into a great chasm. According to the Pew Research Center in 2009, white households held 18 times as much wealth as Hispanic households, the widest gap in over two decades. The economic crisis hit Hispanic families especially hard. From 2005 to 2009, wealth fell by 66 percent among Hispanic households compared with just 16 percent among white households.[1] More so than white Americans, Hispanic families' assets were predominantly tied up in our homes, making us vulnerable when the housing market crashed.[2]

The income gap between Hispanic Americans and white Americans, while still inequitable, is much smaller than the wealth gap. Median white household income in 2011 was 1.4 times that of Hispanics.[3] In order to bridge the great wealth chasm, we must innovate ways for communities of color to transform our income into wealth. Increased financial literacy and access to safe, affordable financial products are necessary to build greater economic stability within our communities. Financially empowering Hispanic Americans is a top priority for me as the Chairman of the Congressional Hispanic Caucus and the Co-Founder and Co-Chair of the Financial and Economic Literacy Caucus.

Ten million Americans lack a bank account.[4] Nearly 15 percent of Hispanic Americans have never had a bank account.[5] Without a bank account, saving money becomes difficult and also hazardous. Customers of check-cashing establishments, with large amounts of cash on their person, are vulnerable to criminals.

Likewise, if your life savings is hidden under your mattress, not only are you at risk of inflation, but you are at extreme risk of robbery and of becoming destitute overnight. With a federally-insured bank or credit union account, your money is safe. Check-cashing, payday loans, and high-cost remittance services are costly, risky, and do not build assets or credit. One study found that an average unbanked person spent $1,200 on fees a year.[6] This is money that could be saved for retirement or a rainy day.

In my district, Hidalgo County, deep in South Texas, more than one-in-five residents lack a bank account. For many immigrants and their families, misconceptions about the trustworthiness of American financial institutions deter them from opening accounts. In many other countries, there is no government deposit guarantee. The corner bank will disappear overnight, along with all of your savings. Understandably, immigrants and their families will be influenced by these experiences. As community leaders, we must emphasize the importance of using mainstream financial services and clarify misconceptions.

Not only should we extol the value of banking to Hispanic communities, we also need to explain the value of banking Hispanic Americans to mainstream financial institutions. Banks and credit unions can be reluctant to offer affordable, low-barrier financial products in low-income communities. They can be reluctant to accept alternative identification. They cite fraud, a lack of profitability, underwriting issues, lack of consumer financial education, and regulatory challenges as major obstacles to banking the underserved.[7]

As a result, our communities experience many barriers to opening a bank account, from inaccessible branches and language barriers to high initial deposit requirements. The FDIC found that half of all banks require at least a $100 deposit to open a basic checking account.[8]

Additionally, one million consumers find themselves on a banking blacklist called ChexSystems, which leaves them stranded in financial purgatory.[9] Only two out of ten banks offer "Second-Chance Checking" accounts that give consumers in ChexSystems an opportunity to reenter the financial mainstream.[10]

Only four in ten banks develop products for the underserved.[11] Financial institutions should recognize that unbanked and underbanked consumers represent an untapped market that should not be ignored. Together, lawmakers financial regulators, and financial institutions can lower the barriers to banking and offer financial education that is culturally relevant. As Cesar Chavez declared, we cannot allow our "friends and neighbors to be left behind." ★

NOTES

[1] Kochar, R., Fry, R., Taylor P. (2011) Wealth Gaps Rise to Record Highs Between Whites, Blacks, Hispanics Twenty-to-One, Pew Research, Social and Demographic Trends. Retrieved from: http://www.pewsocialtrends.org/2011/07/26/wealth-gaps-rise-to-record-highs-between-whites-blacks-hispanics/.

[2] Ibid.

[3] United States Census Bureau. (2012) American Community Survey. Retrieved from: *https://www.census.gov/acs/www/.*

[4] Federal Deposit Insurance Corporation. (2011) 2011 FDIC National Survey of Unbanked and Underbanked Households. Retrieved from: *http://www.fdic.gov/householdsurvey/.*

[5] Ibid.

[6] Beard, M. (2010) Reaching the Unbanked and Underbanked. Federal Reserve of St. Louis. Retrieved from: *https://www.stlouisfed.org/publications/cb/articles/?id=2039.*

[7] Federal Deposit Insurance Corporation. (2011) 2011 Survey of Unbanked and Underbanked Households. Retrieved from: *http://www.fdic.gov/householdsurvey/.*

[8] Ibid.

[9] Silver-Greenberg, J. (2013, July 30). Over a Million Are Denied Bank Accounts for Past Errors. New York Times. Retrieved from: *http://dealbook.nytimes.com/2013/07/30/over-a-million-are-denied-bank-accounts-for-past-errors/.*

[10] Federal Deposit Insurance Corporation. (2011) 2011 Survey of Unbanked and Underbanked Households. Retrieved from: *http://www.fdic.gov/householdsurvey/.*

[11] Ibid.

A WATERSHED YEAR FOR BIPARTISANSHIP
IN CRIMINAL JUSTICE REFORM

WADE HENDERSON, ESQ.

For decades, overwhelming growth in our nation's prison population has been a defining issue for Black America. But 2014 marks a watershed moment for hopes to reform our criminal justice system at the state and federal level.

The War on Drugs has decimated Black and Latino communities. One out of every three Black men will be incarcerated at some point in their lives, and the majority of those arrests will be drug-related.[1] Mandatory minimums and disparities in crack-cocaine sentencing incarcerated countless African Americans for an inhumane length of time and have made the U.S. the world leader in prison population.[2]

This has created a modern day caste system in America where millions of people—mostly African Americans, Latinos, and low-income whites—are marked with a scarlet letter that creates permanent barriers to voting, getting a job or an education, and reintegrating into society. It has also led to a criminal justice system that is unfair, discriminatory, and expensive.

But actions in Congress, the states, and by the Department of Justice are marking a seachange in how our nation views criminal justice issues. The emotional and reactive "tough on crime" approach has given way to a more practical, fair, and economical "smart on crime" consensus.

This bipartisan convergence marks the most significant and coordinated advance in reforming our criminal justice system that we've seen in years.

The Department of Justice is acting decisively to implement the "Smart on Crime" initiative, which seeks to avert mandatory minimum sentences, works to rehabilitate drug users instead of warehousing them in expensive and often violent prisons, and removes barriers to re-entering society. The Justice Department is also revisiting the sentences of some non-violent inmates who have already paid their debt to society and is creating a formal process for these prisoners to apply for clemency.

In a congressional environment that has never been more polarized, an unprecedented bipartisan consensus has lined up behind bills like the Smarter Sentencing Act[4] and the Second Chance Act,[5] which would make sentencing more humane and ease the re-entry process for the formerly incarcerated. Tea party favorites in Congress like Senators Rand Paul (R-KY) and Mike Lee (R-UT) and Congressman Raul Labrador (R-WY) have co-introduced these proposals together with noted progressives like Senators Patrick Leahy (D-VT) and Dick Durbin (D-IL) and Congressman Bobby Scott (D-VA).

States across the country have embarked on ambitious plans to reduce prison populations. Places as diverse as Texas, South Carolina, and New York have all begun to shift their priorities away from expensive and overly punitive sentencing and toward the rehabilitation and re-integration of former convicts into communities.

Taken together, these reforms can help our justice system become more fair, affordable, and responsive to the needs of Black America. But we still have a very long way to go. We must continue to advocate at every level of government if we hope to see progress continue. ★

NOTES

[1] NAACP, Criminal Justice Fact Sheet, Retrieved from: *http://www.naacp.org/pages/criminal-justice-fact-sheet.*

[2] Ibid.

[3] Department of Justice, Smart on Crime. Retrieved from: *http://www.justice.gov/ag/smart-on-crime.pdf.*

[4] See H.R. 3382 Smarter Sentencing Act of 2013. Retrieved from: *http://thomas.loc.gov/cgi-bin/bdquery/D?d113:1:./temp/~bdgYQE::|/home/LegislativeData.php|.* See S. 1410 Smarter Sentencing Act of 2013. Retrieved from: *http://thomas.loc.gov/cgi-bin/bdquery/D?d113:2:./temp/~bdgYQE::|/home/LegislativeData.php|.*

5 See H.R. 3465 Second Chance Reauthorization Act of 2013. Retrieved from: *http://thomas.loc.gov/cgi-bin/bdquery/D?d113:2:./temp/~bdMrh7::|/home/LegislativeData.php|.* See S. 1690 Second Chance Reauthorization Act of 2013. Retrieved from: *http://thomas.loc.gov/cgibin/bdquery/D?d113:4:./temp/~bd6317::|/home/LegislativeData.php|.*

AMERICA INCARCERATED: WHO PAYS & WHO PROFITS

HILL HARPER

"You can't be free if the cost of being you is too high." This is the most quoted line from my book, *Letters to an Incarcerated Brother.* There undoubtedly exists a heavy cost that we as a community and country are bearing for our misguided criminal justice system. Incarceration is not cheap, and the prices we pay come in many different forms.

When I call our criminal justice system misguided, know that I am not suggesting that we stop penalizing people for crimes. I believe firmly in justice and in rehabilitation. However, while crime rates have been dropping over the last 30 years, our nation's prison population has quintupled to over 2 million people—more than a quarter of the world's prison population.[1] The most affected places are the poorest neighborhoods of cities, and more than 1.7 million children are growing up in homes where one parent is behind bars.[2] Recidivism rates are higher than ever, proving that prisons don't solve the problem of crime—they perpetuate it.

In African American communities, in particular, mass incarceration is a serious problem. African Americans are imprisoned at a rate that is, staggeringly, seven times higher than that of white, non-Hispanic Americans.[3] We have locked up a larger percentage of our Black community than South Africa did at the height of apartheid.[4] Our prisons are overpopulated and understaffed. Our prisoners are mistreated and malnourished. Our government is at best inactive and at worst criminally negligent in regards to this matter.

Most solutions proposed involve the privatization of prisons, an effort to keep taxpayers from having to support the "undesirable" prisoners. Of course, taxpayers will take on some of the costs either way, but privatization raises more problems than it solves. Prison privatization provides a financial incentive for the owners to ensure a steady influx of prisoners, which means there are few, if any, recidivism-reduction and education programs offered. Also worth mentioning are the companies that profit by charging exorbitant amounts of money to allow prisoners to stay in touch with loved ones. Calls from the prisoners that I work with often cost as much as a dollar a minute, and some families end up paying upward of $1,000 annually just to show their incarcerated loved ones support.

I wrote this in *Letters to an Incarcerated Brother* and I will write it again: I am incapable of ignoring this. We have to see the current state of our criminal justice system not as the way things are, but as a call to action. I chose to write about the problems of the prison industrial complex because they are not, as many seem to believe, self-repairing concerns; they are not going to disappear unless we *make them disappear*. This is the issue of our time, and I believe that if Dr. Martin Luther King Jr. were alive today, he would be sending out a rallying cry to end this out of control mass incarceration problem.

In 2013, we finally started to talk about the elephant in the room: my book was released; the Netflix adaptation of Piper Kerman's *Orange Is the New Black* saddened and thrilled us; the FCC instituted a long overdue cap on per minute call rates in prisons; and the Federal Prison Reform Act of 2013 was brought before Congress. But talk, at this point, is not enough. We need to take action. So, I ask you: are you willing to step up to the challenge of repairing this nation's faltering criminal justice system? ★

NOTES

[1] King's College London. (2009) World Prison Population List (8th ed.) Retrieved from: *https://www.kcl.ac.uk/depsta/law/news/news_details.php?id=203.*

[2] Glaze, L., Maruschak L. (2008). Bureau of Justice Statistics Special Report: Parents in Prison and Their Minor Children. U.S. Department of Justice Office of Justice Programs. Retrieved from: *http://www.bjs.gov/content/pub/pdf/pptmc.pdf.*

[3] New Century Foundation (2005) The Color of Crime: Race, Crime and Justice in America. Retrieved from: *http://colorofcrime.com/colorofcrime2005.html.*

[4] Abbott, R., (2013, September 19). Congress Takes on Swollen Prison Populations. Courthouse News Service. Retrieved from: *http://www.courthousenews.com/2013/09/19/61291.htm.*

THE EVOLVING FIGHT TO PROTECT THE VOTE

TANYA CLAY HOUSE, ESQ.

"[T]he vote is the most powerful instrument ever devised by man for breaking down injustice and destroying the terrible walls which imprison men because they are different from other men."

—*President Lyndon Johnson, Washington D.C., August 6, 1965*

Our country's history is a testament to not only the power of the right to vote but also the importance of protecting that right. Dating back to the American Revolution, the fight to protect and expand this right has shaped the American experience and particularly that of the African American community. Be it the past violent attacks against the Freedom Riders, more recent misleading voting billboards placed in predominately Black neighborhoods in Ohio and Wisconsin, burdensome photo ID requirements in Texas or North Carolina or restrictions on early voting in Florida and other states, the nature of the attacks against the right to vote continues to evolve and with it so must the weapons we use to combat them.

The vote is unique in that it does not draw its power solely from the affirmative act itself, but also the absence of the act. Growing up in Louisville, Kentucky, I witnessed the alarming effects of the absence of participation—roads left unrepaired, schools underfunded, district boundaries manipulated. Furthermore, Kentucky remains one of three remaining states that permanently disenfranchise formerly incarcerated persons with felony convictions. Sadly, the cycle of voter disenfranchisement continues to occur across the country. The Voting Rights Act has been an essential tool against a wave of legislation that targets many of the most vulnerable voters. However with its decision in the *Shelby County v. Holder* case invalidating section 4 of the Act, the Supreme Court dealt a tremendous blow to the fight to protect the vote.

Remarkably, just six months after this decision, the bipartisan Voting Rights Amendments Act (VRAA) was introduced to remedy this setback. It is critical that both the House and Senate move quickly to pass this legislation especially as the extremely important midterm elections approach. Yet, this is only one tool of many in the toolbox to protect the vote. We must be proactive in empowering ourselves with other necessary tools by passing legislation that will allow us to expand the opportunity to vote, criminalize deceptive voting practices, and facilitate a modern voter registration system.

We must recognize the importance of compounding the power of our vote by being active participants in the democratic process. The process does not end once we cast our ballot. After we vote, it is our responsibility to hold our representatives accountable—during every election—federal, state and local. Our engagement has the power to change outcomes and make history—it can move legislation, change lives and influence decisions. The silver lining of Bloody Sunday was that more than 7,000 Black citizens were added to the voting rolls in Selma after the passage of the Voting Rights Act. Consequently, the Sheriff who terrorized and arrested so many was voted out of office. The vote is the most powerful right we as a democracy have to fight and preserve our own rights and those of others. Today more than ever, we must aggressively seek to exercise our right to vote in order to protect it. ★

A HEALTHIER NATION

THE HONORABLE DONNA M. CHRISTENSEN

"The arc of the moral universe is long, but it bends towards justice."
—Dr. Martin Luther King, Jr.

Achieving justice in health care requires that we eliminate health disparities. Unfortunately, health disparities are not new in this nation. Studies documenting these trends began in 1899 with the release of Dr. W.E.B. DuBois' *The Philadelphia Negro*. Numerous studies followed, but the issue remained under the sociopolitical radar until the 1985 Heckler Report—issued by then-Department of Health and Human Services (HHS) Secretary Margaret Heckler that detailed the extent and impact of racial and ethnic health disparities in the nation.[1]

Fortunately, awareness about health disparities grew and today we are well-versed on the negative civil rights and health repercussions of health disparities, as well as their economic consequences. In fact, a recent report found that the total costs of health disparities over just a three-year period was $1.24 trillion.[2]

The momentum to achieve health equity received a boost when the Affordable Care Act (ACA)—which promises to improve the health not just for Black Americans, but for all Americans—was signed by President Obama in 2010.

There are myriad provisions in the ACA that are pivotal to ongoing and future efforts to eliminate health disparities. Most of these provisions were modeled after the legislative effort that the Congressional Black Caucus, the Congressional Hispanic Caucus, and the Congressional Asian Pacific American Caucus, (collectively known as the Congressional TriCaucus) championed for numerous Congresses. These provisions include:

- *More robust investment in all public health programs;*
- *Standardized data collection and reporting provisions across a broad range of demographic data;*
- *Language services and cultural competency education provisions;*
- *Health workforce provisions, especially those that aim to recruit, train, retain and graduate health care providers from under-served communities;*
- *Community health centers, community health workers and healthier community provisions, as well as the expansion of prevention information and services that aim to reduce health disparities; and*
- *Increased accountability (through the elevation of the Office of Minority Health (OMH) at HHS, the establishment of additional OMHs across other federal agencies, and the elevation to an Institute of the National Center on Minority Health and Health Disparities at the National Institutes of Health).*

While health disparity trends have not improved much, the promising news is that the health equity-related provisions in the ACA could play an integral role in curbing some of these harmful trends.

An African proverb goes: "Those who dig the well should not be denied a drink from the well." But, it's not the passage of the ACA that ends disparities; those details lie in how the health equity provisions are implemented and how the health equity movement continues in the coming years. Health care reform passage is one thing; implementation and long-term progress to improve outcomes is altogether different. Needless to say, the truly hard work is only now beginning.

It is imperative that we all recognize the need to stand up and work to ensure that the health equity provisions included in the ACA are implemented as intended. As I have said numerous times, it is up to the bearers of this torch to demand that the health equity provisions that this law promises come to full fruition.

If we do not come together and stand firm on the front lines of the health equity movement, then we have failed those who have the greatest need—those who have been denied a drink for far too long. That is a legacy that we—as a nation, as a community and as human beings—simply cannot and should not accept. ★

NOTES

[1] U.S. Department of Health and Human Services. (1985) Report of the Secretary's Task Force on Black and Minority Health. Retrieved from: *https://archive. org/details/reportofsecretar00usde.*

[2] LaViest,T., Gaskin D., Richard P. (2009) The Economic Burden of Health Inequalities in the U.S. Joint Center for Political and Economic Studies. Retrieved from: *http://www.jointcenter.org/hpi/sites/all/files/ Burden_Of_Health_FINAL_0.pdf.*

[3] Abbott, R., (2013, September 19). Congress Takes on Swollen Prison Populations. Courthouse News Service. Retrieved from: *http://www.courthousenews. com/2013/09/19/61291.htm.*

YOUR ID WILL BE REQUIRED TO VOTE TODAY

ATTENTION: Pursuant to Act 2003-381 one of the followin identification is required in order for you to vote.

A. Current Valid Photo Identification
1. Governmentally Produced Photo Identifications (curren
2. Employee Identification for Employee w/Photo of Emplc duced by the Employer (current and valid)
3. College or University (within Alabama) Photo Identifica (current and valid)
4. Post Graduate Technical or Professional School (within Photo Identification Card (current and valid)

OR

B. One of the following:
5. Utility Bill of Voter with Voter's name and address (curre
6. Bank Statement with Voter's name and address (curre
7. Government Check with Voter's name and address (cui
8. Paycheck with Voter's name and address (current)
9. Valid Identification card (authorized by law) issued by t Alabama (including any branch, department, agency, or State of Alabama)
10. Valid Identification card (authorized by law) issued by a other 49 states (including any branch, department, or e State)
11. Valid Identification card (authorized by law) issued by t States of America "Federal Government" (including any department, agency, or entity of the Federal Governme
12. Valid United States Passport
13. Valid Alabama Hunting License
14. Valid Alabama Fishing License
15. Valid Alabama Pistol/Revolver Permit
16. Valid Pilot's License issued by the FAA or other author of the Federal Government
17. Valid United States Military Identification
18. Birth Certificate (Certified Copy)
19. Valid Social Security Card
20. Naturalization documentation (Certified Copy)
21. Court Record of Adoption (Certified Copy)
22. Court Record of name change (Certified Copy)
23. Valid Medicaid Card
24. Valid Medicare Card
25. Valid Electronic Benefits Transfer Card
26. Valid Voter Registration Card
27. Other Government Document that shows the name an the voter (valid or certified document issued by a gove agency)

NOTE: Those items listed in 5-27 can be the original docum card, etc.) or a photocopy of that document (license,

IF YOU DO NOT HAVE ONE OF THESE FORMS OF IDENTIFI PLEASE SEE THE CHIEF INSPECTOR. In addition, an indivi does not have identification in his or her possession at the be permitted to vote if the individual is positively identified tion officials as a voter on the poll list who is eligible to vot election official signs the voters list by where the voter sign

OVER 100 YEARS AGO, THE U.S. SUPREME COURT DECLARED THE RIGHT TO VOTE "PRESERVATIVE OF ALL RIGHTS."[1] NOTWITHSTANDING THAT REALITY, THE SUPREME COURT'S TERM, ENDING IN 2013, WILL BE REMEMBERED AS A YEAR OF CHALLENGE TO THE PANOPLY OF CIVIL RIGHTS THAT LIE AT THE HEART OF EQUAL CITIZENSHIP AND OPPORTUNITY FOR AFRICAN AMERICANS.

STANDING IN THE BREACH:
THE SUPREME COURT & SHELBY

SHERRILYN IFILL, ESQ.

In 2013, in *Shelby County, Alabama v. Holder*, the Supreme Court removed the 48-year protection provided by Section 5 of the Voting Rights Act. Congressman John Lewis (D-GA), a former leader of the Student Non-Violent Coordinating Committee (SNCC), and a survivor of the infamous 1965 Bloody Sunday March from Selma to Montgomery, Alabama for voting rights, described the Court's ruling as having "stuck a dagger into the heart of the Voting Rights Act."[2]

// SHELBY COUNTY, ALABAMA V. HOLDER

There was no more significant decision during the 2012–2013 term than the Supreme Court's decision in *Shelby County, Alabama v. Holder*.[3] In that case, the Court essentially eviscerated Section 5 of the Voting Rights Act—our democracy's most effective discrimination checkpoint for millions of voters of color—by striking down as unconstitutional Section 4(b), the "coverage" provision of the Act. Section 4(b) identified the states and localities throughout our nation with the worst histories and ongoing records of racial discrimination in voting. Section 5 placed the burden (of time and expense) on those serially bad-acting jurisdictions—rather than on the victims of discrimination—to demonstrate to the Department of Justice or a federal court in Washington, D.C. that their proposed voting changes would not be harmful to voters of color. Crucially, before the *Shelby* decision, the showing that a proposed law would not put voters of color in a disadvantageous position needed to be made before the law's implementation and the discrimination could take root.

In *Shelby*, NAACP Legal Defense and Educational Fund (LDF) represented Black voters, including a Black elected official in Calera within Shelby County, whose city council seat was eliminated after a 2008 redistricting reduced the Black population in his district from 70 percent to 29 percent.[4] A challenge brought under Section 5 in 2009 resulted in the restoration of the majority-Black voting district from which he was elected.

Significantly, the majority-Black, single-member district that elected LDF's client had been electing candidates preferred by Black voters for more than 20 years. That is because a federal court created that remedial district after recognizing that Alabama had, for over 100 years, intentionally maintained systems of at-large voting with the purpose of denying Black voters access to the political process in the state.[5]

In reaching its decision in *Shelby*, the Court ignored this and other irrefutable evidence that racial discrimination in voting persists in Alabama and the other places covered by Section 4(b) to this day. The Court also ignored record evidence showing that Section 5's protections blocked over 1,000 proposed voting changes between 1982 and 2005—a substantial portion of which were motivated by intentional discrimination. The Court's decision did not address how or why these facts failed to justify the continuing need for Section 5's preclearance scrutiny.

The Supreme Court's decision in *Shelby* also turned its back on an unbroken line of cases, from 1965 through as recently as 2009, upholding on four occasions the constitutionality of the Voting Rights Act. The *Shelby* decision inexplicably disregarded the virtually-unprecedented mandate that a bipartisan Congress issued in 2006 when it voted nearly unanimously (98–0 in the Senate and 390–33 in the House) to reauthorize the Voting Rights Act.

Just eight years ago, in 2006, Congress held 20 hearings and heard testimony from 90 witnesses, each with distinct views, over ten months, ultimately amassing a 15,000 page record (i.e., a gold star congressional record) demonstrating the ongoing reality of racial discrimination experienced by Black, Latino, Asian American, American Indian, and Alaskan Native voters. In 2006, as it did in 1965 with its original enactment and each subsequent reauthorization, Congress acted at the height of its power to cure an infection in Section 5-covered places, which continue to suffer from the most concentrated, adaptive, and persistent racial discrimination in voting. With utter "hubris," as stated by Justice Ginsburg in her scathing and apposite dissent, the Court deemed irrational Congress's resounding recognition of an ongoing and unconstitutional reality faced by millions of voters of color, and instead substituted its judgment for that of Congress.[6]

The *Shelby* decision is without question, devastating. It leaves voters of color unprotected from discriminatory voting measures in jurisdictions throughout the South (and other places of our country) where voting discrimination has been persistent and ongoing. Without the preclearance requirements of Section 5, jurisdictions are now free to adopt discriminatory voting practices. The burden rests with voters—the victims of racial discrimination—and civil rights lawyers to file claims and challenge those practices in court. Voting litigation of this kind is expensive and can take years before coming to a final resolution. The simple, cost-effective, and timely preclearance process of Section 5, which put the burden on jurisdictions to report voting changes, has been removed with a stroke of the Supreme Court's pen.

In the wake of the *Shelby* decision, LDF's charge and that of other civil rights organizations is to continue to protect voters of color in formerly covered jurisdictions by forcefully pushing a proactive agenda. For example, relying on

another provision of the Voting Rights Act, Section 2,[7] as well as the U.S. Constitution and other applicable laws, LDF and other civil rights legal groups already are aggressively responding to attempts by formerly covered jurisdictions to disfranchise voters of color now that Section 5 is no longer a checkpoint.

> **THE *SHELBY* DECISION IS, WITHOUT QUESTION, DEVASTATING. IT LEAVES VOTERS OF COLOR UNPROTECTED FROM DISCRIMINATORY VOTING MEASURES IN JURISDICTIONS THROUGHOUT THE SOUTH (AND OTHER PLACES OF OUR COUNTRY) WHERE VOTING DISCRIMINATION HAS BEEN PERSISTENT AND ONGOING.**

For example, LDF, in *United States v. Texas, et al.*,[8] represents Black college students at historically Black Prairie View A&M and Texas Southern universities, and an organization that engages young people of color to participate in the political process. Among other claims, the lawsuit raises a Section 2 challenge against Texas's racially discriminatory photo ID law, which a federal court previously blocked under Section 5 in 2012 as the most strict photo ID law in the country,[9] a law which poised "unforgiving" burdens (in both time and expense) on poor, disabled, elderly, and people of color in Texas.[10] Within hours of the *Shelby* decision, however, the Texas Attorney General tweeted his intention to activate that state's restrictive photo ID law.

Along with LDF, civil rights organizations, such as the Lawyers' Committee for Civil Rights Under Law, the American Civil Liberties Union, and the Advancement Project have fanned across the south, responding to concerns raised by communities of color about voting changes planned by jurisdictions in the wake of *Shelby*. Communities have reported the sudden adoption of polling place closures, efforts to change district elections to at-large elections, restrictions on early voting, and a wealth of other measures that Section 5 likely would have stopped prior to *Shelby*, but which now must be aggressively challenged by time-consuming and expensive litigation. With communities being our eyes and ears on the ground, litigation also is underway to stop North Carolina from implementing an omnibus, draconian voting law that imposes strict photo ID requirements, limits early voting, and eliminates same-day voter registration, among other provisions harmful to voters of color. That litigation also is harnessing the efforts of the Moral Monday movement, which continues to galvanize hundreds of thousands of people in North Carolina (and across the country) to fight for issues like the right to access the ballot box free from discriminatory restrictions.[11]

In addition to protecting voters of color in the courts post-*Shelby*, the civil rights community has united in its efforts to press Congress to aggressively respond to the Court's decision by amending the Voting Rights Act to restore the preclearance protections that protected voters of color for nearly 50 years. Importantly, just seven months after the Supreme Court's *Shelby* decision, in a strong bipartisan showing, Members of Congress introduced the Voting Rights Act Amendment of 2014, which reflects the first step in protecting the millions of voters of color made vulnerable by the *Shelby* decision.

The civil rights community was galvanized, forceful, engaged, and aggressive in 2013, particularly in defending the right of all Americans to vote, unimpeded by discriminatory and restrictive measures. In light of the Supreme Court's devastating ruling in *Shelby*, If the Supreme Court's admonition in 1888 in *Yick Wo* is true, then we may remember 2013 as a time when civil rights itself was threatened.

But with every threat, there also is opportunity.

We are facing an important moment in our democracy. While America has twice elected an African American president, there remain far too many places in this country that have never elected an African American judge, commissioner, or board of education member.

It is up to us to continue the important work of expanding our democracy. We call on you, in 2014 and beyond, to stand with us in the ongoing fight for full and lasting equality. ★

NOTES

[1] *Yick Wo v. Hopkins*, 118 U.S. 356, 370 (1886).

[2] Lewis, J. (2013, June 25). Press Release: *Rep. John Lewis Calls Court Decision "a Dagger" in the Heart of Voting Access.* Retrieved from: *http://johnlewis.house.gov/press-release/rep-john-lewis-calls-court-decision-"-dagger"-heart-voting-access.*

[3] 133 S. Ct. 2612 (2013).

[4] Brief for Respondent-Intervenors Earl Cunningham, Harry Jones, Albert Jones, Ernest Montgomery, Anthony Vines, and William Walker, *Shelby County, Alabama v. Holder,* No. 12–96 (Jan. 25, 2013). Retrieved from: *http://www.naacpldf.org/files/case_issue/12-96%20bs%20Earl%20Cunningham%20et%20al.pdf.*

[5] *Dillard v. Crenshaw County,* 640 F. Supp. 1347, 1357 (M.D. Ala. 1986) ("From the late 1800s through the present, [Alabama] has consistently erected barriers to keep Black persons from full and equal participation in the social, economic, and political life of the state.").

[6] 133 S. Ct at 2648 (J., Ginsburg, dissenting).

[7] Section 2 of the Voting Rights Act prohibits voting practices that were either enacted with a racially discriminatory *intent*, or that have racially discriminatory *results.* 42 U.S.C. § 1973(a) (2000 ed.).

[8] Civil Action Nos. 2:13-cv-00263; 2:13-cv-193; 2:13-cv-291 (NGR) (S.D. Tex. Aug. 22, 2013).

[9] *Texas v. Holder,* 888 F.Supp.2d 113, 128 (D.D.C. Aug. 30, 2012)

[10] Ibid. at 144.

[11] Fuller, J., (2014, February 10). 80,000 people protested in NC this weekend. Here's why. *The Washington Post.* Retrieved from: *http://www.washingtonpost.com/blogs/the-fix/wp/2014/02/10/why-tens-of-thousands-of-people-were-rallying-in-raleigh/.*

AFFORDABLE HEALTHCARE IS A CIVIL RIGHT

THE HONORABLE KATHLEEN SEBELIUS

"OF ALL FORMS OF INJUSTICE,"
DR. MARTIN LUTHER KING,
JR. ONCE TOLD THE MEDICAL
COMMITTEE FOR HUMAN
RIGHTS, "INJUSTICE IN HEALTH
CARE IS THE MOST SHOCKING
AND INHUMANE."

// UNACCEPTABLE DISPARITIES

As we marked the 50th anniversary of the March on Washington in 2013, we did so against the backdrop of some startling disparities:

African Americans are 55 percent more likely to be uninsured than white Americans.[1] An unacceptable 6.8 million African Americans do not have the security of health coverage, and an unconscionable 732,000 of these Americans are younger than age 19.[2]

Cancer claims the lives of a higher percentage of African Americans than any racial or ethnic group.[3] African American women, who tend to be diagnosed at later, more serious stages, are 40 percent more likely to die from breast cancer, although they are 10 percent less likely to be diagnosed with it.[4]

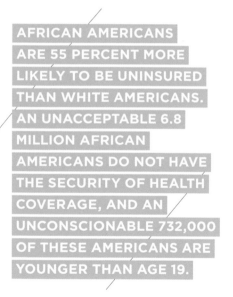

AFRICAN AMERICANS ARE 55 PERCENT MORE LIKELY TO BE UNINSURED THAN WHITE AMERICANS. AN UNACCEPTABLE 6.8 MILLION AFRICAN AMERICANS DO NOT HAVE THE SECURITY OF HEALTH COVERAGE, AND AN UNCONSCIONABLE 732,000 OF THESE AMERICANS ARE YOUNGER THAN AGE 19.

At the same time, African Americans are twice as likely to be diagnosed with diabetes, and 40 percent more likely to have high blood pressure.[5]

Moreover the infant mortality rate among African Americans is more than twice that of non-Hispanic whites.[6]

As a country, we pay dearly for these disparities. We pay in the heartbreak of the lives we have lost, as our friends, relatives and neighbors have been unable to afford care and preventive services. We pay in the economic inefficiency of a system, which—before the Affordable Care Act—saw us spend more each year, only to attain lesser outcomes. We pay in a loss of opportunity and freedom for so many of our fellow Americans.

Without the opportunity to live a healthy life, there is no opportunity to live the American dream or participate fully in our communities. Without the freedom which comes from having access to quality health care, there is no freedom to reach our full potential in the workforce or watch our kids or grandkids grow up. Without the security of health insurance, there is no economic security for middle-class families, and for so many other families working their way into the middle class.

Affordable health coverage is therefore linked to each pillar of the mission that the National Urban League has fought so hard for: economic self-reliance, parity, power, and civil rights.

At the same time, our nation's urban areas are home to some of the highest concentrations of uninsured Americans. One-fifth of uninsured African American citizens and legal residents live in the Atlanta, New York, Chicago, Dallas, Houston, and Detroit metropolitan areas.[7]

// A NEW DAY

For all the adversity we face, the Affordable Care Act gives us the unprecedented opportunity to close some of our worst health disparities.

Because of the new law, Americans who are insured have new rights and protections, including access to preventive services like cancer and cholesterol screenings with no out-of-pocket fees.[8] Young adults can now stay on their parents' plans until age 26 (and 500,000 young African Americans have gained coverage as a result). No one can be denied coverage because of a pre-existing condition.[9]

At the same time, the 4.5 million elderly and disabled African Americans on Medicare have access to many preventive services with no cost-sharing.[10] Many have told me that they are finally able to fill the prescriptions their doctors write them because we are closing the donut hole in prescription drug coverage.

For those who do not have insurance, the Health Insurance Marketplace is an opportunity to purchase affordable, quality coverage—with real choice that was previously unavailable or unaffordable for so many. An estimated 2 million African Americans are eligible for financial assistance to help pay for the costs of their new insurance.[11]

You can shop and sign up for coverage at *HealthCare.gov*, by phone at 1-800-318-2596; through an insurer, agent, or broker; by mail; and with in-person help in your community (See *LocalHelp.HealthCare.gov*).

// MEDICAID EXPANSION

Medicaid expansion is another way the Affordable Care Act is helping more African Americans get covered. If every state were to expand Medicaid, 95 percent of uninsured African Americans would be eligible for assistance with a Marketplace plan, Medicaid, or CHIP.[12] With 25 states (and D.C.) expanding so far, an estimated 60 percent are eligible today.[13]

// SERVING UNDERSERVED COMMUNITIES & DIVERSIFYING OUR WORKFORCE

The Affordable Care Act is investing in more than 1,100 Community Health Centers (where one in five patients is African American). It has also helped nearly triple the size of the National Health Service Corps, which brings health care providers to underserved communities.[14]

One of the great things about the Corps is its diversity: African American physicians make up about 17 percent of Corps physicians (compared to 6 percent of the national physician workforce).[15]

In exchange for serving in the Corps, physicians, nurses and other health care providers are offered help with their student loans. So not only do we bring services to underserved communities, we help build an American workforce that reflects the diversity which makes our country strong.

As we reflect on the March on Washington—and what it means to our country's ever evolving march toward justice—another big anniversary is in our sights. In 2015, we will mark 50 years since the Voting Rights Act became law. It will also be the 50th anniversary of the creation of Medicare and Medicaid.

My father was serving in Congress at the time. He was very involved in the Civil Rights movement, and he was good friends with Reverend Fred Shuttlesworth, the co-founder of the Southern Christian Leadership Conference.

My dad strongly supported the Voting Rights Act, and he helped write the Medicare and Medicaid laws. He saw all these struggles as connected to the broader goal of a more perfect union.

Today, this legacy continues. The Affordable Care Act is the most powerful law for reducing health disparities and expanding opportunity since Medicare and Medicaid were created: The opportunity to live healthier, happier lives. The opportunity to reach our greatest potential. The opportunity to achieve our dreams. The opportunity to contribute fully to community and country.

For these and so many other reasons, affordable health care—as Dr. King taught us—is a civil right. ★

NOTES

[1] U.S. Department of Health and Human Services. (2012) The Affordable Care Act and African Americans. Retrieved from: *http://www.hhs.gov/ healthcare/facts/factsheets/2012/04/aca-and-african-americans04122012a.html.*

[2] Ibid.

[3] Ibid.

[4] Ibid.

[5] Ibid.

[6] Ibid.

[7] Gee, E. (2012) Eligible Uninsured African Americans: 6 in 10 Could Receive Health Insurance Marketplace Tax Credits, Medicaid or CHIP. U.S. Department of Health and Human Services. Retrieved from: *http://aspe.hhs.gov/health/ reports/2013/UninsuredAfricanAmericans/ ib_UninsuredAfricanAmericans.cfm.*

[8] U.S. Department of Health and Human Services. (2012) The Affordable Care Act and African Americans. Retrieved from: *http://www.hhs.gov/ healthcare/facts/factsheets/2012/04/aca-and-african-americans04122012a.html.*

[9] Ibid.

[10] Ibid.

[11] Ibid.

[12] Ibid.

[13] Gee, E. (2012) Eligible Uninsured African Americans: 6 in 10 Could Receive Health Insurance Marketplace Tax Credits, Medicaid or CHIP. U.S. Department of Health and Human Services. Retrieved from: *http://aspe.hhs.gov/health/ reports/2013/UninsuredAfricanAmericans/ ib_UninsuredAfricanAmericans.cfm.*

[14] U.S. Department of Health and Human Services. (2012) The Affordable Care Act and African Americans. Retrieved from: *http://www.hhs.gov/ healthcare/facts/factsheets/2012/04/aca-and-african-americans04122012a.html.*

[15] Ibid.

AS THE UNITED STATES EMERGES FROM
THE GREAT RECESSION WHILE NAVIGATING
THE POLITICAL WATERS OF EXTENDING
HEALTH CARE TO 48 MILLION AMERICANS,
MANY POLICY MAKERS RECOGNIZE A
CONNECTION. UNQUESTIONABLY, THERE
IS AN OPPORTUNITY IN URBAN AMERICA
FOR JOB CREATION AND EXPANSION
SPURRED BY THE ECONOMIC IMPACT OF
THE AFFORDABLE CARE ACT (ACA).

THE AFFORDABLE CARE ACT & HOW IT CAN FUEL ENTREPRENEURISM IN URBAN COMMUNITIES

THE HONORABLE
JABAR SHUMATE

NATIONAL URBAN LEAGUE

As an elected official, I have seen first hand the transformative impact of the Affordable Care Act (ACA). I represent an economically challenged urban district in a largely rural state. Nonetheless, I was afforded an opportunity to orchestrate both the expansion of health care services and opportunities for entrepreneurial growth.

In response to a study that showed people living in the northern section of the city of Tulsa had a shorter life expectancy than residents in other areas, The University of Oklahoma (OU) established the OU—Tulsa Wayman Tisdale Specialty Clinic.[1] The clinic offers treatment in 16 medical specialties ranging from dermatology to pediatric gastroenterology.

The $20 million clinic was built with a combination of public and private funds, combining $10 million from the Oklahoma Legislature and $10 million from Tulsa's philanthropic community. Without question, the clinic was built in anticipation of the scores of the medically underserved slated to receive coverage under the ACA. In fact, my legislative colleagues' questions and subsequent financial support depended on sustainability of the clinic. Nonetheless, the clinic has seen 12,000 patients since opening in January 2013, and that number is expected to easily double next year because of the impact of ACA.[2]

What makes this situation unique and possibly a model for economically depressed urban areas all across America is that this clinic caused an economic resurgence in a largely economically distressed area. The clinic, named for Tulsa native and NBA standout, the late Wayman Tisdale, was built with the highest minority construction participation ever in the city of Tulsa at 25 percent. In fact, OU President David L. Boren stated recently that the first eight members of the construction crew could walk to work. More than $5 million of this project

circulated among those living within a five-mile radius of the building. In addition, minority contractors that worked on the project have been successful at obtaining work on other projects in the city.[3]

The OU—Tulsa School of Urban Design and local community activists collaborated on a re-development plan to beautify neighborhoods and ripen the area around the clinic for economic growth. In response to their work, the city of Tulsa approved $5 million in funding to enact the plan and present another opportunity for local contractors.[4]

This notable success story didn't happen without push from community leaders and elected officials like myself who saw the connection between health conditions and economic outlook. In retrospect, economically depressed communities across the nation should prepare for countless opportunities for job creation and growth spurred directly by the millions of newly insured under the Affordable Care Act.

In the same way, African Americans and other minorities must prepare future generations for the jobs and entrepreneurial opportunities that lie ahead over the next 20 years because of the expansion of the health care industry. It is expected over the next decade that the health care sector could add 4.6 million jobs and one-third of the workforce will be made up of people of color.[5]

Moreover, the field of nursing will see the most explosive growth. By 2020, 712,000 additional jobs will be created and 34 percent of those positions will be directly attributed to ACA. Workforce trends indicate that nursing will continue to be a lucrative career for people of color, especially those that seek to develop staffing firms that specialize in nursing and medical office support.[6]

MedTrust, LLC, originally a traveling nursing service in San Antonio, is one of the leading minority-owned staffing firms in the nation. Rick Martinez, a registered nurse, started the company in his apartment almost 10 years ago. In 2009, as a participant in the SBA 8(a) Business Development Program, MedTrust was awarded an $87 million contract from the U.S. Army. This company personifies the possibilities for minorities in the nursing field.[7]

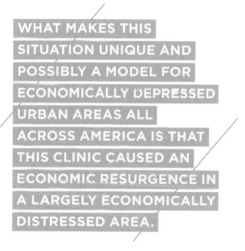

WHAT MAKES THIS SITUATION UNIQUE AND POSSIBLY A MODEL FOR ECONOMICALLY DEPRESSED URBAN AREAS ALL ACROSS AMERICA IS THAT THIS CLINIC CAUSED AN ECONOMIC RESURGENCE IN A LARGELY ECONOMICALLY DISTRESSED AREA.

Without question, it is incumbent for leaders in the African American community to push policy makers and educators toward increasing high school graduation rates and expanding college and career programs in allied health. Without question, the new urban economy will depend on anticipation of future workforce needs. Moving forward, we can ill afford to simply work in the new health care economy without capitalizing on it. ★

NOTES

[1] Lewin Consulting Group. (2013) Retrieved from: *http://www.csctulsa.org/files/file/Lewin%20 Report%202006.pdf.*

[2] Morgan, R. (2013, Dec. 2) Friends, Officials Dedicate Wayman Tisdale Clinic Tulsa World. Retrieved from: *http://m.tulsaworld.com/homepagelatest/friends-officials-dedicate-wayman-tisdale-health-clinic/article_e0ed7be8-5bc8-11e3-90e8-0019bb30f31a.html?mode=jqm.*

[3] Black Chronicle Newspaper. (2013, December 5). A Community Bridge" Supporters Say Clinic Long Overdue. Retrieved from: *http://www.blackchronicle.com/news/12-5-13/tisdale.html.*

[4] KTUL. (2013, December 2) OU Formally Dedicates Specialty Health Clinic to Wayman Tisdale. Retrieved from: *http://www.ktul.com/story/24116458/ou-formally-dedicates-specialty-health-clinic-to-wayman-Tisdale.*

[5] Childers, L. (2005).Traveling Our Own Road. Minority Nurse. Retrieved from: *http://www.minoritynurse.com/article/traveling-our-own-road*

[6] Frogner, B., Spetz, J. (2013) the Affordable Care Act of 2010: Creating Job Opportunities for Racially and Ethnically Diverse Populations. Retrieved from: *http://www.jointcenter.org/research/affordable-care-act.*

[7] United States Small Business Administration. (2013) SBA 100. Retrieved from: *http://www.sba.gov/sba-100.*

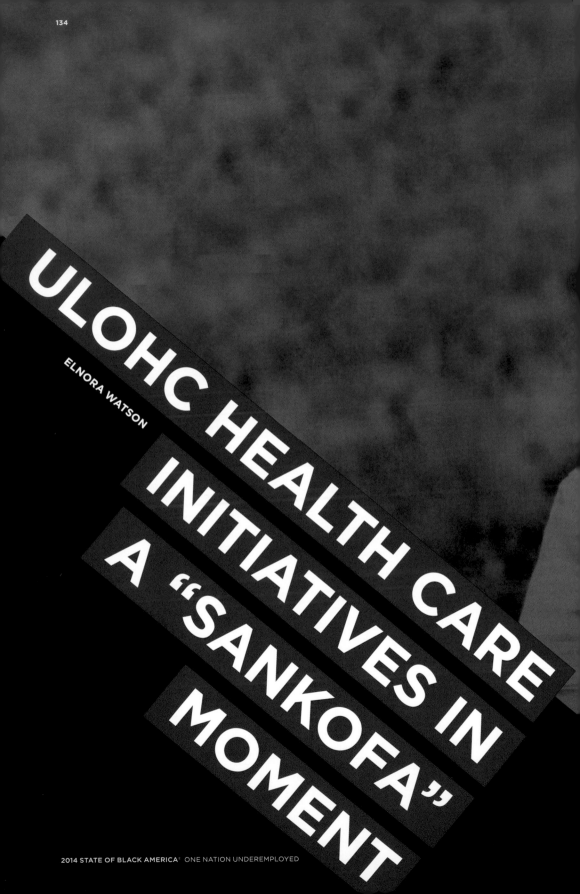

ELNORA WATSON

ULOHC HEALTH CARE INITIATIVES IN A "SANKOFA" MOMENT

ONE HUNDRED AND FIFTY YEARS
AFTER EMANCIPATION, BLACK AMERICA
IS EXPERIENCING A "SANKOFA MOMENT."
COLLECTIVELY WE HAVE THE SENSE OF
BEING AT A CROSSROADS. IN OUR HOMES,
CHURCHES AND COMMUNITY INSTITUTIONS,
WE CAST OUR EYES OVER THE MANY RIVERS
WE HAVE CROSSED TO GATHER WISDOM
FOR THE JOURNEY AHEAD. THERE IS TALK
OF THE NEED FOR A NEW PARADIGM.

The Urban League of Hudson County's current and planned health initiatives reflect this need to empower people to tackle today's health challenges while looking ahead to developing approaches to dealing with those disparities in a holistic and effective way.

// THE AFFORDABLE CARE ACT— EMPOWERMENT FOR TODAY

As one of the five Navigator Organizations funded by the Centers for Medicare and Medicaid Services for the state of New Jersey, the Urban League of Hudson County, Inc. is working to address health disparities in Hudson County and beyond. The League is the lead organization in a consortium comprising the Urban Leagues of Morris, Union and Bergen counties. As Navigators, the consortium organizations are charged with conducting community outreach, providing unbiased and accurate information about the Affordable Care Act and facilitating the public's enrollment in a Quality Health Plan (QHP).

The focus in our work to implement the Affordable Care Act is on the uninsured. Over a million New Jersey residents younger than 65 years old lack health insurance.[1] Most are working. Many are minorities. Two of the four counties covered by the ULOHC's Navigator Consortium—Hudson and Union—are home to over 100,000 uninsured residents each.[2]

In the days leading up to the start of the open enrollment period for the Healthcare Marketplace, the ULOHC joined with Congressman Donald Payne Jr., representatives of the Insurance industry and the Department of Health and Human Services to present an Affordable Care Act Community Forum. Since then, the consortium has conducted over one hundred outreach events, ranging from providing information at a Fugitive Safe Surrender, to assisting Arabic speaking parents at a local

day care center. To date, the consortium has reached over 2,000 consumers, dispelling myths, answering questions and providing clarity about the new health insurance options. About 10 percent of those we reached began the process of enrolling via paper applications.

Located in one of the most diverse counties in the nation, we are also forming collaborations to bring the message of affordable health care to the widest possible audience. A recently formed partnership with Korean Community Services, whose service population makes up a large portion of the uninsured in Bergen County, reflects steps in that direction.

// RECLAIMING COMMUNITY HEALTH—A HOLISTIC APPROACH TO CHANGING LIVES

Another effect of this "Sankofa Moment" is the realization that emotional and social health is as important as physical health, and that all these forms of health are interconnected. Many of the difficulties experienced by members of our community are exacerbated by poverty, community violence and the daily stresses of being members of an oppressed minority. These vestiges of chattel slavery and colonialism manifest as a form of trauma that requires specialized, integrative, holistic and culturally astute responses. A new Emancipation is needed in the modern era, one based on personal, familial and community empowerment that can lead to individual, familial, and community health, healing and wholeness.

The reclamation of Black families and communities from the siege of violence requires a multi-system TRAUMA response at the local level and a connection to cultural pride at the global level. The ULOHC plans to develop a culturally rooted pilot program aimed at improving the coping skills and resilience of children and families of African descent—The Sankofa Project. This will be a research project

ANOTHER EFFECT OF THIS "SANKOFA MOMENT" IS THE REALIZATION THAT EMOTIONAL AND SOCIAL HEALTH IS AS IMPORTANT AS PHYSICAL HEALTH, AND THAT ALL THESE FORMS OF HEALTH ARE INTERCONNECTED. MANY OF THE DIFFICULTIES EXPERIENCED BY MEMBERS OF OUR COMMUNITY ARE EXACERBATED BY POVERTY, COMMUNITY VIOLENCE AND THE DAILY STRESSES OF BEING MEMBERS OF AN OPPRESSED MINORITY.

NOTES

[1] Henry J. Kaiser Foundation (2013) State Health Facts. Retrieved from: *http://kff.org/state-category/health-coverage-uninsured/.*

[2] Ibid.

aimed at testing the impact of an array of culturally rooted interventions on mediating the negative impact of trauma operating in the lives of youth and families. It will aim to reclaim and use the cultural strengths that brought the community thus far to tackle and solve today's problems. Emphasizing the primary cultural value "I is We," the project will aim to reclaim and use traditional cultural strengths to tackle today's problems. Staff will be trained in strength-based assessment and will use evidence-based protocols with demonstrated efficacy. Our interventions will aim to foster a true sense of connection and community among the people being served. Through The Sankofa Project, the Urban League of Hudson County will continue to be a beacon of hope, empowering the community and changing lives. ★

THE CIVIL RIGHTS VOICE IN EDUCATION REFORM

RUFINA A. HERNÁNDEZ, ESQ.

IT'S BEEN NEARLY 60 YEARS SINCE CHIEF JUSTICE WARREN DECLARED, IN THE LANDMARK *BROWN V. BOARD OF EDUCATION* CASE, THAT "IN THE FIELD OF PUBLIC EDUCATION, THE DOCTRINE OF 'SEPARATE BUT EQUAL' HAS NO PLACE."

The U.S. Supreme Court in 1954[1] confirmed what many civil rights leaders saw then, and what many teachers, students and parents are seeing now: that discrimination in our education system deprives students— our nation's most precious treasure and investment—of the chance at an excellent education and future economic opportunities.

Decades later, the fight for quality and equitable education for our children rages on and is one of the great civil rights issues of our time. Joining this fight is the Campaign for High School Equity (CHSE)—a coalition of the nation's leading civil rights and education advocacy organizations. Formed years ago to amplify the civil rights voice in the education space, we are a partnership (including the Alliance for Excellent Education, League of United Latin American Citizens, Mexican American Legal Defense and Educational Fund, National Association for the Advancement of Colored People, National Association of Latino Elected and Appointed Officials Educational Fund, National Council of La Raza, National Indian Education Association, National Urban League, Southeast Asian Resource Action Center, The Leadership Conference on Civil and Human Rights/The Leadership Conference Education Fund), united under the banner of addressing the racial and economic inequalities within the American public high school education system.

Together we advocate on behalf of millions of students of color, Native, English Language Learners (ELL) and low-income students. The terrain on which we fight continues to shift. It now focuses on closing achievement gaps for students within the accountability systems established under the No Child Left Behind Act (NCLB), and strongly advocating for the effective implementation of Common Core State Standards (CCSS), which seeks to ensure that all students are prepared for college and career, regardless of their zip code, income, race or ethnicity.

While the latest reports show that high school graduation rates for America's students are improving, the achievement gaps between racial groups persist and none more explicitly seen than among Black students. Black students have the lowest high school graduation rate among all the racial groups; at 66.1 percent, compared to white students at 83 percent.[2] Without a high school diploma, these students can expect fewer job opportunities, much lower wages and over the long term, a shaky path to career and economic security.

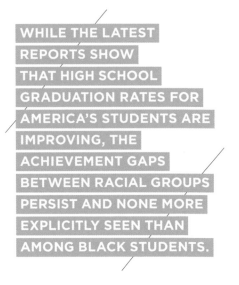

WHILE THE LATEST REPORTS SHOW THAT HIGH SCHOOL GRADUATION RATES FOR AMERICA'S STUDENTS ARE IMPROVING, THE ACHIEVEMENT GAPS BETWEEN RACIAL GROUPS PERSIST AND NONE MORE EXPLICITLY SEEN THAN AMONG BLACK STUDENTS.

CHSE is fighting to ensure that our students have the support and interventions they need to succeed. Key to this has been our push for, and support of, accountability provisions within the education reforms of NCLB and now CCSS. When the Department of Education announced that states agreeing to certain requirements would become eligible for waivers from core accountability provisions in the NCLB law, CHSE sought to ensure that our students' needs would not be lost and our communities' voices were heard. CHSE's analysis of the Elementary and Secondary Education Act waivers, published in "Maintaining a Focus on Subgroups in an Era of ESEA Waivers," raised serious questions about state accountability plans under the ESEA waivers—including whether the use of "super subgroups" could lead to fewer students of color, Native, ELL and low-income students receiving the supports and interventions they need to succeed.[3] The coalition called national attention to the idea that these waivers could "weaken efforts to highlight inequities, narrow achievement gaps, and improve education for our students."[4] Our analysis helped to amplify the discussion of whether struggling students, particularly those historically underserved, would receive the support, interventions and services they desperately need and deserve.

When the Supreme Court made its landmark decision, it shined a bright light on education inequalities and gave voice to the hope of millions of students and their families seeking better opportunities. CHSE, along with our partners, continues to shine that light within U.S. education reform. Recognizing the importance of having the civil rights voice heard, and what our efforts mean for the dreams and aspirations of millions of Black students—America's students—we continue the fight that arose so many decades ago.

As we celebrate the 60th anniversary of the *Brown* decision, we reaffirm our commitment to making the quality and equitable education proclaimed in *Brown v. Board of Education* a reality for our students. Working together— parents, teachers, education and civil rights advocates—we can ensure that this nation's promise of educational excellence is finally fulfilled for all our students. ★

NOTES

[1] *Brown v. Board of Education*, 347 U.S. 483 (1954).

[2] Stillwell, R., and Sable, J. (2013). Public School Graduates and Dropouts from the Common Core of Data: School Year 2009–10: First Look (Provisional Data) (NCES 2013-309rev). U.S. Department of Education. Washington, D.C.: National Center for Education Statistics. Retrieved from: *http://nces. ed.gov/pubsearch.*

[3] Campaign for High School Equity (2013). Maintaining a Focus on Subgroups in an Era of ESEA Waivers. Retrieved from: *http://www.highschoolequity.org/ images/WaiversReport_ExecSum_R3.pdf.*

[4] Campaign for High School Equity. (n.d.). CHSE White Paper on Subgroups. Retrieved December 2, 2013. Retrieved from: *http://www.highschoolequity.org/ media-room/media-resources/reports/385-esea- waivers-white-paper.html#fbid=mZsySGJlvlc.*

GETTING KIDS TO & THROUGH COLLEGE: OUR KIDS, OUR JOB

MICHAEL L. LOMAX, PH.D.

WE ALL KNOW IT: WE NEED MORE AFRICAN AMERICAN COLLEGE GRADUATES. WE KNOW THAT OUR KIDS NEED COLLEGE DEGREES SO THEY CAN QUALIFY FOR JOBS THAT LEAD TO BETTER FUTURES.

A survey performed by our UNCF Frederick D. Patterson Research Institute found that 87 percent of all low-income Black parents want their children to go to and through college.[1] Almost as many, 80 percent, said they thought the education their sons and daughters were getting was preparing them for college.[2]

But the facts tell a different story. Only 66 percent of African American students enrolled in ninth grade will graduate with their class compared to 78 percent for the nation.[3] About a third of the Black students who enroll in college need to take remedial courses in their first year to learn what they should have been taught in high school and before.[4]

Our children have a right to a rigorous academic education, from pre-kindergarten through high school graduation, an education that prepares them for college success, college graduation and rewarding careers. They have a right to excellent teachers. They have a right to learn in a safe school environment and a safe community.

They have a right to rely on their community, the African American community, to lead the way— the way we did in the struggle for civil rights. That's not happening enough today. Others are fighting for educational reforms that would benefit our children—more school choice, better teachers, and public school accountability. We honor their work and welcome their efforts.

But these are our children. When their futures are at stake, we—African American parents, leadership organizations and institutions—must be at the table, even at the head of the table, when and where decisions are made. We have to invest our time and our effort in better futures for our children and for all of us.

Getting students to and through college is UNCF's mission—our North Star, our commitment to fulfilling the promise of our motto, "A mind is a terrible thing to waste."[®] Helping to bring African American communities together to get our children the education they need and deserve is a priority. We're investing our 70 years of experience, our record of helping more than 400,000 students graduate from UNCF colleges with UNCF scholarships, and our credibility in communities across the country. We are calling for others to join us.

The Black community and Black leaders cannot sit on the sidelines, listening to adults argue while our children's futures hang in the balance. We cannot allow ourselves and our institutions—like our HBCUs, like UNCF— to be dismissed and marginalized in the battle for the futures of our own children, not after producing the doctors, teachers, ministers, entrepreneurs and civil rights leaders who are the backbone of our communities.

More Black civil rights organizations, churches, business leaders and institutions have to invest in education reform and understand the issues. We must take prominent leadership roles in activating African Americans because there is so much to gain if we can close the current education attainment gaps and produce significantly more college graduates.

What can we do—together?

- *We can become our own children's strongest advocates for education, making sure that they understand how important education is and going to bat for them with their teachers and principals.*

- *We can make sure that education reform works for our community—that education reform is done with us, not to us. Schools need to be located and structured so that students can attend and parents can engage.*

- *We can hold both school systems and education reformers accountable to the communities and people they purport to serve by demanding excellent schools with passionate and proficient teachers in Black communities regardless of income level.*

- *We can give parents and students the guidance they need to navigate critical decisions along the PK-12 journey, such as selecting quality schools, understanding their full breadth of choices, learning how to secure financial support for college, and how to be positioned for college and career success.*

- *Most of all, we must create a college-going culture, a culture in which going to college and graduating are not the exceptions but the expectation. A culture where individuals and institutions are all pulling in the same direction and conveying the same message— toward college opportunities for all.*

We must invest, as well, in making sure our children can afford to go to college. We have to begin saving for college as early as possible and no later than middle school. Even small regular deposits, kept up over the years, can mount up by freshman year in college. College saving programs, like the UNCF College Account Program, can make savings grow even faster. They can also increase the likelihood that student-savers will go to college, because a student who has a savings account is 4 times more likely to attend college—7 times more likely if the account is in the student's name.[5]

We also need to make sure that our federal, state and local governments maintain funding for higher education. We need to let our elected representatives know that they cannot let Pell Grant buying power shrink, or allow a vital program like Parent PLUS Loans to be restricted, and expect our support.

Because the cost of college continues to increase, we have to invest in college scholarships by responding generously to requests for support from organizations like the National Urban League and UNCF for the scholarship programs they sponsor.

> ## WE MUST CREATE A COLLEGE-GOING CULTURE, A CULTURE IN WHICH GOING TO COLLEGE AND GRADUATING ARE NOT THE EXCEPTIONS BUT THE EXPECTATION.

College attainment must become a metric on the Black community's dashboard. We must do all we can to ensure that our community knows why college is important and what all of us must do to increase the annual numbers of Black college graduates. As with every other historic achievement, African Americans must invest time, commitment and resources in building the transformative movement that will produce an enduring legacy of college graduates. That is why UNCF has expanded its historic motto to issue a national call to action: "A mind is a terrible thing to waste, but a wonderful thing to invest in."™ ★

NOTES

[1] Bridges, B.K., Awokoya, J.T., & Messano, F. (2012). Done to us, not with us: African American parent perceptions of K-12 education. Washington, D.C.: Frederick D. Patterson Research Institute, UNCF.

[2] Ibid.

[3] Stillwell, R., & Sable, J. (2013). Public school graduates and dropouts from the Common Core of Data: School Year 2009–10: First Look (Provisional Data) (NCES 2013-309 rev). U.S. Department of Education. Washington, D.C.: National Center for Education Statistics. Retrieved from: *http://nces. ed.gov/pubsearch*.

[4] U.S. Department of Education, National Center for Education Statistics, 2011-12 National Postsecondary Student Aid Study (NPSAS:12).

[5] Elliott, W. & Beverly, S. (2011). The role of savings and wealth in reducing "wilt" between expectations and college attendance. *Journal of Children & Poverty*, 17(2), 165-185.

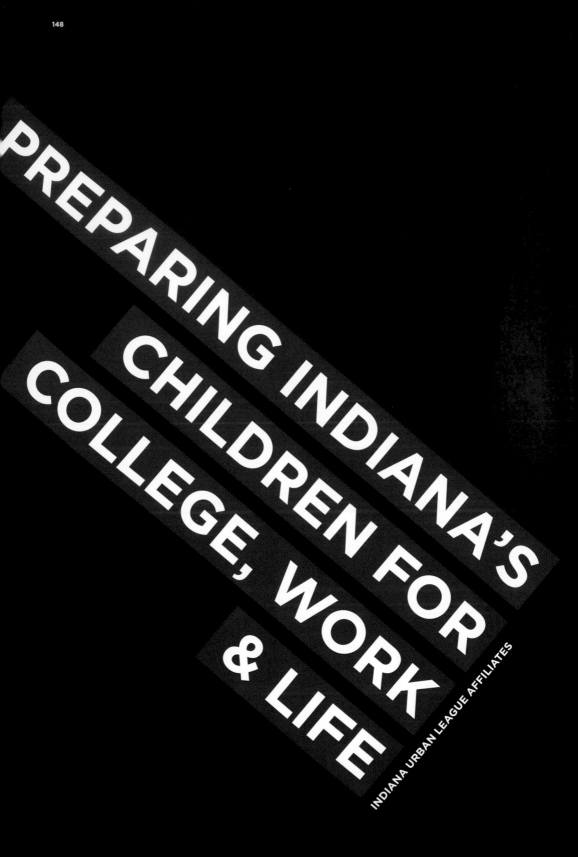

PREPARING INDIANA'S CHILDREN FOR COLLEGE, WORK & LIFE

INDIANA URBAN LEAGUE AFFILIATES

FOR YEARS, INDIANA STUDENTS HAVE GRADUATED FROM HIGH SCHOOL UNPREPARED FOR THE NEXT PHASE IN THEIR LIVES. ONLY ABOUT A THIRD OF HOOSIER HIGH SCHOOL GRADUATES ARE READY FOR COLLEGE, AND ABOUT A THIRD OF THOSE WHO DO ENTER COLLEGE REQUIRE REMEDIATION IN MATH AND ENGLISH.[1]

The Urban League's Indiana affiliates, located in Indianapolis, Fort Wayne, Anderson and Gary,[2] are working to alleviate these deficiencies through education and workforce support services in our respective communities. From the "Read and Rise" program at the Urban League of Madison County to the "In-Power Youth Mentoring Program" at the Urban League of Northwest Indiana—we have made a commitment to empower young people to reach their full potential.

In 2010, the state of Indiana took an important step to ensure all our students graduated from high school ready for college and a career by adopting Common Core State Standards (CCSS), which set forth the skills students need to have in English language arts and math from kindergarten to 12th grade.

Common Core State Standards are designed to close cracks in the system by empowering states to truly prepare students in English and math; empowering educators to share best practices in ways that were never possible before; and empowering students with the skills they need to be successful in life.

Forty-five other states, the District of Columbia and the Department of Defense Schools have adopted Common Core State Standards. The higher education community supports the standards, along with teachers, the Chamber of Commerce, the Indiana Urban League Affiliates and most Hoosiers.[3]

Despite the important advantages of this educational shift, some Indiana lawmakers are working to stop our progress. In April, the Indiana legislature passed a law that paused Indiana's transition to the CCSS, prevented Indiana from

> MISINFORMATION AND AGGRESSIVE ATTACKS ON THE COMMON CORE ARE TAKING PLACE AROUND THE COUNTRY. THIS IS NOTHING LESS THAN PLAYING POLITICS WITH OUR CHILDREN'S FUTURES, AND WE MUST TAKE A FIRM STAND AGAINST THESE TACTICS.

continuing to work with other states to develop new assessments[4] and ordered the state to continue using the archaic Indiana Statewide Testing for Educational Progress-Plus (ISTEP) exam. Sadly, it's our children who will suffer the consequences of these decisions.

Together we are advocating for Indiana to keep CCSS by educating our communities about how these standards will help improve education and equity in our state.

In June 2013, the Fort Wayne Urban League and the Indianapolis Urban League—with assistance from the National Urban League—prepared written testimony in support of maintaining Indiana's participation in CCSS for legislative hearings held by the Joint Education Committees of the Indiana House and Senate.

The Fort Wayne Urban League also participated in a summit, "The Future of Education," to commemorate the 50th Anniversary of Dr. Martin Luther King's visit to Fort Wayne. With more than 1,000 teachers and community leaders present, Fort Wayne Urban League President & CEO Jonathan Ray highlighted the importance of

Common Core State Standards and how they will positively impact the state of Indiana. Additionally, the Fort Wayne Urban League is preparing parents for the Common Core at its charter school and educating over 100 parents whose children participate in its Project Ready program.

Additionally, the Indiana Chamber of Commerce invited the Indianapolis Urban League to join its consortium of organizations advocating for the Common Core. As a part of their efforts, the Indianapolis Urban League began using its existing community forums[5] on education quality and choice to educate the public about Common Core State Standards. This past summer, the Indianapolis Urban League participated in three separate hearings on CCSS held by the Joint Education Committees.

The Indiana Urban League affiliates wrote a joint editorial that ran in the *Indianapolis Star*, the nation's 45th largest newspaper, in support of CCSS and urging community action.

This past summer, the Indianapolis Urban League participated in three separate hearings on the Common Core held by the Joint Education Committees. However, the Committee failed to make a recommendation to support or oppose the standards.

Indiana is not alone in the fight to implement the standards. Misinformation and aggressive attacks on the Common Core are taking place around the country. This is nothing less than playing politics with our children's futures, and we must take a firm stand against these tactics.

Despite these efforts to stop educational progress, we will continue to advocate for these standards to increase equity in our schools and prepare Hoosiers for a brighter future. ★

NOTES

[1] Indiana Commission for Higher Education. (2010). College Readiness Reports. Retrieved from: *http://www.in.gov/che/2687.htm.*

[2] Stillwell, R., and Sable, J. (2013). Public School Graduates and Dropouts from the Common Core of Data: School Year 2009–10: First Look (Provisional Data) (NCES 2013-309rev). U.S. Department of Education. Washington, D.C.: National Center for Education Statistics. Retrieved from: *http://nces.ed.gov/pubsearch.*

[3] Campaign for High School Equity (2013). Maintaining a Focus on Subgroups in an Era of ESEA Waivers. Retrieved from: *http://www.highschoolequity.org/images/WaiversReport_ExecSum_R3.pdf.*

[4] Campaign for High School Equity. (n.d.). CHSE White Paper on Subgroups. Retrieved December 2, 2013, from: *http://www.highschoolequity.org/media-room/media-resources/reports/385-esea-waivers-white-paper.html#fbid=mZsySGJIvIc.*

[5] These forums are supported by the Alliance for School Choice and the Friedman Foundation.

LEAVING NO BRAINS BEHIND

URSULA M. BURNS

MY STORY COULD PROBABLY ONLY
HAPPEN IN AMERICA. I HAVE TWO
SIBLINGS—AN OLDER BROTHER AND A
YOUNGER SISTER. WE WERE RAISED
BY A SINGLE MOTHER IN THE HOUSING
PROJECTS ON THE LOWER EAST SIDE
OF MANHATTAN. THIS WAS THE 1960S.

We were poor, but we didn't know it. Just about everyone in our world was in the same boat, and we made due. Then there was my mother whose generous heart and indomitable spirit protected and nurtured us.

She gave me courage, will and love. I can still hear her telling me that circumstances don't define anyone. It's the content of your character. Mom couldn't do a whole lot about our circumstances, but she sure did shape my character—a gift of immeasurable value.

Like so many others, my mom saw education as the way up and out, and she insisted that we take school seriously. I was a good student and came to love it. Although my teachers kept steering me toward a career as a nurse or teacher, those choices didn't seem quite right for me.

I spent endless afternoons in the library searching through career directories and learned that chemical engineers made a lot of money. We needed the money so I figured what the heck—I'd become a chemical engineer.

Wrong. I hated it, and truth be told, I wasn't very good at it. Rather than abandon engineering, I shifted and changed my major to mechanical engineering which I loved. That led to a summer internship with Xerox, and the rest, as they say, is history.

Now, I tell you that story for a point. If I didn't have the mother I had, if she hadn't sacrificed to send me to the right school and if Xerox hadn't taken an interest in me, there is no way this poor Black girl from the projects would have ever become a mechanical engineer.

Multiply that by the thousands of young women and people of color who have the innate talent to become an engineer or scientist, but lack the motivation and help. Think of all the talent that

is wasted. Think of all the talent that could be harnessed to keep our nation on the leading edge of innovation and technology.

Why does this matter? Because the number of jobs in the U.S. economy that require science, engineering, math and innovation is growing, and the number of people prepared to fill these jobs is shrinking.

IF I DIDN'T HAVE THE MOTHER I HAD, IF SHE HADN'T SACRIFICED TO SEND ME TO THE RIGHT SCHOOL AND IF XEROX HADN'T TAKEN AN INTEREST IN ME, THERE IS NO WAY THIS POOR BLACK GIRL FROM THE PROJECTS WOULD HAVE EVER BECOME A MECHANICAL ENGINEER.

The case for this argument is irrefutable. For much of the 20th century, our economic power and quality of life have depended on innovation. It fueled the automotive and aviation industries, the advent of the computer and information technology, bio-technology, space exploration and a whole lot more. All this innovation led to the creation of millions of high-skill, high-pay jobs.

Many forces are threatening that formula for success. Some—like the rise of economies in China and India—are largely beyond our control. But one is not. Innovation and education are inexorably linked. The pipeline of scientists, engineers and mathematicians—who are at the heart of innovation—is decreasing at a time when the need has never been greater.

Nearly a quarter of a century has passed since the alarm on the crisis was first sounded. In *Winning The Brain Race*, published in 1988, former Xerox CEO David T. Kearns argued that a world-class economy depended on a world-class public education system. Despite a lot of investment directed at the problem in the intervening years, the situation has not gotten any better.

Let's not kid ourselves. This problem has long roots. Scientists and engineers don't get made overnight. They have to be educated through a long process that begins at age 10 to 12, and that takes time. That's why it's so important to America's future that we get serious about leaving no brains behind.

It also takes looking in all the right places. We literally have kids chasing dreams that are attainable only for just a small percentage, yet we need science, technology, engineering and math (STEM) graduates by the hundreds of thousands. Young women and racial minorities are way underrepresented in these areas. As a nation, we need to correct that. The United Negro College Fund tells us that a mind is a terrible thing to waste. Former President Bush started a push to make sure we leave no child behind. President Obama started our schools on the race to the top.

But, we're rapidly running out of time. We need to act in a focused, concerted fashion and we need to do it now. If we don't, we run the very real risk of losing our world leadership. No one sector can fix the problem alone—it's the shared responsibility of business, government and education.

If you talk to just about any company of size, and a lot of smaller ones, too, they will cite

successes and improvements they have helped make possible in public education. So, I've been asking myself: why don't we see the results on a massive scale? I've concluded three things:

- *First, we need to do more, and we need to do it smarter.*
- *Second, business, government and education need to coordinate efforts.*
- *Third, we need to identify programs that are producing measurable, tangible results and leverage them.*

The last point is especially important to me. We may have to create some new initiatives to fill in gaps, but not many. There are hundreds of education programs out there that work. We need to identify them, celebrate them, invest in them and scale them.

I've made it a personal priority to be a vocal advocate for innovation in the U.S. Companies like Xerox succeed through innovation. We need to encourage more investments in STEM education to nurture the next generation of inventors and innovators.

That's precisely what we're attempting to do with Change the Equation (CTE)—an effort I'm leading with several other business leaders at the request of President Obama. It's part of the administration's Race to the Top initiative, and it's focused on rallying business support around STEM education.

CTE is identifying education programs that work—like FIRST, the national robotics competition for high schoolers, and the National Academy Foundation's Academies of Engineering. These programs keep youngsters in school. They motivate them to go to college. They inspire them to careers in innovation. They try to make STEM cool for kids. Just imagine the possibilities if engineers and scientists were adored like athletes and entertainers.

Two great thinkers of the late 18th century had a lot to say about the importance of education. Thomas Jefferson thought it was essential to our experiment with democracy. Adam Smith thought education was critical to economic growth. Both were right, and today we should care deeply about both.

Smith argued that the wealth of a nation resides in its people. This was prior to the Industrial Revolution, so I'm sure he got a lot of push back on that argument. I dare say there is not a person reading this who would argue against that notion that the future success of our country rests in large measure on our people, their brain power and the innovation they are able to create.

That point gets more and more crucial by the day. It's estimated that eight out of every 10 new jobs being created in America require advanced workplace training or formal higher education. No one thinks that trend is likely to reverse itself.

Make no mistake about it. A world-class economy depends on a world-class workforce, and a world-class workforce depends on a world-class education system. If we want a robust economy fueled by an educated work force, we need to invest in our schools. It's as simple—and as hard—as that. ★

MAKING THE GRADE:

PUT THE ARTS BACK IN EDUCATION

WYNTON MARSALIS

FOR YEARS, WE HAVE WITNESSED THE
SLOW, STEADY DETERIORATION OF
AMERICAN PUBLIC EDUCATION AND
HAVE DEBATED AND TESTED MYRIAD
WAYS TO CORRECT IT. IS IT CHARTER
SCHOOLS, COMMON CORE STATE
STANDARDS OR OTHER REFORMS?

When we compare what we are actually providing for many of our children with the promises that our nation must fulfill in order to flourish, it is downright discouraging. We assemble, debate, meet at conferences and other gatherings, and leave feeling inspired and invigorated. We arrive home and face the same old problems that will never be solved with the same old solutions. Those solutions that excited us in conference demonstrate, in practice, the limits of our imagination. In frustration, we become complacent and eventually, we settle.

The answers we seek are to be found in the Arts. Since the Russians launched Sputnik in 1957, there has been a misplaced concentration on math and sciences as the only "real" subjects and an imprudent dismantling of the arts and culture programs in public education. School orchestras are almost non-existent. Millions of dollars in string instruments have rotted away, and even dance, snuck into the curriculum as a physical education requirement, is no longer available.

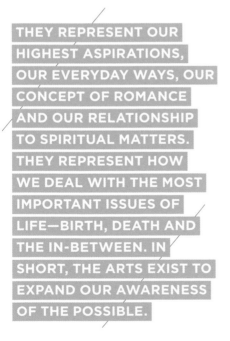

THEY REPRESENT OUR HIGHEST ASPIRATIONS, OUR EVERYDAY WAYS, OUR CONCEPT OF ROMANCE AND OUR RELATIONSHIP TO SPIRITUAL MATTERS. THEY REPRESENT HOW WE DEAL WITH THE MOST IMPORTANT ISSUES OF LIFE—BIRTH, DEATH AND THE IN-BETWEEN. IN SHORT, THE ARTS EXIST TO EXPAND OUR AWARENESS OF THE POSSIBLE.

Generations of neglect have taken the Arts off of our national agenda. Though beset with an abundance of social and cultural ills that distort the national personality, we never consider investing in the very thing designed to call us home, our homegrown Arts. Much like the 14th Century European victims of the Bubonic Plague who looked everywhere for a cure, in the last 50 years, we've looked everywhere to correct our education system except the most obvious place—our way of life. Our internal life and that of our students are under relentless assault by an increasingly crass entertainment and "reality TV" industry that has little to do with reality and is routinely disconnected from any aspirations of quality.

When will it occur to us that there is much in American culture that teaches, unifies and heals us? When will we realize that ultimately, the Arts as representative of cultural solutions have provided a time-tested blueprint of how to face the ever-changing world with class, creativity, confidence, integrity and competence?

It is essential that we identify those aspects of culture that unify. If not, we are lost on the landscape of a variegated country battling over every little issue as separate tribes with different defining characteristics. Our collective heritage should not be considered an elective. My father is a teacher and a musician. I went to great high schools with good teachers and made good grades. Still, I was thoroughly ignorant of the riches of my artistic heritage as an American. Most of us are.

America is still a young country, and for much of our existence, we have had an arts identity crisis—first believing that the only worthwhile art came from Europe. Then, we believed art exacerbated class distinctions. Now, many of us believe that the Arts are dreamy, play-time material. This is why they are always the first

AMERICA IS STILL A YOUNG COUNTRY, AND FOR MUCH OF OUR EXISTENCE, WE HAVE HAD AN ARTS IDENTITY CRISIS—FIRST BELIEVING THAT THE ONLY WORTHWHILE ART CAME FROM EUROPE. THEN, WE BELIEVED ART EXACERBATED CLASS DISTINCTIONS. NOW, MANY OF US BELIEVE THAT THE ARTS ARE DREAMY, PLAY-TIME MATERIAL. THIS IS WHY THEY ARE ALWAYS THE FIRST PROGRAM CUT FROM SCHOOLS.

program cut from schools. The misinformed and prevailing thought has been that the Arts are impractical. In reality, art forms contain the collective wisdom of a people.

They represent our highest aspirations, our everyday ways, our concept of romance and our relationship to spiritual matters. They represent how we deal with the most important issues of life—birth, death and the in-between. In short, the Arts exist to expand our awareness of the possible. If they are insightful and well-crafted enough, they can stand as testaments to the grandeur of a people across epochs: Homer, Beethoven, Michealangelo, and Chaucer— all from another place and time, whose achievements are part of the international lingua franca of contemporary civilization. That is the power of the Arts.

We all know that civilization requires a supreme effort. But whereas the technology of people

becomes outmoded, the technology of the human soul does not change. Technology is not the marvel; people are.

In the simplest and most innate context, creativity and innovation reiterate the importance of soul. We talk a lot about innovation in the realm of science and technology. But we also have an artistic imperative to understand and reengage creativity and innovation not merely as tools for technological and economic development and increase, but also as tools for democracy and accomplished citizenship— demonstrating a cooperative effort to excel.

In this era of technology and the belief that our technology makes us modern, Jazz and the Arts point to one thing—the undisputed importance of our humanity and of the human being. It's most appropriate to have a cultural component to our education system because the Arts let us know who we are in all of our glory—the best of who we are in all aspects. As we now clearly see, our political power and financial might are greatly diminished when put to the service of an impoverished cultural agenda.

Perhaps our preoccupation with technological progress has overshadowed our concern with human progress. Whatever the cause, we are more than that.

I think we all yearn for a new American mythology, another national narrative that elevates adult tastes and behavior over adolescent impulses.

We want to embrace one another and also our generations, but don't know how. The answer is not more education, but more substantive and more culturally-rooted education. The primary justification for the value of education is not competition with other countries for technological jobs or winning in the so-called science race. In this time, we also need to be

educated in who we are, and with the Arts,
education extends far outside the classroom.

In response to the lack of culture and integrity
we see in our way of life, now is the time
to fight for quality and excellence in public
education and rebuild our dismantled arts
programs piece by piece. As we do, we will
begin to see a complete transformation of our
education system through the prism and values
of the American arts and culture—creativity,
innovation, democracy, and integrity.

Whether expressed through artists visiting
schools, museum trips, arts curricula, master
classes, community bands, artist diplomats, swing
dance competitions or another form, inherent in
the Arts is a transcendence and a togetherness
that is larger than our collective ignorance.

It only stands to logic and reason that a complex
nation with many, diverse people must develop
an understanding of its collective heritage to
find that which we seek. ★

WINNING TRIFE³CTA FOR COMMUNITY EMPOWERMENT: EDUCATION, EMPLOYMENT, ENTREPRENEURSHIP

ERIKA MCCONDUIT-DIGGS, ESQ.

IN THE YEARS SINCE HURRICANE KATRINA, NEW
ORLEANS HAS CLAWED ITS WAY BACK TO THE TOP
OF ALL THE LISTS THAT MATTER IN THIS COUNTRY—
FROM ECONOMIC GROWTH POTENTIAL TO
EDUCATION REFORM. YET, OUR GREAT CITY IS STILL
CHALLENGED BY ISSUES SURROUNDING EQUITY.

Indeed, every inclusion metric underscores the difficulties minorities face in economic advancement. Black men of working age face a 52 percent unemployment rate.[1] Only 11 percent of Black men earn bachelor's degrees.[2] While our rate of business startups is 56 percent higher than the national average, only 2 percent of business receipts accrued to minority-owned businesses.[3] We must shift our focus to empower all segments of our community if we are to become as great as our legacy dictates.

The National Urban League's Jobs Rebuild America investment supports programs in job training and certification, employment, college readiness, mentorship, STEM enhancements, and increased business opportunities. Utilizing the "trifecta" approach of *Education, Employment and Entrepreneurship* (E[3]), the Urban League of Greater New Orleans has embraced this opportunity to integrate these investments and to maximize outcomes in these programs: Project Ready—Urban League College Track Program; the Urban Youth Empowerment Program (UYEP) and Training 2 Work (T2W) program; and the Women's Business Resource and Entrepreneurship Center.

// EDUCATION—URBAN LEAGUE COLLEGE TRACK: PROJECT READY

New Orleans' youth are some of the most at-risk and underserved in the nation. Fully 34 percent of the children in New Orleans live in poverty, compared to the national average of 20 percent.[4] Youth in New Orleans are twice as likely to live in poverty and drop out of school without a high school diploma than youth elsewhere in Louisiana and four times more likely than youth living in other parts of the United States.[5]

Our Urban League College Track: Project Ready Initiative aims to reverse this tide through this program which offers 200 underserved

youth college readiness, academic mentoring and STEM exposure to help them get through high school and college.

Through Project Pipeline, a program of the Louisiana Chapter of the National Organization of Minority Architects, Project Ready students receive hands-on training in the fundamentals of design. Discussions are supplemented with site visits to prominent works of architecture in New Orleans, many of which were crafted and built by African American artisans.

Urban League College Track educational activities are coupled with our Project Ready

THE NATIONAL URBAN LEAGUE'S JOBS REBUILD AMERICA INVESTMENT SUPPORTS PROGRAMS IN JOB TRAINING AND CERTIFICATION, EMPLOYMENT, COLLEGE READINESS, MENTORSHIP, STEM ENHANCEMENTS, AND INCREASED BUSINESS OPPORTUNITIES. UTILIZING THE "TRIFECTA" APPROACH OF EDUCATION, EMPLOYMENT AND ENTREPRENEURSHIP (E[3]), THE URBAN LEAGUE OF GREATER NEW ORLEANS HAS EMBRACED THIS OPPORTUNITY TO INTEGRATE THESE INVESTMENTS AND TO MAXIMIZE OUTCOMES.

Mentor Program, which incorporates a holistic suite of support services including personal and academic goal setting and character development. Outperforming the national, state, and city of New Orleans averages, 100 percent of our graduating seniors have been accepted to four-year colleges and universities, with a 76 percent persistence rate for our college students. Our class of 2013 boasted an average ACT (American College Testing) score of 20, on a scale of 1 to 36, with more than 75 percent earning college scholarships and currently attending 23 universities regionally and across the nation.

// EMPLOYMENT: URBAN YOUTH EMPOWERMENT PROGRAM (UYEP WORKS) AND TRAINING 2 WORK (T2W)

Our UYEP Works and T2W programs help to address problems associated with low participation in school or work of youth between the ages of 16–19—along with high rates of serious crime, incarceration and recidivism for youth and young adults. The Urban League's Office of Workforce Development acts as a conduit to bridge gaps in education, socialization, and job training, while creating a pipeline of skilled workers for the new and emerging regional economy. More than 350 jobseekers have participated in customized training; 44 percent were connected to employment with earnings at more than $10/hour; GED participants increased their knowledge by more than one grade level; and our Core Level Construction graduates boast an overall grade average of 91 percent.

// ENTREPRENEURSHIP: WOMEN'S BUSINESS RESOURCE AND ENTREPRENEURSHIP CENTER

Through our Women's Business Resource and Entrepreneurship Center, we are providing technical assistance to over 1,100 small businesses each year. In 2013, 28 new businesses were established with our assistance; 106 new jobs were created by our business clients; and 23 jobs were saved in declining businesses that were aided by the Center. Business owner clients received loans totaling $1.6 million; contracts totaling $3.6 million; and were issued bonding in excess of $31 million.

Collectively, our Education, Employment and Entrepreneurship trifecta approach will help usher in the next phase of our city's rebirth and ensure the future growth and development of our most treasured existence—our people. ★

NOTES

[1] Rainey, R. (2013, June 12) African-American men in New Orleans are an untapped workforce, new report says. *The Times Picayune*. Retrieved from: *http://www.nola.com/politics/index.ssf/2013/06/african_american_men_in_new_or.html*.

[2] Plyer, A., Ortiz, E., Horwitz, B., Hobor, G. (2013, August 14) The New Orleans Index at Eight: Measuring Greater New Orleans' Progress toward Prosperity. Retrieved from: *http://www.gnocdc.org/TheNewOrleansIndexAtEight/index.html*.

[3] Ibid.

[4] Annie E. Casey Foundation (2011) Kids Count Data Book: State Profiles in Child Well-Being. Retrieved from: *http://www.aecf.org/KnowledgeCenter/Publications.aspx?pubguid=%7BE78A80B5-988E-4FB5-A070-8279A5170B35%7D*.

[5] Ibid.

21ST CENTURY JOBS & CLIMATE CHANGE:

A CURSE & A BLESSING FOR AFRICAN AMERICANS

J. MARSHALL SHEPHERD, PH.D.

CLIMATE CHANGE AND RELATED EXTREME
WEATHER EVENTS WILL HAVE A FAR WORSE
IMPACT ON CERTAIN SEGMENTS OF OUR
POPULATION, ACCORDING TO MANY STUDIES.[1,2]
IF YOU WANT A POIGNANT EXAMPLE, LOOK
NO FURTHER THAN FACES HUDDLED IN THE
SUPERDOME OR ON BUSES HEADED TO
HOUSTON AFTER HURRICANE KATRINA

The storm affected the entire Gulf Coast region irrespective of race, origin, or status. Yet African Americans were particularly vulnerable and less resilient to the hazard. Many residents lost jobs or essentially became "hurricane refugees."

Virtually all major scientific studies and organizations[3,4,5] continue to affirm that our climate is changing and that manifestations are apparent in today's weather. This century, the United States has experienced Hurricane Katrina, a Superstorm, unprecedented drought, "biblical" scale flooding, brutal heat waves, and unusually intense blizzards. One day at church, an elderly gentleman approached me and said, "Doc, what's going on? Things are different with the weather now." He was right.

Climate change, partially caused by increased greenhouse gas emissions, affects the economy, public health, water resources, energy, and many facets of society. The ultimate irony is that African Americans, per capita, have smaller emission "footprints" than the white population according to a 2004 Congressional Black Caucus report.[6]

Still, many African Americans perceive climate change as an issue (1) about polar bears or environmentalists and (2) far into the future with no immediate consequences. These are flawed and very dangerous assumptions. African Americans are at greater risk from weather and climate related disasters, both episodic and long-term, than white Americans.[6] Studies[7, 8, 9, 10] even affirm that vulnerable groups such as racial minorities, the poor, and elderly are more likely to fear great risks form natural disasters, but are less likely to act on warnings; experience significant psychological-physical impacts; and are slower to bounce back. African Americans also experience, at a greater rate, a multitude of extreme weather climate health issues like heat stress, upper respiratory illnesses, waterborne disease, and

post-traumatic stress. Along with these stressors, weather-climate price inflation and loss of job/ work hours tend to compound other impacts in the long-term. Herein, the focus is on challenges and opportunities surrounding climate change and the African American job market.

// JOBS: CHALLENGES

Climate vulnerability defines susceptibility of social systems to harmful effects of climate extremes and variability as well as ability to cope with them. Texas Southern University Dean Robert Bullard, father of the modern environmental justice movement, has long argued that racial or poor groups face economic, health, and place-based disparities because of environmental degradation, industrial negligence, and social vulnerability.[11] Many scholars[12] now refer to the disparities in climate vulnerability by race as the "Climate Gap."

Roughly 55–60 percent of the Black population lives in the South and coastal regions,[13] which are particularly susceptible to droughts, floods, hurricanes, sea level changes and heat waves. Dean Bullard has estimated that the South is more prone to climate-related disasters, in scale and magnitude, by a ratio of 4 to 1. This has several implications on employment and under-employment of Blacks. When a storm like Hurricane Katrina or Sandy happens, many people temporarily or permanently lose their jobs and in some cases must be relocated completely. Of concern, scientists expect more intense hurricanes and continued sea level rise.[14]

The economies of the South and other parts of the United States are highly dependent upon agriculture. Studies continue to warn that more frequent and intense drought and reduced agricultural productivity will be a by-product of climate warming.[15, 16] Reduced crop yields are correlated with reduced labor needs in the fields, processing facilities, and other sectors of the agrarian supply chain. A significant number of African Americans and other minorities, primarily Latinos, are employed in the agriculture industry.

Economic market forces impacted by climate change (e.g. energy policy, cap and trade policies, regulation and market disruption due to extreme events) affect supply, demand, and price for services and commodities. Hoerner and Robinson's 2008 report points out that energy prices are a significant driver of recession and subsequent job reductions. Climate or weather related "inflation" (e.g. spikes of gas prices when hurricanes shutter off-shore oil rigs) stresses African Americans disproportionately because a significant income and employment gap exists between African Americans and white Americans.[17, 18] As I stated in a 2013 Senate Briefing,[19] the 2012 Midwest drought caused U.S. citizens to pay more for bread, cereals, and meat.

// JOBS: THE OPPORTUNITIES

There is a bright side. The "green" economy promoted by President Obama will reflect a new job market and a generation of professionals that understand climate science, weather, renewable engineering, conservation practices, mitigation-adaptation strategies, and environmental sustainability. It is important to note that the green economy is upon us. For example, Washington state already produces a Green-Economy Jobs Report each year.[20]

Conservative ideology characterizes the "green" economy as expensive or job killing, but the President's Climate Action Plan[21] and other studies note that millions of American workers stand to benefit. Most green jobs will be anchored around strategies that seek to mitigate carbon emissions or adapt to climate change. According to the University of Massachusetts-Amherst and the Center for American Progress,[22] jobs will emerge

centered around six green strategies: "building retrofitting, mass transit, energy-efficient automobiles, wind power, solar power, and cellulosic biomass fuels." Weather, climate, and environmental scientists will be required as well as a new generation of environmental engineers, planners, and business practitioners that understand the new green economy.

Pollin and Wicks-Lim[22] point out that many jobs will require the same skillsets already possessed by many laborers. For example, constructing a hydroelectric dam or wind farm still requires skilled labor, sheet metal workers, truck drivers, construction workers and electricians. Even with the durability of some jobs, African Americans must overcome the aversion to STEM to be positioned for the new opportunities that will emerge.[23] Yet, African Americans are severely under-represented in degree programs aligned with many future STEM careers.

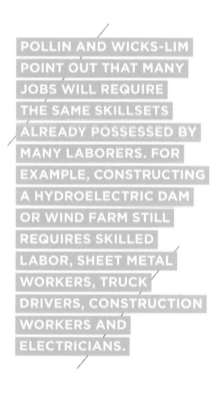

POLLIN AND WICKS-LIM POINT OUT THAT MANY JOBS WILL REQUIRE THE SAME SKILLSETS ALREADY POSSESSED BY MANY LABORERS. FOR EXAMPLE, CONSTRUCTING A HYDROELECTRIC DAM OR WIND FARM STILL REQUIRES SKILLED LABOR, SHEET METAL WORKERS, TRUCK DRIVERS, CONSTRUCTION WORKERS AND ELECTRICIANS.

African Americans will need to:

- *Understand that there are "good" jobs outside of business, law, and medicine.*
- *Develop a network or pipeline of mentors for young scientists or engineers to aspire to.*
- *Overcome the stigma that STEM excellence is nerdy or uncool.*
- *Find ways to make science accessible and fun for younger generations in their day-to-day lives and through broader exposure to opportunities.*

In some cases, this will mean some adults and students will have to move beyond cultural, academic, or geographic comfort zones. After all, our future job security may depend on it. ★

NOTES

[1] Hoerner, J., Robinson, N. (2008 July) A Climate of Change African Americans, Global Warming, and a Just Climate Policy for the U.S. Retrieved from: http://rprogress.org/publications/2008/climateofchange.pdf.

[2] Shepherd, J. (2013, February 11) Are African-Americans More Vulnerable to Climate Change? Ebony. Retrieved from: http://www.ebony.com/news-views/are-african-americans-more-vulnerable-to-climate-change-352#ixzz2qN5qdDXN.

[3] Allen, S., Bex, V., Boschung, J., Midgley, P., Nauels, A., Plattner, G., Qin, D., Stocker, T., Tignor M. (2013) Climate Change 2013: The Physical Science Basis. Retrieved from: http://www.ipcc.ch/report/ar5/wg1/.

[4] American Meteorological Society. (2012) Climate Change: An Information Statement of the American Meteorological Society. Retrieved from: http://www.ametsoc.org/policy/2012climatechange.html.

[5] National Academy of Sciences. Climate Change: Evidence, Impacts, and Choices. Retrieved from http://nas-sites.org/americasclimatechoices/more-resources-on-climate-change/climate-change-lines-of-evidence-booklet/.

[6] Congressional Black Caucus Foundation. (2014, July 21) African Americans and Climate Change: An Unequal Burden. Retrieved from: http://rprogress.org/publications/2004/CBCF_REPORT_F.pdf.

[7] Hoyle, Z. (2013, June 13) Hot Time in the City: In Georgia, Atlanta residents could be hit hardest by climate change. United States Department of Agriculture. Retrieved from: http://www.srs.fs.usda.gov/compass/2013/06/13/hot-time-in-the-city/.

[8] Polsky, C., R. Neff, and B. Yarnal, (2007) Building comparable global change vulnerability assessments: The vulnerability scoping diagram. Global Environmental Change, 17, 472-485.

[9] Cutter, S. L., and C. Finch, (2008) Temporal and spatial changes in social vulnerability to natural hazards. Proceedings of the National Academy of Sciences, 105, 2301–2306.

[10] Wood, N., C. Burton, and S. Cutter, (2010) Community variations in social vulnerability to Cascadia-related tsunamis in the U.S. Pacific Northwest. Natural Hazards, 52, 369–389.

[11] Bullard, R., Wright, B., (2012, July) The Wrong Complexion for Protection: How the Government Response to Disaster Endangers African American Communities. New York: NYU Press. Retrieved from: http://nyupress.org/books/book-details.aspx?bookid=1183.

[12] Morello-Frosch, R., Pastor, M, Sadd, J., Shonkoff, S. (2013) Climate Change: Inequalities in How Climate Change Hurts americans & How to Close the Gap. Retrieved from: http://dornsife.usc.edu/assets/sites/242/docs/The_Climate_Gap_Full_Report_FINAL.pdf.

[13] Social Science Data Analysis Network. CensusScope. Retrieved from: *http://www.censusscope.org/us/map_nhblack.html*.

[14] Knutson, T., McBride, J. Chan, J., Emanuel, K., Holland, G., Landsea, C., Held, I., Holland, G., Kossin, J., Srivastava, A.K., Sugi, M. (2010, February 21) Tropical cyclones and climate change. Nature GeoScience. Retrieved from: *http://www.nature.com/ngeo/journal/v3/n3/abs/ngeo779.html*.

[15] *http://www.nature.com/nclimate/journal/v3/n1/full/nclimate1633.html*.

[16] Betts, R., Burke, E., Clark, R., Camp, J., Gornall, J., Willett, K., Wiltshire, A. (2010, August) Implications of climate change for agricultural productivity in the early twenty-first century. Retrieved from: *http://rstb.royalsocietypublishing.org/content/365/1554/2973.full*.

[17] Plumer, B. (2013, August 28) These ten charts show the Black–white economic gap hasn't budged in 50 years. *WashingtonPost.com*. Retrieved from: *http://www.washingtonpost.com/blogs/wonkblog/wp/2013/08/28/these-seven-charts-show-the-black-white-economic-gap-hasnt-budged-in-50-years/*.

[18] Woodruff, M. (2013, August 29) The Income Gap Between Blacks and Whites Has Only Gotten Worse Since the 1960s. Business Insider. Retrieved from: *http://www.businessinsider.com/the-income-gap-between-blacks-and-whites-2013-8" \I "ixzz2udwkqfj2" http://www.businessinsider.com/the-income-gap-between-blacks-and-whites-2013-8#ixzz2udwkqfj2 http://www.businessinsider.com/the-income-gap-between-blacks-and-whites-2013-8*.

[19] U.S. Senate Committee on Environment and Public Works. (2013, February 13) Retrieved from: *http://www.epw.senate.gov/public/index.cfm?FuseAction=Hearings.Hearing&Hearing_ID=cf67a715-fca1-8682-f7dd-13242e8035d1*.

[20] Washington State Employment Security Department. (2011) Green-Economy Jobs Report. Retrieved from: *https://fortress.wa.gov/esd/employmentdata/reports-publications/special-reports/green-economy-jobs-report*.

[21] Executive Office of the President. (2013, June) The President's Climate Action Plan. Retrieved from: *http://www.whitehouse.gov/sites/default/files/image/president27sclimateactionplan.pdf*.

[22] Pollin, R., Wicks-Lim, J. (2008 June) Job Opportunities for the Green Economy: A State-by-State Picture of Occupations that Gain From Green Investments. Retrieved from: *http://www.peri.umass.edu/fileadmin/pdf/other_publication_types/Green_Jobs_PERI.pdf*.

[23] Shepherd, J. (2013, April, 15) Why African Americans May be Left Out of the 21st Century Job Market. Ebony. Retrieved from: *http://www.ebony.com/career-finance/why-african-americans-may-be-left-out-of-the-21st-century-job-market-498" \I "axzz2qK5CEzP7" http://www.ebony.com/career-finance/why-african-americans-may-be-left-out-of-the-21st-century-job-market-498#axzz2qK5CEzP7*.

ENTREPRENEURSHIP

RANDAL D. PINKETT, PH.D. &
JEFFREY A. ROBINSON, PH.D.

& ECONOMIC

DEVELOPMENT

EVER SINCE WE CO-FOUNDED
OUR FIRST COMPANY WHILE
UNDERGRADUATES AT RUTGERS
UNIVERSITY, ENTREPRENEURSHIP
HAS BEEN AT THE CENTER OF OUR
COMMUNITY BUILDING STRATEGIES.

Entrepreneurship is about creating value in the world. In our book, *Black Faces in White Places: 10 Game Changing Strategies to Achieve Success and Find Greatness,* we further describe entrepreneurship as follows:

"Entrepreneurship is about using your talents to make a positive impact in your areas of influence, and then leveraging all of the resources at your disposal to create value in the world...For those that find themselves looking to create new schools, new nonprofits, new businesses, and new religious institutions, we encourage you to 'think and act entrepreneurially'—to apply the principles of the entrepreneurial mindset to creating new entities...People who create new entities and apply the entrepreneurial mindset to their work are entrepreneurs."

We believe that this entrepreneurial mindset is the key to the future economic development of the Black community. Entrepreneurs are the major wealth creators in America, but unfortunately less than 5 percent of the Black population is self-employed or engaged in founding and running registered businesses. Furthermore, the entrepreneurs who are making money in Black communities are not Black. Often, the wealth that is created through entrepreneurship doesn't stay in the Black

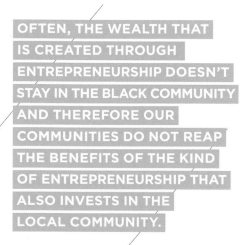

OFTEN, THE WEALTH THAT IS CREATED THROUGH ENTREPRENEURSHIP DOESN'T STAY IN THE BLACK COMMUNITY AND THEREFORE OUR COMMUNITIES DO NOT REAP THE BENEFITS OF THE KIND OF ENTREPRENEURSHIP THAT ALSO INVESTS IN THE LOCAL COMMUNITY.

community and, therefore, our communities do not reap the benefits of the kind of entrepreneurship that also invests in the local community.

We see three strategies to increase the effectiveness of entrepreneurship as an economic development tool for the Black community:

// 1. WE MUST RECOGNIZE THE IMPORTANCE OF ENTREPRENEURSHIP AS THE MOST IMPORTANT VEHICLE OF ECONOMIC DEVELOPMENT IN THE BLACK COMMUNITY.

In a study conducted by the Kauffman Foundation, it was noted that Black Americans, and in particular Black males, were the most likely to say they wanted to open their own business. Unfortunately, the statistics also tell us that Blacks are the least likely to actually open a business. There may be several explanations for this paradox, but it points towards the untapped potential for entrepreneurial activity in our community. In fact, based on a study conducted by the U.S. Minority Business Development Agency, if we raised the participation rate of Black and other minority entrepreneurs to a level even with our percentage of the U.S. population, we would not only create more wealth in the community,[1] but we would wipe out the unemployment problem in minority communities. When we ran the same models specifically on Black entrepreneurship in New Jersey, we found that by doubling the number of Black-owned businesses, we would create an additional 56,000 jobs in the state. These findings should make building entrepreneurs and supporting entrepreneurship a priority in our community.

// 2. WE MUST SHIFT THE MINDSET FROM BEING SMALL BUSINESS OWNERS TO BEING EXECUTIVES OF BUSINESS ENTERPRISES.

We meet many "solo-preneurs" who are running small businesses without any business partners, and we know that their potential is limited. In order to truly transform our neighborhoods into thriving communities, we need to build more "business enterprises." A business enterprise is an entity that builds wealth that can be shared in future generations or simultaneously creates community wealth through job creation and other social impacts. In fact, the most impactful entrepreneurship occurs when teams of entrepreneurial individuals join together to create enterprises that leverage the five "M"s—money, marketing, management, mentors and mergers/acquisitions—to create wealth. For example, Oprah Winfrey and Jeff Jacobs formed a partnership that catapulted Oprah to becoming the first Black female billionaire. When Bert Mitchell invited Robert Titus, a colleague working as a sole practitioner to join his firm as a partner, they created Mitchell & Titus, which is now the largest minority-controlled accounting firm in the United States. Lastly, David Steward and James Kavanaugh joined forces to establish World Wide Technology, which has grown to become the largest Black-owned business in the country.

// 3. WE MUST USE DOUBLE- AND TRIPLE-BOTTOM LINE LOGIC TO MAKE ECONOMIC PROGRESS, SOCIAL IMPACT, AND ADDRESS ISSUES OF ENVIRONMENTAL JUSTICE AND DEGRADATION.

To use this kind of logic in your business endeavors means achieving financial goals and social and/or environmental goals simultaneously. These "social entrepreneurs" blur the lines between making a profit and making a difference by combining them into a holistic agenda. Just as entrepreneurs change the face of industry by focusing on the bottom line of making a profit, social entrepreneurs change the face of society by focusing on the "double-bottom line" of making a profit *and* making a difference; building organizations *and* building communities; doing good business *and* goodwill; and implementing solid business practices and socially responsible behavior (*and* environmentally-

friendly practices, which reflects a triple-bottom line). In this age of "buying local" and building "sustainable" communities, this double- and triple-bottom line logic is a must for all, but especially for our Black businesses. Several good examples of this model exist. In Chicago, IL, Brenda Palms Barber founded Sweet Beginnings LLC as a business that would hire the graduates of their U-Turn Permitted Program. Sweet Beginnings hires people who were formerly incarcerated and interested in turning their lives around to create natural bath and beauty products derived from the honey and beeswax harvested from beehives they host on abandoned properties and rooftops in Chicago's West Side. The products, known as BeeLove, are sold in Whole Foods, Hudson Bookseller Shops and boutiques around the county. Other examples include companies such as City Fresh Foods in Boston, MA and Brotherhood Brewing Company in St. Paul, MN, which are similar to Sweet Beginnings because they function as for-profit companies that have specific local community impact goals that are tied to their business model. This double-bottom line logic must be taken up by more businesses in our community if we are ever going to make a significant impact on the social and economic problems we face in our communities.

These examples underscore the need to support Black social entrepreneurs in every community. If we want to see significant economic improvement across our nation in the 21st century, we must increase the number of Black business enterprises, entrepreneurs and social entrepreneurs in our communities. ★

NOTES

[1] U.S. Department of Commerce, Minority Business Development Agency (2007) 2007 Survey of Business Owners. Retrieved from: *http://www.mbda.gov/node/671.*

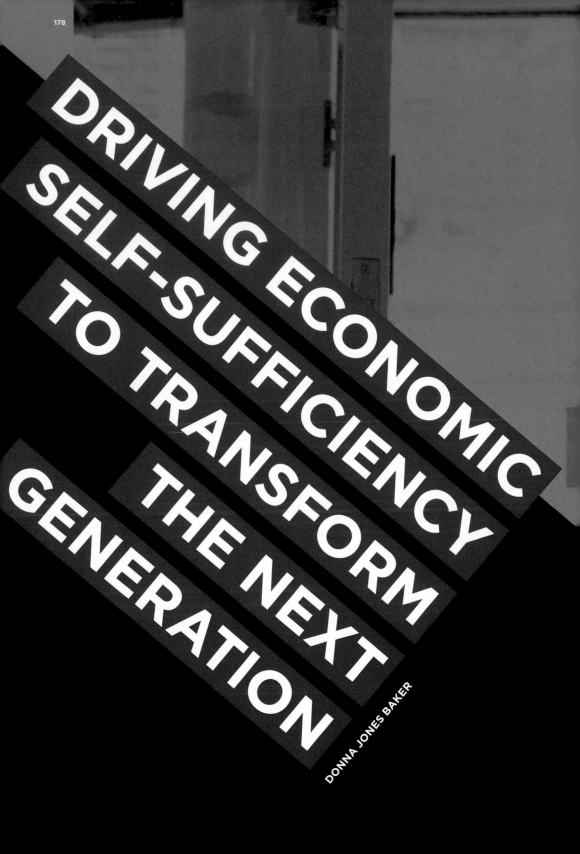

DRIVING ECONOMIC SELF-SUFFICIENCY TO TRANSFORM THE NEXT GENERATION

DONNA JONES BAKER

ECONOMIC SELF-SUFFICIENCY MAY BE DEFINED AS THE ABILITY OF A PERSON OR THE ABILITY OF A FAMILY TO MAINTAIN A REASONABLE STANDARD OF LIVING THAT IS INDEPENDENT OF ASSISTANCE FROM OTHERS.

NATIONAL URBAN LEAGUE

To be economically self-sufficient is to have the ability to provide basic needs such as adequate food, clothing, shelter, healthcare, and transportation without the benefit of financial assistance from others, including institutions and government agencies. With this definition of economic self-sufficiency in mind, in 2012 our Urban League launched a comprehensive strategic plan that guides our programming and allows us to directly impact the lives of hundreds of families in our service area. The mission of the Urban League of Greater Southwestern Ohio is *"to transform generations by promoting personal empowerment and economic self-sufficiency."* Our vision is vibrant communities with thriving individuals, families, and businesses.

Changing the paradigm has not been easy. In 2005–2009, there were 13,772 families below the poverty level in Cincinnati.[1] Seventy-six percent of those families were African American. The Urban League maintains a commitment to changing that paradigm by focusing on the key areas of Workforce Development and Business Development/Entrepreneurship with workforce programs comprising 29.5 percent of our overall agency budget. Both programs are roads to economic self-sufficiency.

The creation of jobs is critical to economic self-sufficiency and can be the first step toward building generational wealth. Our workforce programs are designed to prepare participants for success in the work arena by providing free programs that teach and reinforce soft skills, basic job readiness and provide an entrée into the various skilled trades. All of our workforce programs are built upon the foundation of our flagship program: Solid Opportunities for Advancement and Retention (SOAR). In 2013, SOAR and our Accelerated Call Center Education Program (ACE) were the gateways to employment for 650 men and women with jobs paying an average of $10.50 an hour and

providing participants a pathway to specialized and seasonal industry-specific training programs and employment. Recognizing the link between poverty and education, the League annually co-hosts youth-oriented pathways to specialized and seasonal industry-specific training programs and employment.

Being economically self-sufficient through owning your own business is not a new concept in the African American community. We have traditionally owned the neighborhood grocery, the barber shop, the beauty parlor and the funeral home—all providing needed services and specializing in serving the African American community. We recognize such businesses as the backbone of America in general. Many of our small businesses die due to the lack of operating capital. Through our Business Development &

BEING ECONOMICALLY SELF-SUFFICIENT THROUGH OWNING YOUR OWN BUSINESS IS NOT A NEW CONCEPT IN THE AFRICAN AMERICAN COMMUNITY. WE HAVE TRADITIONALLY OWNED THE NEIGHBORHOOD GROCERY, THE BARBER SHOP, THE BEAUTY PARLOR AND THE FUNERAL HOME; ALL PROVIDING NEEDED SERVICES AND SPECIALIZING IN SERVING THE AFRICAN AMERICAN COMMUNITY.

Entrepreneurship programs, we meet the needs of both established and aspiring entrepreneurs. We include as a part of our program a Small Business Development Center and the regional office of the Women's Business Enterprise National Council (WBENC) women's business certification program.

Founded in 2010, our League's African American Business Development Program (AABDP) provides technical assistance, mentoring, encouragement and hope for individuals and families as they pursue their own path to the American Dream. To date, 46 companies have participated in the program with a 93 percent completion rate. Of the companies starting the program, 88 percent are still in business. Training and success go hand-in-glove. Twenty-three of our AABDP companies report having received 351 contracts for a total of $66,788,633. Small business growth has a domino effect; companies participating in our AABDP program have been able to hire additional employees, frequently hiring from one of our workforce development programs. The steady company growth of these businesses has resulted in their receiving approximately $7,492,863 in small business loans. In an effort to help support and grow this program, AABDP received a five-year grant from Hightowers Petroleum Company, a local multi-generational family-owned group of companies—proof that generational wealth is the key to creating an economically stable community.

The League also engages in social entrepreneurship with an on-site call center that will eventually provide employment to more than 150 people making a minimum wage of more than $10.50 per hour. ★

NOTES

[1] Social Areas of Cincinnati (2009) Poverty, Race and Gender in Cincinnati. Retrieved from: *http://www.socialareasofcincinnati.org/files/FifthEdition/TableofContents_color.pdf.*

FACTS VS. FICTION: BUYING BLACK AS AN ECONOMIC EMPOWERMENT STRATEGY

MARGARITA "MAGGIE" ANDERSON

THE FACT IS THAT WE HAVE ECONOMICALLY EMPOWERED THE AFRICAN AMERICAN COMMUNITY BEFORE VIA STRATEGIC ENTREPRENEURSHIP AND THE PROACTIVE SUPPORT OF OUR BUSINESSES.

The fact is that our friends from other racial and ethnic communities still do this and have realized great cultural, political and economic empowerment. The fiction is that segregation was the necessary impetus and context for self-help economics and community unity. The fiction is that integration killed the African American community's economic potential.

Demand. Self-help economics. Buying Black. Buying power. Conscious consumerism. While I use, promote, and teach these concepts every day, they are woefully and conspicuously underutilized in the Black community's economic empowerment conversation. While "buying Black" is at least as old and undeniable in our history as Emancipation,[1] "buying Black" has not been a highlight of the modern, post-Civil Rights era struggle for economic empowerment, much less a noticeable movement or public approach embraced by our community's institutions, professional and civic organizations, universities, or churches.

// WHERE WE BUY HAS A LOT TO DO WITH WHERE WE ARE

In order for the proactive, public, strategic and intentional support of Black-owned businesses (i.e., "buying Black") to work as a viable strategy for Black economic empowerment, it must first be acknowledged, proven and promoted that business power, community power, financial power and economic power are all a function of buying power.

In practice, self-help economics seems to be more proactively and effectively leveraged by other ethnic groups. For example, in Asian communities, a dollar circulates among the community's banks, retailers, and business professionals for up to 28 days before it is spent outside the community. In the Jewish community, the circulation period is 19 days; in the White Anglo-Saxon Protestant (WASP)

community, it's 17 days; and in the Hispanic community, it's 7 days. Yet, in the Black community, the dollar lives only six hours before it leaves the community.[2]

That recycling of the dollar is important to communities because it gives children a chance to see business owners who look like them every day—in the neighborhood, on TV, on the billboards, and in the stores and franchises. As neighborhood families support these businesses, the businesses in turn support the neighborhood by employing local residents. This is classic self-help economics.[3]

Though self-help economics, as defined above, was more commonly practiced by the Black

THAT RECYCLING OF THE DOLLAR IS IMPORTANT TO COMMUNITIES BECAUSE IT GIVES CHILDREN A CHANCE TO SEE BUSINESS OWNERS WHO LOOK LIKE THEM EVERY DAY— IN THE NEIGHBORHOOD, ON TV, ON THE BILLBOARDS, AND IN THE STORES AND FRANCHISES. AS NEIGHBORHOOD FAMILIES SUPPORT THESE BUSINESSES, THE BUSINESSES IN TURN SUPPORT THE NEIGHBORHOOD BY EMPLOYING LOCAL RESIDENTS.

community before integration, the once Black-owned pharmacies, beauty supply stores, grocers, hotels, banks and convenience stores no longer exist in Black neighborhoods on that same scale.[4] Consequently, those who now own these businesses in Black neighborhoods hardly invest in and employ from the local community.[5]

Additionally, most of the products and services African Americans now consume—Black media and entertainment, Black dating websites, Black hair and skin care, Black toys, and Black fashion—are neither produced nor distributed by Black-owned firms.[6] Behind this consumption are billions of dollars in business contracts, business growth, advertising revenue, entrepreneurial opportunity and economic empowerment that, while driven by Black consumer spending, are not empowering the Black community.[7] Still today, we as African American thought leaders and policymakers have not asserted, and have just begun to imply, that the success or demise of our businesses, the ability to create jobs, the opportunity to close the wealth gap, and the idea of building and maintaining self-sustaining communities and strong, financially secure families has anything to do with how Black consumers spend their money. Without that confession, perspective and ultimate consensus, it will be impossible to build an economic empowerment strategy around self-help economics or "buying Black."

My insights as to why self-help economics as a practice has diminished and not been revived in the African American community, and how conscious consumerism or "buying Black" can still be a viable solution to our economic crises, are informed by personal experiences. Namely, conceiving and conducting The Empowerment Experiment (my family's historic and highly publicized stand and social experiment of completely living off Black businesses and professionals and buying only Black-made products for one year) and all the subsequent opportunities to share and expound upon this experiment.

// SEGREGATION VS INTEGRATION— COMMITMENT, COMMON SENSE, AND CONSCIOUSNESS ARE NOT DRIVEN BY OPPRESSION AND INSULT

Historically, the laws of this nation segregated Black communities to the extent that Black people "had" to support each other. But, I don't believe this to be the only reason for such legendary Black-owned business successes as the North Carolina Mutual Insurance Company, the largest Black-owned company in America and the anchor of Durham, North Carolina's Black Wall Street of the 1910s and 20s, or Madam CJ Walker, the first Black woman millionaire who revolutionized the Black hair care industry. Segregation did not compel the ingenuity, intelligence, and investment that created those businesses, nor did unjust laws force Black people to believe in each other. To accept that the viability of a consumer-driven economic empowerment strategy depends on segregation or oppression of a community is to fall prey to the notion that the Black community must be forced into greatness. This paradigm curtails the capacity of any kind of economic empowerment plan or discussion in a legally integrated society. On the contrary, I believe we can bring back the economic empowerment that sustained the Black community before and until integration.

// ECONOMIC EMPOWERMENT IN AN INTEGRATED CONTEXT—SOLIDARITY AND SMART, STRATEGIC SPENDING THAT IS DRIVEN BY INNOVATION AND COMPELS INCLUSION

The innovation needed to enable consumer-driven economic empowerment is found when we choose to leverage what modern-day progress has given us—technology, diverse networks, more transparency, more connections and more access to information. It is now easier than ever before to learn about, mobilize, seek and support Black-owned businesses. Therefore, technology enables us to involve consumers in an economic empowerment strategy by educating, inspiring and facilitating their practice of self-help economics.

The inclusive component of a modern day "buy Black" economic empowerment strategy comes from driving more Black-owned business representation and success in corporate America—a huge, but under-appreciated opportunity space. Too many brands and retailers thrive off the Black consumer dollar but have zero minority inputs in their supply chains. For instance, according to my research and the *Wall Street Journal*, over 60 percent of Hennessy's global market share comes from African Americans in the United States; yet, the company has no Black distributors and lacks a supplier diversity program.[8] However, more supplier, franchisee, agent and vendor diversity could create hundreds of thousands of jobs.[9]

Harnessing this potential is both an opportunity and a challenge, but there is a way forward. First, we have to hold corporations accountable for investing in our economic empowerment by cultivating solid business relationships with Black-owned firms.[10] Second, we must demonstrate the economic impact that supplier diversity can have on their bottom line and within our communities. Third, we have to prove that everyday consumers are willing to do more to support the mainstream corporations that do business with Black-owned firms as opposed to simply marketing to Black consumers.

// CONCLUSION—PROOF PLUS POTENTIAL EQUALS POWER

According to the landmark Northwestern University Kellogg Business School study based on The Empowerment Experiment, out of the close to $1 trillion in Black buying power, maybe 3 percent of that goes to Black professionals, suppliers and firms. But, if Black households with annual income of $75,000 or more—middle and upper income African Americans—were to increase spending with Black professionals and firms from 3 percent to just 10 percent, we could create close to 1,000,000 jobs.[11] This 10 percent includes direct spending with local Black-owned businesses, as well as indirect spending through the support of Black vendors, agents, dealers and franchises of mainstream firms. The new jobs would be created from the money we already have and currently spend—no government program and no corporate social responsibility outlay necessary.

This is a doable, inclusive economic empowerment strategy. Buying Black in an integrated society can work, but we all must do our part to improve the presence of Black firms in the American economy. ★

NOTES

[1] The concept of buying Black might trace its formal introduction to the last day of summer, 1832, when Maria Stewart stood in front of Boston's Franklin Hall and confronted Blacks and whites about race, gender and economic solidarity. "Daughters of Africa, awake!" she exhorted. "It is of no use for us to sit with our hands folded, hanging our heads...Let us make a mighty effort and arise...and let us raise a fund ourselves. Do you ask, what can we do? Unite and build a store of your own." [Source: Jorgensen-Earp, Cheryl R. (2006, Sep). Maria W. Miller Stewart Lecture Delivered at Franklin Hall. *Voices of Democracy*.]

[2] Muhammad, Cedric. (2007, Dec 28). Ending 'Leakage' In Black America. *Final Call magazine*. Stephens, Brooke. (1997). *Talking Dollars and Making Sense: A Wealth Building Guide for African-Americans*. New York, NY: McGraw-Hill.

[3] Clingman, James. (2000). *Blackonomic$: The Way to Psychological and Economic Freedom for African Americans*. Los Angeles, CA: Milligan Books.

[4] All those concerned with the evolution and empowerment capacity of Black business and entrepreneurship in America will cite the history and economic impact of Tulsa Oklahoma in the early 1900s. Called the first "Black Wall Street," hundreds of locally owned businesses, including banks, insurance companies, hotels, real estate and construction firms, clinics, manufacturers, grocers, bakeries, apparel outlets and hardware stores thrived, hundreds of millions were recycled, the dollar lived for up to three years before going outside the community, dozens of Black millionaires were created, and unemployment was statistically insignificant.

[Sources: Boyd, William K. (1927). *The Story of Durham, City of the New South, 2nd ed.* Durham, NC: Duke University Press.

Stephens, Brooke. (1997). *Talking Dollars and Making Sense: A Wealth Building Guide for African-Americans*. New York, NY: McGraw-Hill.]

[5] Bogan, V. & Darity, W. Jr. (2008). Culture and entrepreneurship? African American and immigrant self-employment in the United States. *The Journal of Socio-Economics*, 37, 2000–2019

Anderson, M. & Gregory, T. (2012). *Our Black Year: One Family's Quest to Buy Black in America's Racially Divided Economy*. New York, NY: Public Affairs Books.

Chicago Urban League. (2008, Feb). *The Future of Economic Development for African Americans in the Chicago Metropolitan Area: The Next Ten Years*. Chicago, IL: Chicago Urban League.

[6] The Nellsen Company. (2012). African American Consumers: Still Vital, Still Growing, 2012 Report.

The Neilsen Company. (2013). Resilient, Receptive and Relevant: The African-American Consumer, 2013 Report.

[7] Anderson, M. & Gregory, T. (2012). *Our Black Year: One Family's Quest ot Buy Black in America's Racially Divided Economy*. New York, NY: Public Affairs Books.

Rogers, Steven. (2010). The Empowerment Experiment: The Findings and Potential Impact on Black-Owned Businesses in *Our Black Year: One Family's Quest to Buy Black in America's Racially Divided Economy*, pp. 233–260. New York, NY: Public Affairs Books.

DiversityBusiness.com. (2009, Sep 21). *Supplier Diversity Notes: Spend Doesn't Matter*. Retrieved from: *http://www.diversitybusiness.com/news/supplierdiversity/45200980.asp*.

[8] Bialik, Carl. (2009, Mar 2). A (Slightly) Exaggerated Trend: Blacks and Cognac. *Wall Street Journal*. Retrieved from: *http://blogs.wsj.com/numbersguy/a-slightly-exaggerated-trend-blacks-and-cognac-609/*.

[9] Rogers, Steven. (2010). The Empowerment Experiment: The Findings and Potential Impact on Black-Owned Businesses in *Our Black Year: One Family's Quest to Buy Black in America's Racially Divided Economy*, pp. 233–260. New York, NY: Public Affairs Books.

[10] Ibid.

[11] Ibid.

"THE DIFFERENCE BETWEEN FAILURE AND SUCCESS REVOLVES AROUND TWO CONNECTED INGREDIENTS—THE QUALITY OF YOUR PEOPLE AND THE AMOUNT OF INNOVATION THEY BRING TO THE MARKET."

— *Ursula M. Burns, Chairman & CEO, Xerox*
   First African American woman to lead a Fortune 500 company

TRANSFORMING FUTURES FOR A DARING TECH TOMORROW:

AFRICAN AMERICAN ENTREPRENEURS, BROADBAND & THE COMING COMMUNITY BENEFITS

TANYA LEAH LOMBARD

NATIONAL URBAN LEAGUE

We're living in exciting times. The spread of high-speed Internet service is spurring benefits in nearly every aspect of our community, from education to healthcare to social entrepreneurship. It's creating dazzling opportunities for a new generation of African American innovators.

For African American entrepreneurs, this Digital Revolution offers dramatic potential to expand creative energies. These smart, savvy men and women are the new face of African American tech leaders in the 21st century.

IN THE HIGH-TECH WORLD, NOT EVERYTHING IS IDEAL. AFRICAN AMERICAN START-UPS STILL HAVE DIFFICULTY ATTRACTING CAPITAL. YET THE POWER OF BROADBAND TECHNOLOGY ALSO ALLOWS NEW WAYS TO GAIN FUNDING, WHICH MAKES IT POSSIBLE FOR OUR BEST MINDS TO PURSUE THEIR INNOVATIVE DREAMS, WHILE ADDING JOBS AND VALUE IN OUR COMMUNITIES.

AT&T has invested $96 billion in infrastructure during the past five years—more than any other private company. This transformation is critical for America's future. The growth of high-speed broadband, especially mobile, and the ongoing transition to Internet Protocol (IP) systems fulfill our promise to make broadband affordable and accessible to urban and rural communities.

In education, high-speed broadband offers Historically Black Colleges and Universities (HBCUs) a roadmap to reach students hungry to improve their education, but unable to afford going to school on campus.

Last year, AT&T and Georgia Tech announced the nation's first online master's program in computer science. Students with a broadband connection and a willingness to study can earn their computer science degree for about $6,600.

In the high-tech world, not everything is ideal. African American start-ups still have difficulty attracting capital. Yet, the power of broadband technology also allows new ways to gain funding, which makes it possible for our best minds to pursue their innovative dreams, while adding jobs and value in our communities.

This change also has the power to close the digital divide, especially as it applies to science, technology, engineering, arts and mathematics (STEAM) fields. These subjects are vital and the number of jobs requiring this knowledge is growing exponentially.

For 140 years, a succession of African American inventors shaped the growth of the telephone system into today's global communications network. The early telephone owes much of its existence to a young African American inventor, Lewis Latimer, who worked closely with Alexander Graham Bell, providing the blueprint for the early telephone.

Most recently, American business magnate, innovator, philanthropist, and artist, Beyoncé Knowles, shattered records by harnessing the power of technology to sell nearly one million digital copies of her new recording in three days without marketing and promotional efforts— making it the fastest selling album in iTunes history.[1] This was a game-changing example of true innovation.

Embrace innovation—Black history is still being written. The true power lies within the technology you hold in your hands—use it wisely. ★

NOTES

[1] Caulfield, K. 2013, (December 16). Beyoncé Fastest-Selling Album Ever In iTunes Store: 828,773 In Three Days. *Billboard Magazine*. Retrieved from: *http://www.billboard.com/articles/news/5839825/ beyonce-fastest-selling-album-ever-in-itunes-store-828773-in-three-days.*

CHALLENGES & OPPORTUNITIES

FOR AFRICAN AMERICANS IN COMMUNICATIONS & TECHNOLOGY

HONORABLE MIGNON L. CLYBURN

AS A FEDERAL COMMUNICATIONS
COMMISSIONER, I AM OFTEN ASKED TO
OPINE ON A WIDE RANGE OF ISSUES
REGARDING REGULATIONS, LAWS
AND PUBLIC POLICY IN THE AREAS OF
COMMUNICATIONS AND INFORMATION
TECHNOLOGY. MY WORK IS BOTH
REWARDING AND CHALLENGING, AND I
CONSIDER IT A HIGH HONOR TO SERVE.

However, as the only African American on the FCC, I see my responsibilities through a unique set of lenses because I know all too well that our community suffers disproportionately from the lack of access to capital and critical resources. This is why, as a public servant, I strive to be a "facilitator of opportunities" and a "connector of the disconnected."

As a general rule, I am of the opinion that the marketplace should be left alone when things are working well. But when the market does not operate fairly or efficiently, those of us in government should not hesitate to step in judiciously to ensure fairness and competition or restore foreclosed opportunities. It is important to make certain that there is not only a level playing field, but that the game is open to every player who wants to step onto that field.

Today, the communications landscape is replete with activity, investment, innovation and change. Yet, with all of this positive momentum, major disconnects remain.

Although African Americans have the perennial distinction of being among the heaviest consumers of mobile, internet and social media services, we are woefully underrepresented

THERE IS NO DENYING THAT TECHNOLOGY CAN HELP POSITIVELY TRANSFORM ALMOST ANY SET OF CONDITIONS WE FACE TODAY. BUT STANDING ON ITS OWN, TECHNOLOGY—WHILE POWERFUL—IS ONLY AS EFFECTIVE AS HOW WE CHOOSE TO USE IT.

when it comes to employment throughout the communications and technology industries, especially at the upper ranks. Likewise, our communities have a high level of need and demand for broadband services, yet huge gaps remain between the dollars invested in comparison with the general market. Not insignificantly, there are far too few partnerships between African American enterprises and entrepreneurs and major industry providers.

Whether it is broadcast, cable, satellite, online, software, wireless or any other major communications or technology platform, we have much to do to bridge the divide between aspiration and implementation.

There is no denying that technology can help positively transform almost any set of conditions we face today. It allows us to tackle many of our most vexing problems—from multi-generational poverty, to chronically failing schools, to longstanding healthcare disparities—in more efficient ways. It has the potential to break down barriers, create jobs and build wealth. But standing on its own, technology—while powerful—is only as effective as how we choose to use it.

One important area, which presents both a critical challenge and a tremendous opportunity, is Health IT.

When we look at the needs of the historically marginalized, communications technology can be empowering. It enables us to tailor unique responses to meet the most critical of needs, and broadband-enabled health solutions can be acute care equalizers in poor and underserved communities. However, the infrastructure needed to support all of this must be widely available, accessible and affordable to all.

Improvements in Health IT will address several notable concerns. First, it will help eradicate those health disparities which continue to plague minority communities. Second, connections can generate entrepreneurial opportunities for minority business enterprises, allowing innovative partnerships with established technology, healthcare and service companies. Third, improved health communications can lead to higher levels of employment, as more networks and services are expanded to include new families and consumers.

While these outcomes are important and achievable, their success hinges on the participation and partnership of three key stakeholders—government, industry, and communities. Each key stakeholder must provide the leadership, insights and initiatives to expand opportunities for African Americans. We should not expect government, alone, to solve the problem. Industry, or the corporate sector, most often has ample resources, but not always the will. Communities may have the willingness, but too often lack the means and wherewithal to go it alone. Only by working collectively and collaboratively, can we truly hope to achieve enduring success.

Personally, I will be focused on three areas to meet and address these challenges:

First, I will continue to work tirelessly for the widespread deployment and adoption of broadband services to African Americans and other underserved communities. This alone has the potential to yield more information, which can lead to greater employment and entrepreneurial opportunities for those who are facing a world where technological skills are essential to compete locally and globally.

Second, I will work to make sure that the marketplace of ideas, goods and services is open to entrepreneurs and businesses from every community and that more opportunities for contracts, deals, and business exchanges are freely and fairly made available.

Third, I will continue to identify resources and see that they are publicized, made available, and leveraged to create win-win-win solutions for the private sector, the policymakers, and those who stand to benefit the most.

Our nation is undergoing a series of transformational changes and is moving from an analog to a fully digital world. Improvements and opportunities abound. But as policy makers and community leaders, we would fall painfully short if we fail to ensure that no one and no community is left behind. My pledge to each of you is that I will use the time and talent entrusted to me to pursue each of these necessary and noteworthy goals. ★

ABOUT THE AUTHORS

// VANESSA ALLEN, M.D., PH.D.

Dr. Vanessa Allen serves as President and CEO of the Urban League of Northwest Indiana, which covers Lake, Porter, and LaPorte counties.

Dr. Allen has worked as an administrator at Purdue University Calumet, South Suburban College, and the Gary Community School Corporation. A 1977 graduate of Horace Mann High School in Gary, Indiana, she would earn her Associate of Arts degree in Sociology from Purdue Calumet, a Bachelor of Science in Organizational Management from Calumet College, and Master's degree in Education from Purdue University Calumet—all while working full-time during the day and raising two daughters. Just recently, Dr. Allen earned her Doctorate in Educational Leadership at Argosy University located in Chicago, IL.

Dr. Allen serves on several national boards, supports civic and charitable endeavors, promotes education, life skills strategies, and career advancement. She is a choir member and praise team leader. She loves the Lord and gives Him the praise for all His many blessings. She has two adult children and three grandchildren.

// MARGARITA "MAGGIE" ANDERSON

Margarita "Maggie" Anderson is the author of *Our Black Year,* the CEO of Economic Empowerment for Powered By Action, Inc., and the Founder of The Empowerment Experiment (EE).

Margarita Anderson and her family made history and dominated headlines as national media covered their year-long stand in honor of Black professionals, entrepreneurs, businesses and neighborhoods. The Anderson family lived exclusively off Black business and talent, and bought only Black-made products for an entire year. This first-ever, real-life case study in self-help economics was called The Empowerment Experiment (EE). Their experiment resulted in a landmark study conducted by Northwestern University's Kellogg School of Business which proved—with the data from the Anderson's journey—how incremental support of Black businesses can rescue the Black community and improve the American economy as a whole.

Margarita, a first-generation Cuban-American, has a B.A. in Political Science from Emory University; and earned a J.D. and M.B.A. from the University of Chicago, where President Barack Obama was her law professor and mentor. Before the experiment, she was an aide to Congressman John Lewis, a political speechwriter, a corporate strategy executive at McDonald's Corporation, and the speechwriter for the mayor of Atlanta.

Since the experiment, Margarita has become the face of a conscious consumerism movement uniting consumers, corporations, and the quality Black businesses that can rescue struggling communities and provide role models to Black youth.

// DONNA JONES BAKER

Donna Jones Baker has more than 25 years of nonprofit leadership experience. She is the President and CEO of the Urban League of Greater Southwestern Ohio, the parent organization for the Dayton area's Miami Valley Urban League and the Greater Cincinnati Urban League. Mrs. Baker has held this position since November 2003. The Urban League is a high profile, community-based, organization dedicated to developing and delivering high quality programs and services for the underserved that develops a multitude of opportunities for individuals and families.

Prior to serving with the Urban League, Ms. Baker was Executive Director of Associated Black Charities, headquartered in Baltimore, Maryland since 1989. Under Ms. Baker's leadership, Associated Black Charities, a fundraising and grant making organization, grew from a $500,000 organization to a $26,000,000 organization. She led the organization in making grants totaling more than $60 million and increased its endowment to over a million dollars.

The Urban League board of trustees and the community benefit from Ms. Baker's educational mix of a Bachelor's degree in Social Work earned at Murray State University and a Master's degree in Business Administration, earned at the University of Baltimore.

In addition to numerous speaking engagements, examples of her considerable community involvement include serving as a board member of Xavier University-Cincinnati and co-chairperson of Cincinnati Mayor Mark Mallory's Complete Count Committee (an initiative designed to ensure an accurate 2010 Census count) and of the Cincinnati Chamber's Diverse by Design Committee.

// THE HONORABLE ALVIN BROWN

On May 17, 2011 Alvin Brown was elected to lead Jacksonville, FL as its Mayor. Prior to the election, Brown served as an Executive in Residence at Jacksonville University's Davis School of Business. He is the past president and CEO of the Willie Gary Classic Foundation, an organization that helps to provide scholarships for historically Black colleges.

Brown came to Washington, D.C. to work as an intern in the House of Representatives, and eventually became a senior member of the Clinton-Gore Administration in 1993. As Vice President Al Gore's senior advisor for urban policy and vice chair of the White House Community Empowerment Board, Brown advised both the vice president and President Clinton on a wide range of domestic issues, including community revitalization, job creation, new business development and expansion of the supply of affordable housing.

Brown was also co-chair of the White House Task Force on Livable Communities focusing on urban sprawl and smart growth. He also held a number of key positions within the administration, including senior advisor to the late Commerce Secretary Ron Brown and senior advisor to former U.S. Secretary of Housing and Urban Development Andrew Cuomo.

A graduate of Jacksonville University, Brown earned a Bachelor of Science and a Master's in Business Administration there and completed postgraduate work at the Kennedy School of Government at Harvard University.

Brown is the recipient of numerous awards including the Frederick Douglass Award from the Southern Christian Leadership Conference, the Excellence in Community Service Award from 100 Black Men of America, and the Chairman's Award from the Congressional Black Caucus.

// LINDSAY D. BROWN

Lindsay D. Brown serves as the interim President/CEO of the Urban League of Madison County. During his time in this office, Lindsay has put together several programs to benefit the youth of our community, including programs like Read and Rise, a summer reading program geared for youth ages from five through 12; After School Tutoring Sessions which targets all students elementary to high school, and the Talented Tenth Leadership Program which targets a group of youth from tenth grade to seniors in High School.

Brown is a native of Anderson, Indiana. He graduated from Anderson High School and has his Bachelor's degree in Business Management from Indiana Wesleyan University. After graduation he worked in the management field for Ford Motor Company and Nestle USA.

Brown has become a trailblazer in the Anderson Community. He is currently participating on several community organization boards, which consist of United Way of Madison County, Black Chamber of Commerce, and Madison County Council of Government. Most recently Brown was named the chairman of the African American Leadership Coalition.

Brown is committed in serving his community and is truly a role model for all young men. He is the father of two sons: Landon and Lathan Brown, and has been married to his beautiful wife Janna Brown for three years.

// URSULA M. BURNS

Ursula M. Burns is Chairman and CEO of Xerox, the world's leading enterprise for business process and document management.

Burns joined Xerox in 1980 as a mechanical engineering summer intern, and later assumed roles in product development and planning. From 1992 through 2000, Burns, at a pivotal point in the company's history, led several business teams including the company's color business and office network printing business.

In 2000, Burns was named senior vice president, Corporate Strategic Services, and, alongside then-CEO Anne Mulcahy, worked to restructure Xerox through its turnaround to emerge as a leader in color technology and document services. In April 2007, Burns was named president of Xerox, expanding her leadership to also include the company's IT organization, corporate strategy, human resources, corporate marketing and global accounts.

Burns was named CEO in July 2009, and on May 20, 2010, became chairman of the company, leading the 140,000 people of Xerox who serve clients in more than 160 countries.

Burns earned a bachelor of science degree in mechanical engineering from Polytechnic Institute of NYU and a master of science degree in mechanical engineering from Columbia University.

In addition to the Xerox board, she is a board director of the American Express Corporation and Exxon Mobil Corporation. Burns also provides leadership counsel to community, educational and nonprofit organizations including FIRST—For Inspiration and Recognition of Science and Technology—National Academy Foundation, MIT, and the U.S. Olympic Committee, among others. She is a founding board director of Change the Equation, which focuses on improving the U.S.'s education system in science, technology, engineering and math (STEM). In March 2010, U.S. President Barack Obama appointed Burns vice chair of the President's Export Council.

// THE HONORABLE DONNA M. CHRISTENSEN

The Honorable Donna M. Christensen is the first woman Delegate from the United States Virgin Islands. She serves as an Assistant Minority Whip in the Democratic Caucus.

With her election to Congress in 1996, Delegate Christensen became the first female physician to serve as a Member in the history of the U.S. Congress and the first woman to represent an offshore Territory.

In the 113th Congress, Delegate Christensen serves on the Committee on Energy and Commerce; its Subcommittees on Health, on Energy and Power and on Commerce, Manufacturing and Trade. She is the first Delegate to Congress to serve on this exclusive committee.

Delegate Christensen chairs the Congressional Black Caucus' Health Braintrust, which oversees and advocates minority health issues nationally and internationally. She is a member of the Congressional Caucus for Women's Issues and a number of other caucuses and taskforces.

Delegate Christensen earned a Bachelor of Science from St. Mary's College in Notre Dame, Indiana. She earned an M.D. from George Washington University School of Medicine in Washington, D.C.; interned at Pacific Medical Center in San Francisco, and completed her residency in family medicine at Howard University Medical Center. She became a board certified family physician in 1977.

She began her medical career in the Virgin Islands in 1975 as an emergency room physician and staff physician at the Maternal & Child Health program. Her career highlights include leadership roles in healthcare administration and a private practice in family medicine from 1975 until her election to Congress.

// THE HONORABLE MIGNON L. CLYBURN

The Honorable Mignon L. Clyburn served as Acting Chairwoman of the Federal Communications Commission, following her appointment by President Barack Obama on May 20, 2013. As Commissioner, she is serving a second term as a Democrat on the Commission, for which she was sworn in on February 19, 2013 following her re-nomination by the President and confirmation by the United States Senate.

Clyburn began her service at the FCC in August, 2009, after spending 11 years as a member of the sixth district on the Public Service Commission (PSC) of South Carolina. She served as its chair from July 2002 through June 2004. Prior to her service on the PSC, Clyburn was the publisher and general manager of *The Coastal Times*, a Charleston-based weekly newspaper that focused primarily on issues affecting the African American community. She co-owned and operated the family-founded newspaper for 14 years.

A longtime champion of consumers and a defender of the public interest, Commissioner Clyburn approaches every Commission proceeding with an eye toward how it will affect all Americans. She has pushed for media ownership rules that reflect the demographics of American, affordable universal telephone and high-speed internet access, greater broadband deployment and adoption throughout the nation, and transparency in regulation.

Clyburn is a graduate of the University of South Carolina, and holds a Bachelor of Science degree in Banking, Finance and Economics.

// THE HONORABLE MICHAEL B. HANCOCK

Michael B. Hancock was born in Fort Hood, Texas, and moved to Denver when he was just 10 months old. A graduate of Denver's Manual High School, Hancock attended Hastings College in Nebraska, working summers in Denver as an intern for then-Mayor Federico Peña's office before graduating in 1991 with a B.A. in political science and minor in communications. He earned a master's degree in public administration from the University of Colorado-Denver in 1995.

Hancock started his career working at both the Denver Housing Authority and National Civic League, where he designed, implemented and oversaw the first-ever athletic, cultural and leadership-training programs in public housing and helped replicate similar programs throughout the country. He joined Metro Denver's Urban League affiliate in 1995 as program director before becoming president in 1999, becoming the youngest president of an Urban League affiliate. During his tenure, Hancock created an award-winning job-training program and developed long lasting private-sector partnerships.

In 2003, Hancock was elected to represent Denver City Council's District 11, serving two terms as council president, from 2006–08. He presided over the creation of the Denver Preschool Program; spearheaded efforts to expand economic opportunities; fought to end the foreclosure crisis and mortgage fraud; and helped guide the Better Denver Bond program.

Mayor Hancock is the proud father of three children—Alayna, Jordan and Janae—and he and his wife, Mary, have been married for 20 years after first meeting in middle school.

// CHANELLE P. HARDY, ESQ.

Chanelle P. Hardy, a passionate advocate for economic opportunity and civil rights for African Americans, leads the policy, research and advocacy activities of the National Urban League as SVP for Policy and Executive Director of the Washington Bureau. She represents the League before the Congress and at federal agencies on all Urban League priorities, including the federal budget, job creation and entrepreneurship, asset-building and homeownership, education and training, and access to quality healthcare. She is particularly focused on telecommunications and technology policy, which she believes is a key driver of community empowerment through access to information, culture and opportunity.

During her tenure, Ms. Hardy has led the growth and expansion of the "NUL on the Hill" Legislative Policy Conference; worked with the Association of (Urban League) Executives to launch Affiliate Policy Task Forces in Jobs, Housing & Asset-Building, Education and Healthcare; and launched Project Advocate—an initiative to promote civic engagement and non-partisan voter registration and education activities across the affiliate movement. She is also the Editor-in-Chief of *The State of Black America* and Equality Index, which is going into its thirty-eighth publication. She also established the Urban Solutions Council to explore areas of strategic policy alignment between the National Urban League and private sector.

Prior to joining the League, Ms. Hardy served as a Counsel and Chief of Staff to a Democratic Member of the U.S. Congress, as a Staff Attorney in the Federal Trade Commission Bureau of Consumer Protection, as a Policy Fellow and Legislative Counsel to Consumers Union, and as a Teach for America Corps member, teaching fifth graders in Washington, D.C. She received her J.D. from the Howard University School of Law.

Ms. Hardy has been quoted as a policy expert and offered commentary in numerous media outlets, including *The Root,* National Public Radio, *The Washington Post* and the *Associated Press.*

Ms. Hardy is a member of the boards of Excel Academy Public Charter School, the first all-girls public school in Washington, D.C.; and the Congressional Black Caucus Institute; and is a member of the Alfred Street Baptist Church in Alexandria, VA.

// HILL HARPER

Hill Harper is an award-winning actor, bestselling author and philanthropist. A star of the TV drama "CSI: NY" and the author of four *New York Times* bestsellers, he has earned seven NAACP Image Awards for his writing and acting.

Mr. Harper is also the founder of the Manifest Your Destiny Foundation, dedicated to empowering under-served youth through mentorship, scholarship and grant programs. Harper graduated magna cum laude as valedictorian of his department with a B.A. from Brown University, and cum laude with a J.D. from Harvard Law School. He also holds a Master's Degree with honors from Harvard's Kennedy School of Government and honorary doctoral degrees from Howard University, Winston-Salem State University, Cheyney University, Westfield State College, Tougaloo College and Dillard University.

Hill Harper travels frequently as a motivational speaker addressing a wide range of audiences including youth, adults, couples and business leaders. In July 2010, Harper was diagnosed with thyroid cancer. His bestselling book *The Wealth Cure* chronicles the cancer diagnosis and his journey to health.

// WADE HENDERSON, ESQ.

Wade Henderson is the president and CEO of The Leadership Conference on Civil and Human Rights, the nation's premier civil and human rights coalition, and The Leadership Conference Education Fund. Under his stewardship, The Leadership Conference has become one of the nation's most effective advocates for civil and human rights. Mr. Henderson is also the Joseph L. Rauh, Jr., Professor of Public Interest Law at the David A. Clarke School of Law, University of the District of Columbia. Prior to his role with The Leadership Conference, Mr. Henderson was the Washington Bureau director of the NAACP. Mr. Henderson is a graduate of Howard University and the Rutgers University School of Law. He is a member of the Bar in the District of Columbia and the United States Supreme Court. Mr. Henderson has received countless awards and honors, including the prestigious Eleanor Roosevelt Award for Human Rights and the Charles Hamilton Houston Medallion of Merit from the Washington Bar Association.

// RUFINA A. HERNÁNDEZ, ESQ.

Rufina A. Hernández, Esq., is executive director of the Campaign for High School Equity (CHSE), a coalition of the nation's most prominent civil rights and education advocacy organizations focused on high school education reform.

A leading voice on solutions to the challenges facing African American, Asian, Latino, and Native students, Hernández has a long record of civil rights and education reform advocacy. Prior to joining CHSE, she served as associate director of the National Education Association's (NEA) External Partnerships and Advocacy department. As director of NEA's Human and Civil Rights department she developed strategies to promote culturally competent teaching aimed at improving academic achievement among students from diverse backgrounds.

Before coming to Washington, D.C., Hernández was executive director of the Latin American Research and Service Agency (LARASA), a Colorado-based civil rights organization. During her tenure there, she advocated for policy reform in civil rights issues affecting the Latino community, including health, education, employment, and immigration.

A native of New Mexico, Hernández holds a Bachelor of Arts degree from the University of New Mexico and a Juris Doctor from the Georgetown University Law Center.

// THE HONORABLE RUBÉN HINOJOSA

Congressman Rubén Hinojosa (D-TX) was elected to Congress in 1996 and is serving his ninth term as the representative of the 15th District of Texas. Congressman Hinojosa is a champion for the disadvantaged and has distinguished himself as a strong advocate for education, housing and economic development. His primary goal in Congress has been to reduce the chronic unemployment rate by focusing on developing a highly educated, well-trained workforce, modernizing local infrastructure including roads and highways, and creating new job opportunities. He co-founded the House Financial Literacy and Economic Education Caucus in 2004, which currently numbers 87 members from both sides of the aisle. He is the Chairman of the Congressional Hispanic Caucus for the 113th Congress.

Prior to his election, Congressman Hinojosa served 20 years as President & Chief Financial Officer of a family-owned food processing company, H&H Foods. He earned a Bachelor's degree in Business Administration and a Master's degree in Business Administration from the University of Texas in Austin and in Edinburg, respectively.

He is married to Martha Lopez Hinojosa and has one son, Rubén Jr., and four daughters, Laura, Iliana, Kaitlin and Karén.

// THE HONORABLE MIKE HONDA

U.S. Congressman Mike Honda represents the 17th Congressional District of California and has served in the U.S. House of Representatives for over twelve years. In Congress, Rep. Honda is a member of the powerful House Appropriations Committee, Chair Emeritus of the Congressional Asian Pacific American Caucus, Co-chair of the Democratic Caucus' New Media Working Group, and House Democratic Senior Whip.

Rep. Honda's district includes Silicon Valley, the birthplace of technology innovation and now the country's leading developer of green technology. He has dedicated his life to public service and is lauded for his work on education, civil rights, national service, immigration, transportation, the environment, and high-tech issues.

Serving as a California State Assembly member, Santa Clara County Board Supervisor, San Jose Planning Commissioner, San Jose Unified School Board Member, Peace Corps Volunteer in El Salvador, and with over 30 years in education as a teacher, principal and school board member, Rep. Honda's commitment to serving the people of California's 17th district is unwavering and unparalleled.

// TANYA CLAY HOUSE, ESQ.

Tanya Clay House is the Director of the Public Policy Department at the Lawyers' Committee for Civil Rights Under Law where she serves as the principal representative for the Lawyers' Committee on Capitol Hill and policy liaison with state and local legislative bodies, the White House, and federal and state agencies.

Mrs. House formerly served as the Public Policy Director at People For the American Way (PFAW). She also served as the policy liaison for the African American Ministers Leadership Council, a program of PFAW Foundation.

In 2000, Mrs. House began her political career as Legislative Counsel for Representative Sheila Jackson Lee (D-TX), serving as staff counsel in, among other areas, the full Judiciary Committee and the Subcommittee on Crime. From there, she moved to the Senate to work for Senator Barbara

Boxer (D-CA) focusing on civil rights and social policy issues. Before working on the Hill and prior to attending law school, she worked for the Kentucky Department of Education, focusing on the KY Education Reform Act.

Mrs. House is a recognized expert on civil rights issues, and has testified before Congress; and offered insight and analysis in print and broadcast media. She was selected as a 2010 NGen (Next Generation) Fellow with the Independent Sector Foundation, and as one of the "Top 100 African Americans to Watch for 2010" by *TheRoot.com.*

A native of Louisville, Kentucky, Mrs. House earned her B.A. cum laude in political science from the University of Michigan and her J.D. from the University of Texas, School of Law in 1999.

// SHERRILYN IFILL, ESQ.

Sherrilyn Ifill is the seventh president and director-counsel of the NAACP Legal Defense and Educational Fund, Inc. and is a long-time member of the LDF family. After graduating law school, Ms. Ifill served first as a fellow at the American Civil Liberties Union and then as an assistant counsel in LDF's New York office, where she litigated voting rights cases. Among her successful litigation was the landmark Voting Rights Act case *Houston Lawyers' Association vs. Attorney General of Texas*, in which the Supreme Court held that judicial elections are covered by the provisions of section 2 of the Voting Rights Act.

In 1993, Ms. Ifill joined the faculty of the University of Maryland School of Law, where, in addition to teaching Civil Procedure, Constitutional Law and variety of seminars, she continued to litigate and consult on a broad range of civil rights cases. Ms. Ifill launched several innovative legal offerings while at Maryland Law School, including an environmental justice course in which students represented rural communities in Maryland. Ms. Ifill has emerged as a highly regarded national civil rights strategist and public intellectual whose writings, speeches and media appearances enrich public debate about a range of political and civil rights issues.

Ms. Ifill is a graduate of Vassar College, and received her J.D. from New York University School of Law.

// MICHAEL L. LOMAX, PH.D.

Since 2004, Michael L. Lomax, Ph.D. has been president and CEO of the United Negro College Fund (UNCF), the nation's largest private provider of scholarships and other educational support to African American students and a leading advocate of college readiness: students' need for an education, from pre-school through high school, that prepares them for college success. Under his leadership, UNCF has raised $1.5 billion and helped more than 92,000 students earn college degrees and launch careers. Annually, UNCF's work enables 60,000 students to go to college with UNCF scholarships and attend its 37 member historically Black college and universities.

Before coming to UNCF, Dr. Lomax was president of Dillard University in New Orleans and a literature professor at UNCF member institutions Morehouse and Spelman Colleges. He also served as chairman of the Fulton County Commission in Atlanta, the first African American elected to that post.

At UNCF's helm, Lomax oversees the organization's 400 scholarship programs, which award 10,000 scholarships a year worth more than $100 million. He also launched the UNCF Institute for Capacity Building, which helps UNCF's 37 member historically Black colleges and universities become stronger, more effective and more self-sustaining. Under Dr. Lomax's leadership, UNCF has fought for college readiness and education reform in through partnerships with reform-focused leaders and organizations. He serves on the boards of Teach For America, the KIPP Foundation, the National Alliance for Public Charter Schools and Stand for Children. He also co-chaired the Washington, D.C. mayoral education transition team and the search committee for a new D.C. school chancellor.

// TANYA LEAH LOMBARD

Tanya Leah Lombard serves as Assistant Vice President of Public Affairs at AT&T. She is charged with creating, promoting and managing AT&T's brand-messaging to minority communities through the development and stewardship of strategic community-based relations and projects. Ms. Lombard is a native of New Orleans with more than twenty years of experience in public policy development, strategic communications and community development. She is widely recognized as a confidante of leaders at the highest levels of government, business, national, civic and professional organizations.

Ms. Lombard has worked in the field of public policy and government relations for the past twenty years. Prior to joining AT&T, Ms. Lombard was a Principal with Peck, Madigan, Jones & Stewart, Inc., a premier Washington, D.C. government relations firm providing strategic, legislative, regulatory, public policy and communication services.

During the Clinton Administration, Ms. Lombard served in several capacities, including Special Assistant to the President and Director of Political Affairs for the Southern Region. In that role, Ms. Lombard advised President Clinton, Vice President Gore, First Lady Hillary Clinton and Tipper Gore on the national political climate. Ms. Lombard is active in professional and civic leadership. She currently serves on the boards

of directors for the National Action Network, the National Coalition of Black Civic Participation and the NAACP Special Contributions Board.

Ms. Lombard, a native of New Orleans, Louisiana, earned a Bachelor of Arts degree from Xavier University in 1990, and is a former elected official in Louisiana, serving on the Democratic State Central Committee and Orleans Parish Democratic Executive Committee.

// WYNTON MARSALIS

Wynton Marsalis is an internationally acclaimed musician, composer, bandleader, educator and leading advocate of American culture. By creating and performing an expansive range of new music for quartets to big bands, chamber music ensembles to symphony orchestras, tap dance to ballet, Marsalis has expanded the vocabulary for jazz and created a vital body of work that places him among the world's finest musicians and composers. To date, Marsalis has won nine Grammys—being the only artist ever to win for both jazz and classical records—and has produced more than 70 records, selling more than seven million copies worldwide, including three Gold Records.

Marsalis is currently Artistic Director for Jazz at Lincoln Center. Under his leadership, Jazz at Lincoln Center opened Frederick P. Rose Hall in 2004, the world's first institution for jazz which has also become a mecca for learning and a hub for performance.

Marsalis has received honorary degrees from more than 30 of America's leading academic institutions including Columbia, Harvard, Howard, Princeton and Yale. He has been awarded numerous honors for excellence in the Arts, leadership, arts education and community service. *Time Magazine* recognized Marsalis as one of America's most promising leaders under age 40 and as one of America's 25 most influential people.

Marsalis has received The National Medal of Arts, the highest award given to artists by the United States Government, and United Nations Secretary-General Kofi Annan proclaimed Marsalis an international ambassador of goodwill by appointing him a UN Messenger of Peace. The French Ministry of Culture appointed him the rank of Knight in the Order of Arts and Literature, and he also received France's highest distinction, the insignia Chevalier of the Legion of Honor, first awarded by Napoleon Bonaparte.

Marsalis has written five books: *Sweet Swing Blues on the Road*; *Jazz in the Bittersweet Blues of Life*; *To a Young Musician: Letters from the Road*; *Jazz ABZ*; and *Moving to Higher Ground: How Jazz Can Change Your Life*.

// ERIKA MCCONDUIT-DIGGS, ESQ.

Erika McConduit-Diggs, Esq. currently serves as the President and CEO of the Urban League of Greater New Orleans. In her role, she oversees agency operations, strategic planning, partnership development, contract management, and policy initiatives of the agency, whose mission is to Empower Communities and Change Lives. Ms. McConduit-Diggs is heavily engaged in the city and state's education reform, as a representative of the community engagement arm of the movement. In this capacity, she has served on numerous committees including Mayor Landrieu's Education Task Force, Louisiana State Superintendent of Education John White's Student Task Force as co-chair, and the Recovery School District's Charter Application Task Force.

Prior to joining the Urban League, Ms. McConduit-Diggs was the Chief Operating Officer of the YWCA of White Plains and Central Westchester, New York.

A native of New Orleans, Ms. McConduit-Diggs is a pioneering and committed civic and professional leader. Her current and past service includes serving on, among many others, the New Orleans Regional Leadership Institute's Board of Directors, the KID smART Board of Directors, Orleans Parish Education Network's Board of Directors. She is also a graduate of the National Urban League's Emerging Leader program.

Ms. McConduit-Diggs graduated summa cum laude from Howard University with a Bachelor of Arts degree in Communications, and cum laude from Loyola University School of Law in New Orleans, Louisiana. She is married and has three children.

// MARC H. MORIAL

Entrepreneur. Lawyer. Professor. Legislator. Mayor. President, U.S. Conference of Mayors. President and CEO of the National Urban League, the nation's largest historic civil rights and urban advocacy organization.

In a distinguished professional career that has spanned 25 years, Marc Morial has performed all of these roles with excellence and is one of the most accomplished servant-leaders in the nation. As President and CEO of the National Urban League since 2003, he has been the primary catalyst for an era of change—a transformation for the 104-year old civil rights organization. His energetic and skilled leadership has expanded the League's work around an Empowerment agenda, which is redefining civil rights in the 21st century with a renewed emphasis on closing the economic gaps between whites and Blacks, as well as other communities of color, and rich and poor Americans.

During his tenure, the League had record fundraising success with a 280MM, five-year fundraising effort. He has secured the BBB nonprofit certification, which has established the NUL as a leading national nonprofit, and the coveted 4-star rating from Charity Navigator, which has placed the NUL in the top 10 percent of all U.S. charities for adhering to good governance and other best practices, as well as executing its mission in a fiscally responsible way.

Under his stewardship, the League launched a historic $100 million, five-year "Jobs Rebuild America: Educate, Employ, Empower" initiative in 2013—a solutions-based, comprehensive approach to the nation's employment and education crisis that brings together federal government, business, and nonprofit resources to create economic opportunity in 50 cities across the country through the Urban League affiliate network.

His creativity has led to initiatives such as the Urban Youth Empowerment Program to assist young adults in securing sustainable jobs and Entrepreneurship Centers in 10 cities to help the growth of small businesses. Also, Morial helped create the Urban Empowerment Fund, which will lend to urban impact businesses, and helped create the League's New Markets Tax Credits initiative, which has pumped nearly $500 million into urban impact businesses, including minority business, through both debt and equity investments.

As mayor of New Orleans, Morial was a popular chief executive with a broad multi-racial coalition who led New Orleans' 1990's renaissance and left office with a 70 percent approval rating.

As a lawyer, Morial won the Louisiana State Bar Association's Pro Bono Publico Award for his legal service to the poor and disadvantaged. He was also one of the youngest lawyers, at age 26, to argue and win a major case before the Louisiana Supreme Court.

As a professor, Morial served on the adjunct faculty of Xavier University in Louisiana, where he taught Constitutional Law and Business Law.

As a Louisiana state senator, Morial was named Legislative Rookie of the Year, Education Senator of the Year, and Environmental Senator of the Year, while authoring laws on a wide range of important subjects.

A graduate of the University of Pennsylvania with a degree in Economics and African American Studies, he also holds a law degree from the Georgetown University Law Center in Washington, D.C., as well as numerous honorary degrees including Xavier University and Howard University.

Under appointment by President Obama, Morial has served as Chair of the Census Advisory Committee, a member of the President's Advisory Council on Financial Capability, and on the Department of Education's Equity and Excellence Commission. He was also appointed to the Twenty-First Century Workforce Commission by President Bill Clinton.

Morial has been recognized as one of the 100 Most Influential Black Americans by *Ebony Magazine*, one of the Top 50 Nonprofit Executives by the *Nonprofit Times*, and one of the Top 100 Black Lawyers in America.

// RANDAL D. PINKETT, PH.D.

Dr. Randal D. Pinkett is an entrepreneur, speaker, author, scholar and community servant. He is the co-founder, chairman & CEO of BCT Partners, a multimillion dollar management, technology and policy consulting firm based in Newark, NJ. He is a sought-after public speaker for corporate, youth and community groups, and has been featured on nationally televised programs such as "The Today Show" and "Live with Regis and Kelly."

He was the Season 4 winner of NBC's hit reality television show "The Apprentice" with Donald Trump. He is a published writer and academic scholar. His first book, *Campus CEO: The Student Entrepreneur's Guide to Launching a Multimillion-Dollar Business*, was released in February 2007.

Dr. Pinkett holds five academic degrees including: a B.S. in Electrical Engineering from Rutgers University; a M.Sc. in Computer Science from Oxford University, as a Rhodes Scholar; a S.M. in Electrical Engineering from MIT, a M.B.A. MIT Sloan School of Management; and a Ph.D. from the MIT Media Laboratory.

Born in Philadelphia, PA, and raised in New Jersey, he is happily married to Zahara Wadud-Pinkett. They are both proud parents of their daughter, Amira Leslie.

// THE HONORABLE STEPHANIE RAWLINGS-BLAKE

Stephanie Rawlings-Blake was sworn in as Baltimore's 49th mayor on February 4, 2010. In November 2011, she was elected to her first full-term as mayor, receiving 87 percent of the vote in the mayoral general election. Mayor Rawlings-Blake has focused her administration on growing Baltimore's population by 10,000 families over the next decade by improving public safety and public education and strengthening city neighborhoods.

Mayor Rawlings-Blake serves as Secretary of the Democratic National Committee (DNC) as well as in key leadership positions in the U.S. Conference of Mayors (USCM). In 2010, she was elected by her fellow mayors to the USCM Board of Trustees.

In 2013, Mayor Rawlings-Blake presented *Change to Grow: A Ten-Year Financial Plan for Baltimore*, the city's first long-range financial plan. The plan includes a bold set of major reforms that amount to the most significant changes to the way the city does business in generations.

Rawlings-Blake was first elected to the City Council in 1995, at the age of 25—the youngest person ever elected to the Baltimore City Council—and served as the Council's president from January 2007 to February 2010. From 1998 to 2006, Rawlings-Blake was an attorney with the Baltimore Office of the Public Defender.

Rawlings-Blake has been honored with numerous awards including the National Congress of Black Women's Shirley Chisholm Memorial Award Trailblazer and one of Baltimore's "Young Women on the Move" by the National Association of Negro Business and Professional Women's Clubs.

Rawlings-Blake earned a Bachelor of Arts degree in Political Science from Oberlin College in Oberlin, Ohio. She received her Juris Doctor from the University of Maryland School of Law in 1995.

// JONATHAN C. RAY

Jonathan C. Ray serves as President and CEO of the Fort Wayne Urban League. A native of Fort Wayne, Jonathan's parents played an important and key role in his life with his late mother, Mary C. Ray, being his role model and mentor.

Jonathan started his professional career as a house parent for Crossroad Children's Home where he forged his commitment to enrich the lives of children and families. Big Brothers/Big Sisters of Greater Fort Wayne provided Jonathan with his next opportunity to serve people. At Big Brothers/Big Sisters he established an offsite volunteer recruitment office as well as a nationally recognized successful youth program called Project Mentor. Jonathan later accepted the position of Northeast Regional Director at Lutheran Social Services of Indiana where he established, among other things, the court ordered program "Children Cope with Divorce."

Jonathan spent 10 years as the County Director for the Allen County Division of Family and Children. Under his watch, family and youth programs like the intensive intervention team (prevents out of home child placement) were established. He also created several home-based case management programs changing the agency culture to focus on a home and family preservation model. Additionally, Jonathan established the Faith Based Initiative (FBI) program and the Sports Academic Consortium (SAC) program. Every year during his tenure he helped provide more than 200 Allen County children with the opportunity to attend a summer camp.

Jonathan earned a Masters of Social Work degree from Indiana University.

// JEFFREY A. ROBINSON, PH.D.

Jeffrey A. Robinson, Ph.D. is an award-winning business school professor, international speaker and entrepreneur. Since 2008, he has been a leading faculty member at Rutgers Business School where he is an assistant professor of management and entrepreneurship and the founding Assistant Director of The Center for Urban Entrepreneurship & Economic Development.

Dr. Robinson's research describes how business practices and entrepreneurship can impact societal issues. He is the author of books and articles on such topics as social entrepreneurship, African American women in entrepreneurship, and patterns of Black employment.

In 2007, he was selected as the recipient of the Aspen Institute's Social Impact Faculty Pioneer Award for his research, service and teaching activities at the intersection of business and society. In 2011, his course, Urban Entrepreneurship & Economic Development, was recognized as a model of Innovative Entrepreneurship Education by the U.S. Association of Small Business and Entrepreneurship.

Dr. Robinson is the co-author of *Black Faces in White Places: 10 Game-Changing Strategies to Achieve Success and Find Greatness* with Dr. Randal Pinkett. He is a sought after speaker and media commentator and his research has appeared in the *American Journal of Sociology, Business & Society*, the *Journal of Developmental Entrepreneurship*, the *African Journal of Business and Management*, the *International Journal of Entrepreneurship* and the *Annals of the American Academy of Political and Social Science*.

// THE HONORABLE KATHLEEN SEBELIUS

The Honorable Kathleen Sebelius was sworn in as the 21st Secretary of the Department of Health and Human Services (HHS) on April 28, 2009. Since taking office, Secretary Sebelius has led ambitious efforts to improve America's health and enhance the delivery of human services to some of the nation's most vulnerable populations, including young children, those with disabilities, and the elderly.

As part of the historic Affordable Care Act, she is implementing reforms that have ended many of the insurance industry's worst abuses and will help 34 million uninsured Americans get health coverage. She is also working with doctors, nurses, hospital leaders, employers, and patients to slow the growth in health care costs through better care and better health.

Under Secretary Sebelius's leadership, HHS is committed to innovation, from promoting public-private collaboration to bring life-saving medicines to market, to building a 21st century food safety system that prevents outbreaks before they occur, to collaborating with the Department of Education, to help states increase the quality of early childhood education programs, and give parents more information to make the best choices for their children.

Secretary Sebelius served as Governor of Kansas from 2003 until her Cabinet appointment in April, 2009, and was named one of America's Top Five Governors by *Time Magazine*.

// THOMAS M. SHAPIRO, PH.D.

Thomas Shapiro directs the Institute on Assets and Social Policy and is the Pokross Professor of Law and Social Policy at The Heller School for Social Policy and Management, Brandeis University. Professor Shapiro's primary interest is in racial inequality and public policy. He is a leader in the asset development field with a particular focus on closing the racial wealth gap. In February of this year he co-authored a groundbreaking study, *The Roots of the Widening Racial Wealth Gap: Explaining the Black-White Economic Divide*, which statistically validates five "fundamental factors" that together largely explain why white households accumulate wealth so much faster over time than African American households.

// J. MARSHALL SHEPHERD, PH.D.

Dr. J. Marshall Shepherd is the 2013 President of the American Meteorological Society and only the second African American to be elected to head the leading professional society in weather and climate related sciences. He is the Georgia Athletic Association Professor of Geography and Atmospheric Sciences and Director of the Atmospheric Sciences Program at the University of Georgia. Dr. Shepherd is an internationally respected scientist with over 75 publications. The White House, Congress, NASA, NOAA and major media outlets routinely call upon Dr. Shepherd as an expert on weather and climate topics.

Prior to joining the University of Georgia, Dr. Shepherd spent 12 years at NASA Goddard Space Flight Center developing advanced missions and science to study planet Earth. Dr. Shepherd received the Presidential Early Career Award for Science and Engineering at the White House in 2004 and has received numerous other awards.

// THE HONORABLE JABAR SHUMATE

The Honorable Jabar Shumate was elected in November 2012 to serve the people of Oklahoma's Senate District 11. Prior to his election to the state senate, Shumate served four terms in the Oklahoma House of Representatives. Prior to his career he served as press secretary to University of Oklahoma President, David L. Boren.

Senator Shumate has a passion for improving education. He has been an advocate for kids trapped in low performing schools and fought for increased funding for public education.

Sen. Shumate is very active in his community serving as a trustee and usher at his church, Metropolitan Baptist Church; as a member of the board of trustees for the National Urban League; and with his fraternity, Kappa Alpha Psi Fraternity, Inc.

He also serves on the Oklahoma Foundation for Excellence Board of Directors and represents Oklahoma on the legislative advisory committee for the Southern Regional Education Board. Sen. Shumate is a member of the 19th class of Leadership Oklahoma, and while in the House, he was selected for the prestigious Henry Toll Fellowship Program.

Sen. Shumate a native Tulsan, graduated from Tulsa's Booker T. Washington High School and received both his Bachelor's and Master's degrees from the University of Oklahoma.

// JOSEPH A. SLASH

Joseph A. Slash is the President and CEO of the Indianapolis Urban League. He joined the League in 2002 as its Chief Operating Officer, and was appointed President & CEO in 2003.

Mr. Slash is formerly Vice President, Community and Corporate Effectiveness, of Indianapolis Power and Light Company (IPL). Prior to joining IPL, he was Deputy Mayor and Chief of Staff of the City of Indianapolis from 1978–89. Mr. Slash worked as Staff Accountant and then Audit Manager for Ernst & Young.

Mr. Slash serves on the Board of Directors of Fifth Third Bank of Central Indiana, National Government Services, a WellPoint subsidiary, Greater Indianapolis Progress Committee (GIPC), Center for Leadership Development, and the Indiana Historical Society. He is also a member of the Indianapolis Metropolitan Police Department Merit Board and a member of the Board of Visitors of the School of Business at Indiana University Purdue University at Indianapolis (IUPUI). Slash recently served as Co-Chairman of the 2012 Super Bowl Emerging Business Committee.

Mr. Slash is also a Certified Public Accountant earning his degree from Marshall University, and is a lifetime member of Kappa Alpha Psi Fraternity, Inc.

// THE HONORABLE AC WHARTON, JR.

AC Wharton, Jr. was sworn in as the Mayor of the City of Memphis on October 26, 2009. Prior to his election, AC Wharton served as the Mayor of Shelby County for seven years and was the first African American elected to that office.

Twice elected as Shelby County Mayor, Wharton led initiatives that shaped the region's future. He inspired Operation Safe Community, the area's first comprehensive crime-fighting plan; tackled education and early childhood development issues with programs like Books from Birth and Ready, Set, Grow; and reduced the county's inherited debt while limiting citizens to only one tax increase in seven years.

An attorney by trade, Wharton is a former public defender and served as executive director of the nonprofit Memphis Area Legal Services, which received national recognition as a result of his leadership. At a national level, he worked for a special appropriation for one of the nation's first transitional living facilities for juveniles. While serving as a public defender, Wharton's passion for reform in criminal justice system's treatment of the mentally ill led to the nationally renowned Jericho Project.

Mayor Wharton received his law degree in 1971, graduating with honors from the University of Mississippi Law School. He became the University's first African American professor of law, where he taught for 25 years. He earned a political science degree from Tennessee State University and is a native of Lebanon, Tennessee.

The Mayor and his wife, Ruby, have raised six sons in Memphis.

INDEX

OF AUTHORS & ARTICLES

In 1987, the National Urban League began publishing *The State of Black America* in a smaller, typeset format. By doing so, it became easier to catalog and archive the various essays by author and article.

The 2014 edition of *The State of Black America* is the nineteenth to feature an Index of the Authors and Articles that have appeared since 1987. The articles have been divided by topic and are listed in alphabetical order by authors' names.

Reprints of the articles catalogued herein are available through the National Urban League Washington Bureau, 1805 7th Street, N.W., Washington, D.C. 20005.

AN APPRECIATION

Jones, Stephanie J., "Rosa Parks: An Ordinary Woman, An Extraordinary Life," 2006, pp. 245–246.

National Urban League, "Ossie Davis: Still Caught in the Dream," 2005, pp. 137–138.

BLACK MALES

Bell, William C., "How are the Children? Foster Care and African-American Boys," 2007, pp. 151–157.

Carnethon, Mercedes R., "Black Male Life Expectancy in the United States: A Multi-Level Exploration of Causes," 2007, pp. 137–150.

Dyson, Eric Michael, "Sexual Fault Lines: Robbing the Love Between Us," 2007, pp. 229–237.

Edelman, Marian Wright, "Time to Wake Up and Act: The State of Black America," 2013, pp. 68–69.

Hanson, Renee, Mark McArdle, and Valerie Rawlston Wilson, "Invisible Men: The Urgent Problems of Low-Income African-American Males," 2007, pp. 209–216.

Harper, Hill, "America Incarcerated: Who Pays and Who Profits," 2014, pp. 112–113.

Holzer, Harry J., "Reconnecting Young Black Men: What Policies Would Help," 2007, pp. 75–87.

Ifill, Sherrilyn, "Standing in the Breach: The Supreme Court and Shelby," 2014, pp. 118–123.

Johns, David J., "Re-Imagining Black Masculine Identity: An Investigation of the 'Problem' Surrounding the Construction of Black Masculinity in America," 2007, pp. 59–73.

Lanier, James R., "The Empowerment Movement and the Black Male," 2004, pp. 143–148.

———, "The National Urban League's Commission on the Black Male: Renewal, Revival and Resurrection Feasibility and Strategic Planning Study," 2005, pp. 107–109.

McGhee, David, "Mentoring Matters: Why Young Professionals and Others Must Mentor," 2013, pp. 162–165.

Morial, Marc H., "Empowering Black Males to Reach Their Full Potential," 2007, pp. 13–15.

Nutter, Michael A., "Black Men Are Killing Black Men. There, I Said It." 2012, pp. 106–109.

Reed, James, and Aaron Thomas, "The National Urban League: The National Urban League: Empowering Black Males to Reach Their Full Potential," 2007, pp. 217–218.

Rodgers III, William M., "Why Should African Americans Care About Macroeconomic Policy," 2007, pp. 89–103.

Wilson, Valerie Rawlston, "On Equal Ground: Causes and Solutions for Lower College Completion Rates Among Black Males," 2007, pp. 123–135.

BUSINESS

Blankfein, Lloyd, "Creating Jobs and Opportunities Through Minority Owned Businesses," 2012, pp. 70–73.

Bryant, John Hope, "Financial Dignity in an Economic Age," 2013, pp. 134–138.

Cofield, Natalie M. "What's in it for Us? How Federal Business Inclusion Programs and Legislation Affect Minority Entrepreneurs," 2011, pp. 100–109.

Emerson, Melinda F., "Five Things You Must Have to Run a Successful Business," 2004, pp. 153–156.

Glasgow, Douglas G., "The Black Underclass in Perspective," 1987, pp. 129–144.

Henderson, Lenneal J., "Empowerment through Enterprise: African-American Business Development," 1993, pp. 91–108.

Humphries, Frederick S., "The National Talent Strategy: Ideas to Secure U.S. Competitiveness and Economic Growth," 2013, pp. 86–90.

Marshall, Cynthia, "Digitizing the Dream: The Role of Technology in Empowering Communities," 2013, pp. 130–133.

Price, Hugh B., "Beacons in a New Millennium: Reflections on 21st-Century Leaders and Leadership," 2000, pp. 13–39.

Tidwell, Billy J., "Black Wealth: Facts and Fiction," 1988, pp. 193–210.

Turner, Mark D., "Escaping the 'Ghetto' of Subcontracting," 2006, pp. 117–131.

Walker, Juliet E.K., "The Future of Black Business in America: Can It Get Out of the Box?," 2000, pp. 199–226.

CASE STUDIES

Allen, V., Brown, L., Ray, J., Slash, J., "Preparing Indiana's Children for College, Work and Life—Indiana Urban League Affiliates," 2014, pp. 148–151.

Cleaver II, Emanuel, "Green Impact Zone of Kansas City, MO," 2011, pp. 88–93.

McConduit-Diggs, Erika, "Winning TrifE³cta for Community Empowerment: Education, Employment, Entrepreneurship," 2014, pp. 164–167.

Patrick, Deval L., "Growing an Innovative Economy in Massachusetts," 2011, pp. 154–158.

Shumate, Jabar, "The Affordable Care Act and How It Can Fuel Entrepreneurism in Urban Communities," 2014, pp. 130–133.

CHILDREN AND YOUTH

Allen, V., Brown, L., Ray, J., Slash, J., "Preparing Indiana's Children for College, Work and Life—Indiana Urban League Affiliates," 2014, pp. 148–151.

Bell, William C., "How are the Children? Foster Care and African-American Boys," 2007, pp. 151–157.

———, "Community Based Organizations and Child Welfare: Building Communities of Hope," 2013, pp. 166–169.

Bryant, John Hope, "Financial Dignity in an Economic Age," 2013, pp. 134–138.

Burns, Ursula, "Leaving No Brains Behind," 2014, pp. 152–157.

Chávez, Anna Maria, "Helping Girls Make Healthy Choices," 2012, pp. 124–126.

Comer, James P., "Leave No Child Behind: Preparing Today's Youth for Tomorrow's World," 2005, pp. 75–84.

Cox, Kenya L. Covington, "The Childcare Imbalance: Impact on Working Opportunities for Poor Mothers," 2003, pp. 197–224.

Dallas Highlight, "Urban Youth Empowerment Program," 2011, pp. 84–86.

Edelman, Marian Wright, "The State of Our Children," 2006, pp. 133–141.

———, "Losing Our Children in America's Cradle to Prison Pipeline," 2007, pp. 219–227.

———, "Time to Wake Up and Act: The State of Black America," 2013, pp. 68–69.

Fulbright-Anderson, Karen, "Developing Our Youth: What Works," 1996, pp. 127–143.

Hare, Bruce R., "Black Youth at Risk," 1988, pp. 81–93.

Harris, Dot, "Diversity in STEM: An Economic Imperative," 2013, pp. 92–95.

Honda, Mike, "Equity and Excellence Lead to Opportunity," 2014, pp. 104–105.

Howard, Jeff P., "The Third Movement: Developing Black Children for the 21st Century," 1993, pp. 11–34.

Hrabowski III, Dr. Freeman A., "The Power of Education to Empower Our Children," 2013, pp. 82–85.

Humphries, Frederick S., "The National Talent Strategy: Ideas to Secure U.S. Competitiveness and Economic Growth," 2013, pp. 86–90.

Kirk, Ron, "Education: The Critical Link between Trade and Jobs," 2013, pp. 76–80.

Knaus, Christopher B., "Still Segregated, Still Unequal: Analyzing the Impact of No Child Left Behind on African-American Students," 2007, pp. 105–121.

Lomax, Dr. Michael, "Getting Kids To and Through College: Our Kids, Our Jobs," 2014, pp. 142–147.

Marsalis, Wynton, "Making the Grade: Put the Arts Back in Education," 2014, pp. 158–163.

McConduit-Diggs, Erika, "Winning TrifE³cta for Community Empowerment: Education, Employment, Entrepreneurship," 2014, pp. 164–167.

McGhee, David, "Mentoring Matters: Why Young Professionals and Others Must Mentor," 2013, pp. 162–165.

McMurray, Georgia L., "Those of Broader Vision: An African-American Perspective on Teenage Pregnancy and Parenting," 1990, pp. 195–211.

Moore, Evelyn K., "The Call: Universal Child Care," 1996, pp. 219–244.

Murphy, Laura, "Stop the Fast Track to Prison," 2013, pp. 96–100.

Obama, Michelle, "Let's Move Initiative on Healthier Schools," 2011, pp. 138–140.

Shaw, Jr., Lee, "Healthy Boys Stand SCOUTStrong™," 2012, pp. 126–128.

Scott, Kimberly A., "A Case Study: African-American Girls and Their Families," 2003, pp. 181–195.

Special Report. "Partnering to Empower Healthy Kids," 2012, pp. 120–123.

Williams, Terry M., and William Kornblum, "A Portrait of Youth: Coming of Age in Harlem Public Housing," 1991, pp. 187–207.

CIVIC ENGAGEMENT

Alton, Kimberley, "The State of Civil Rights 2008," 2008, pp. 157–161.

Brazile, Donna, "Fallout from the Mid-Term Elections: Making the Most of the Next Two Years," 2011, pp. 180–190.

Brown James, Stefanie, "Black Civic Engagement 2.0: In with the Old, in with the New," 2013, pp. 67–68.

Campbell, Melanie L., "Election Reform: Protecting Our Vote from the Enemy That Never Sleeps," 2008, pp. 149–156.

Capehart, Jonathan, "Race Still Does Matter—A Lot," 2013, pp. 150–153.

Chappell, Kevin, "'Realities' of Black America," 2011, pp. 192–195.

Fauntroy, Michael K., "The New Arithmetic of Black Political Power," 2013, pp. 154–157.

Fudge, Marcia L., "Unfinished Business," 2013, pp. 65.

Hardy, Chanelle P., "Introduction to Lift Ev'ry Voice: A Special Collection of Articles and Op-Eds.," 2013, pp. 60–61.

Holder, Jr., Eric H., "Civil Rights Enforcement in the 21st Century," 2013, pp. 144–148.

House, Tanya Clay, "The Evolving Fight to Protect the Vote," 2014, pp. 114–115.

Lewis, John, "New Tactics, Same Old Taint," 2013, pp. 62–63.

Lindsay, Tiffany, "Weaving the Fabric: The Political Activism of Young African-American Women," 2008, pp. 47–50.

Scott, Robert C. "Bobby," "Minority Voter Participation: Reviewing Past and Present Barriers to the Polls," 2012, pp. 44–47.

Watts, Vincent and White, Edith, "Project Advocate: A Roadmap to Civic Engagement," 2013 pp. 140–143.

White, Edith and Watts, Vincent, "Project Advocate: A Roadmap to Civic Engagement," 2013 pp. 140–143.

Wijewardena, Madura and Kirk Clay, "Government with the Consent of All: Redistricting Strategies for Civil Rights Organizations," 2011, pp. 196–201.

Wijewardena, Madura, "Understanding the Equality Index," 2012, pp. 16–19.

———, "Understanding the Equality Index," 2013, pp. 22–25.

Wilson, Valerie Rawlston, "Introduction to the 2011 Equality Index," 2011, pp. 14–22.

———, "Introduction to the 2012 Equality Index," 2012, pp. 10–15.

———, "Introduction to the 2013 Equality Index," 2013, pp. 12–21.

Yearwood, Jr., Lennox,"The Rise and Fall and Rise Again of Jim Crow Laws," 2012, pp. 48–53.

CIVIL RIGHTS

Alton, Kimberley, "The State of Civil Rights 2008," 2008, pp. 157–161.

Archer, Dennis W., "Security Must Never Trump Liberty," 2004, pp. 139–142.

Brown James, Stefanie, "Black Civic Engagement 2.0: In with the Old, in with the New," 2013, pp. 67–68.

Burnham, David, "The Fog of War," 2005, pp. 123–127.

Campbell, Melanie L., "Election Reform: Protecting Our Vote from the Enemy That Never Sleeps," 2008, pp. 149–156.

Chappell, Kevin, " 'Realities' of Black America," 2011, pp. 192–195.

Edelman, Marian Wright, "Time to Wake Up and Act: The State of Black America," 2013, pp. 68–69.

Fudge, Marcia L., "Unfinished Business," 2013, pp. 65.

Grant, Gwen, "The Fullness of Time for a More Perfect Union: The Movement Continues," 2009, pp. 171–177.

Hardy, Chanelle P., "Introduction to Lift Ev'ry Voice: A Special Collection of Articles and Op-Eds.," 2013, pp. 60–61.

———, "Introduction to the 21 Century Agenda for Jobs and Freedom." 2013, pp. 102–103.

Harper, Hill, "America Incarcerated: Who Pays and Who Profits," 2014, pp. 112–113.

Henderson, Wade, "A Watershed Year for Bipartisanship in Criminal Justice Reform," 2014, pp. 110–111.

Hernández, Rufina, "The Civil Rights Voice in Education Reform," 2014, pp. 138–141.

Holder, Jr., Eric H., "Civil Rights Enforcement in the 21st Century," 2013, pp. 144–148.

Honda, Mike, "Equity and Excellence Lead to Opportunity," 2014, pp. 104–105.

House, Tanya Clay, "The Evolving Fight to Protect the Vote," 2014, pp. 114–115.

Ifill, Sherrilyn, "Standing in the Breach: The Supreme Court and *Shelby*," 2014, pp. 118–123.

Jones, Nathaniel R., "The State of Civil Rights," 2006, pp. 165–170.

———, "Did I Ever" 2009, pp. 213–219.

Jones-DeWeever, Avis A., "The Enduring Icon: Dr. Dorothy Height," 2013, pp. 64.

Lewis, John, "New Tactics, Same Old Taint," 2013, pp. 62–63.

Mack, John W., "Reflections on National Urban League's Legacy and Service," 2013, pp. 66.

Ogletree, Jr., Charles J., "Brown at 50: Considering the Continuing Legal Struggle for Racial Justice," 2004, pp. 81–96.

Sebelius, Kathleen, "Affordable Health Care is a Civil Right," 2014, pp. 124–129.

Sharpton, Al, "Though We Have Achieved Much, the Battle Continues," 2013, pp. 63–64.

Shaw, Theodore M., "The State of Civil Rights," 2007, pp. 173–183.

Wijewardena, Madura and Kirk Clay, "Government with the Consent of All: Redistricting Strategies for Civil Rights Organizations," 2011, pp. 196–201.

CRIMINAL JUSTICE

Curry, George E., "Racial Disparities Drive Prison Boom," 2006, pp. 171–187.

Drucker, Ernest M., "The Impact of Mass Incarceration on Public Health in Black Communities," 2003, pp. 151–168.

Edelman, Marian Wright, "Losing Our Children in America's Cradle to Prison Pipeline," 2007, pp. 219–227.

———, "Time to Wake Up and Act: The State of Black America," 2013, pp. 68–69.

Henderson, Wade, "A Watershed Year for Bipartisanship in Criminal Justice Reform," 2014, pp. 110–111.

Lanier, James R., "The Harmful Impact of the Criminal Justice System and War on Drugs on the African-American Family," 2003, pp. 169–179.

Murphy, Laura, "Stop the Fast Track to Prison," 2013, pp. 96–100.

DIVERSITY

Bell, Derrick, "The Elusive Quest for Racial Justice: The Chronicle of the Constitutional Contradiction," 1991, pp. 9–23.

Burns, Ursula, "Leaving No Brains Behind," 2014, pp. 152–157.

Capehart, Jonathan, "Race Still Does Matter—A Lot," 2013, pp. 150–153.

Cobbs, Price M., "Critical Perspectives on the Psychology of Race," 1988, pp. 61–70.

———, "Valuing Diversity: The Myth and the Challenge," 1989, pp. 151–159.

Darity, Jr., William, "History, Discrimination and Racial Inequality," 1999, pp. 153–166.

Harris, Dot, "Diversity in STEM: An Economic Imperative," 2013, pp. 92–95.

Humphries, Frederick S., "The National Talent Strategy: Ideas to Secure U.S. Competitiveness and Economic Growth," 2013, pp. 86–90.

Jones, Stephanie J., "Sunday Morning Apartheid: A Diversity Study of the Sunday Morning Talk Shows," 2006, pp. 189–228.

Stoute, Steve, "Tanning of America Makes Growth, Prosperity and Empowerment Easier," 2012, pp. 84–89.

Watson, Bernard C., "The Demographic Revolution: Diversity in 21st-Century America," 1992, pp. 31–59.

Wiley, Maya, "Hurricane Katrina Exposed the Face of Diversity," 2006, pp. 143–153.

DRUG TRADE

Lanier, James R., "The Harmful Impact of the Criminal Justice System and War on Drugs on the African-American Family," 2003, pp. 169–179.

ECONOMICS

Alexis, Marcus and Geraldine R. Henderson, "The Economic Base of African-American Communities: A Study of Consumption Patterns," 1994, pp. 51–82.

Anderson, Bernard, "Lessons Learned from the Economic Crisis: Job Creation and Economy Recovery," 2010, pp. 60–65.

———, "William M. Rodgers III, Lucy J. Reuben, and Valerie Rawlston Wilson, "The New Normal? Opportunities for Prosperity in a 'Jobless Recovery,'" 2011, pp. 54–63.

Anderson, Maggie, "Facts Versus Fiction: Buying Black as an Economic Empowerment Strategy," 2014, pp. 182–187.

Atlanta Highlight, "Economic Empowerment Tour," 2011, pp. 118–120.

Baker, Donna Jones, "Driving Economic Self-Sufficiency to Transform the Next Generation," 2014, pp. 178–181.

Bradford, William, "Black Family Wealth in the United States," 2000, pp. 103–145.

———, "Money Matters: Lending Discrimination in African-American Communities," 1993, pp. 109–134.

Bryant, John Hope, "Financial Dignity in an Economic Age," 2013, pp. 134–138.

Buckner, Marland and Chanelle P. Hardy, "Leveraging the Greening of America to Strengthen the Workforce Development System," 2011, pp. 76–83.

Burbridge, Lynn C., "Toward Economic Self-Sufficiency: Independence Without Poverty," 1993, pp. 71–90.

Cleaver II, Emanuel, "Green Impact Zone of Kansas City, MO," 2011, pp. 88–93.

Corbett, Keith, "Economic Innovation: Finance and Lending Initiatives Point Paths to Prosperity for Underserved Communities," 2011, pp. 122–129.

Edwards, Harry, "Playoffs and Payoffs: The African-American Athlete as an Institutional Resource," 1994, pp. 85–111.

Graves, Jr., Earl, "Wealth for Life," 2009, pp. 165–170.

Hamilton, Darrick, "The Racial Composition of American Jobs," 2006, pp. 77–115.

Harris, Andrea, "The Subprime Wipeout: Unsustainable Loans Erase Gains Made by African-American Women," 2008, pp. 125–133.

Harris, Dot, "Diversity in STEM: An Economic Imperative," 2013, pp. 92–95.

Henderson, Lenneal J., "Blacks, Budgets, and Taxes: Assessing the Impact of Budget Deficit Reduction and Tax Reform on Blacks," 1987, pp. 75–95.

———, "Budget and Tax Strategy: Implications for Blacks," 1990, pp. 53–71.

———, "Public Investment for Public Good: Needs, Benefits, and Financing Options," 1992, pp. 213–229.

Herman, Alexis, "African-American Women and Work: Still a Tale of Two Cities," 2008, pp. 109–113.

Hinojosa, Ruben, "Financial Literacy: Investing to Empower," 2014, pp. 108–109.

Holzer, Harry J., "Reconnecting Young Black Men: What Policies Would Help," 2007, pp. 75–87.

Humphries, Frederick S., "The National Talent Strategy: Ideas to Secure U.S. Competitiveness and Economic Growth," 2013, pp. 86–90.

Jeffries, John M., and Richard L. Schaffer, "Changes in Economy and Labor Market Status of Black Americans," 1996, pp. 12–77.

Jones, Stephanie J., "The Subprime Meltdown: Disarming the 'Weapons of Mass Deception,'" 2009, pp. 157–164.

Kirk, Ron, "Education: The Critical Link Between Trade and Jobs," 2013, pp. 76–80.

Malveaux, Julianne, "Shouldering the Third Burden: The Status of African-American Women," 2008, pp. 75–81.

———, "The Parity Imperative: Civil Rights, Economic Justice, and the New American Dilemma," 1992, pp. 281–303.

McConduit-Diggs, Erika, "Winning TrifE3cta for Community Empowerment: Education, Employment, Entrepreneurship," 2014, pp. 164–167.

Mensah, Lisa, "Putting Homeownership Back Within Our Reach," 2008, pp. 135–142.

Morial, Marc H. and Marvin Owens, "The National Urban League Economic Empowerment Initiative," 2005, pp. 111–113.

Myers, Jr., Samuel L., "African-American Economic Well-Being During the Boom and Bust," 2004, pp. 53–80.

National Urban League, "The National Urban League's Homebuyer's Bill of Rights," 2008, pp. 143–147.

National Urban League Research Staff, "African Americans in Profile: Selected Demographic, Social and Economic Data," 1992, pp. 309–325.

———, "The Economic Status of African Americans During the Reagan-Bush Era Withered Opportunities, Limited Outcomes, and Uncertain Outlook," 1993, pp. 135–200.

———, "The Economic Status of African Americans: Limited Ownership and Persistent Inequality," 1992, pp. 61–117.

———, "The Economic Status of African Americans: 'Permanent' Poverty and Inequality," 1991, pp. 25–75.

———, "Economic Status of Black Americans During the 1980s: A Decade of Limited Progress," 1990, pp. 25–52.

———, "Economic Status of Black Americans," 1989, pp. 9–39.

———, "Economic Status of Black 1987," 1988, pp. 129–152.

———, "Economic Status of Blacks 1986," 1987, pp. 49–73.

Patrick, Deval L., "Growing an Innovative Economy in Massachusetts," 2011, pp. 154–158.

Pinkett, Dr. Randal, Robinson, Dr. Jeffrey, "Entrepreneurship and Economic Development," 2014, pp. 174–177.

Reuben, Lucy J., "Make Room for the New 'She'EOs: An Analysis of Businesses Owned by Black Females," 2008, pp. 115–124.

Richardson, Cy, "What Must Be Done: The Case for More Homeownership and Financial Education Counseling," 2009, pp. 145–155.

Rivlin, Alice M., "Pay Now or Pay Later: Jobs, Fiscal Responsibility and the Future of Black America," 2011, pp. 202–206.

Rodgers III, William, M., "Why Should African Americans Care About Macroeconomic Policy," 2007, pp. 89–103.

Shapiro, Thomas M., "The Racial Wealth Gap," 2005, pp. 41–48.

———, "Policies of Exclusion Perpetuate the Racial Wealth Gap" 2014, pp. 106–107.

Sharpe, Rhonda, "Preparing a Diverse and Competitive STEM Workforce," 2011, pp. 142–152.

Shepherd, Dr. J. Marshall, "21st Century Jobs and Climate Change: A Curse and Blessing for African Americans," 2014, pp. 168–173.

Shumate, Jabar, "The Affordable Care Act and How It Can Fuel Entrepreneurism in Urban Communities," 2014, pp. 130–133.

Spriggs, William, "Nothing Trickled Down: Why Reaganomics Failed America," 2009, pp. 123–133.

Stoute, Steve, "Tanning of America Makes Growth, Prosperity and Empowerment Easier," 2012, pp. 84–89.

Taylor, Robert D., "Wealth Creation: The Next Leadership Challenge," 2005, pp. 119–122.

Thompson, J. Phil, "The Coming Green Economy," 2009, pp. 135–142.

Tidwell, Billy J., "Economic Costs of American Racism," 1991, pp. 219–232.

Turner, Mark D., "Escaping the 'Ghetto' of Subcontracting," 2006, pp. 117–131.

Watkins, Celeste, "The Socio-Economic Divide Among Black Americans Under 35," 2001, pp. 67–85.

Webb, Michael B., "Programs for Progress and Empowerment: The Urban League's National Education Initiative," 1993, pp. 203–216.

EDUCATION

Allen, V., Brown, L., Ray, J., Slash, J., "Preparing Indiana's Children for College, Work and Life—Indiana Urban League Affiliates," 2014, pp. 148–151.

Allen, Walter R., "The Struggle Continues: Race, Equity and Affirmative Action in U.S. Higher Education," 2001, pp. 87–100.

Bailey, Deirdre, "School Choice: The Option of Success," 2001, pp. 101–114.

Bradford, William D., "Dollars for Deeds: Prospects and Prescriptions for African-American Financial Institutions," 1994, pp. 31–50.

Burns, Ursula, "Leaving No Brains Behind," 2014, pp. 152–157.

Bush, Esther and Stokes, Patricia, "The Equity and Excellence Project: Community-Driven Education Reform," 2013, pp. 70–74.

Carr, Gregory E., "Sacrifice If You Must—The Reward Is Clear," 2012, pp. 137–139.

Chauhan, Shree, "Bringing Higher Education to the Masses: A Conversation with Coursera Co-Founder Andrew Ng," 2013, pp. 102–106.

Cole, Johnnetta Betsch, "The Triumphs and Challenges of Historically Black Colleges and Universities," 2008, pp. 99–107.

Comer, James P., Norris Haynes, and Muriel Hamilton-Leel, "School Power: A Model for Improving Black Student Achievement," 1990, pp. 225–238.

———, "Leave No Child Behind: Preparing Today's Youth for Tomorrow's World," 2005, pp. 75–84.

Dilworth, Mary E. "Historically Black Colleges and Universities: Taking Care of Home," 1994, pp. 127–151.

Duncan, Arne, "The Path to Success for African Americans," 2010, pp. 92–96.

Edelman, Marian Wright, "Black Children in America," 1989, pp. 63–76.

———, "Time to Wake Up and Act: The State of Black America," 2013, pp. 68–69.

Enyia, Amara, C. "College for All?" 2012, pp. 149–151.

Fattah, Chaka, "Needed: Equality in Education," 2009, pp. 57–60.

Freeman, Dr. Kimberly Edelin, "African-American Men and Women in Higher Education: 'Filling the Glass' in the New Millennium," 2000, pp. 61–90.

Gordon, Edmund W., "The State of Education in Black America," 2004, pp. 97–113.

Guinier, Prof. Lani, "Confirmative Action in a Multiracial Democracy," 2000, pp. 333–364.

Hanson, Renee R., "A Pathway to School Readiness: The Impact of Family on Early Childhood Education," 2008, pp. 89–98.

Hardy, Chanelle P., "Introduction: The Value of College," 2012, pp. 132–135.

Harris, Dot, "Diversity in STEM: An Economic Imperative," 2013, pp. 92–95.

Hernández, Rufina, "The Civil Rights Voice in Education Reform," 2014, pp. 138–141.

Honda, Mike, "Equity and Excellence Lead to Opportunity," 2014, pp. 104–105.

Hrabowski III, Dr. Freeman A., "The Power of Education to Empower Our Children," 2013, pp. 82–85.

Humphries, Frederick S., "The National Talent Strategy: Ideas to Secure U.S. Competitiveness and Economic Growth," 2013, pp. 86–90.

Jackson, John, "From Miracle to Movement: Mandating a National Opportunity to Learn, 2009, pp. 61–70.

Jackson, Maria Rosario, "Arts, Culture, and Communities: Do Our Neighborhoods Inspire Our Children to Reach Higher?" 2012, pp. 153–154.

Journal of Blacks in Higher Education (reprint), "The 'Acting White' Myth," 2005, pp. 115–117.

Kirk, Ron, "Education: The Critical Link between Trade and Jobs," 2013, pp. 76–80.

Knaus, Christopher B., "Still Segregated, Still Unequal: Analyzing the Impact of No Child Left Behind on African American Students," 2007, pp. 105–121.

Legend, John, "The Show Me Campaign: A Conversation with John Legend," 2012, pp. 151–153.

Lomax, Dr. Michael, "Getting Kids To and Through College: Our Kids, Our Jobs," 2014, pp. 142–147.

Luckey, Desireé, "Communities, Schools and Families Make the Education-Career Connection," 2012, pp. 139–141.

Marsalis, Wynton, "Making the Grade: Put the Arts Back in Education," 2014, pp. 158–163.

McBay, Shirley M. "The Condition of African American Education: Changes and Challenges," 1992, pp. 141–156.

McConduit-Diggs, Erika, "Winning TrifE3cta for Community Empowerment: Education, Employment, Entrepreneurship," 2014, pp. 164–167.

McKenzie, Floretta Dukes with Patricia Evans, "Education Strategies for the 90s," 1991, pp. 95–109.

Morial, Marc H. and Hal Smith, "Education is a Jobs Issue," 2011, pp. 130–137.

Murphy, Laura, "Stop the Fast Track to Prison," 2013, pp. 96–100.

Patrick, Deval L., "Growing an Innovative Economy in Massachusetts," 2011, pp. 154–158.

Perry, Dr. Steve, "Real Reform is Getting Kids One Step Closer to Quality Schools," 2012, pp. 147–149.

Powell, Kevin, "Why A College Education Matters," 2012, pp. 136–137.

Ransom, Tafaya and John Michael Lee, "College Readiness and Completion for Young Men of Color," 2012, pp. 141–147.

Ribeau, Sidney, "Foreword: A Competitive Foundation for the Future," 2011, pp. 8–9.

Robinson, Sharon P., "Taking Charge: An Approach to Making the Educational Problems of Blacks Comprehensible and Manageable," 1987, pp. 31–47.

Rose, Dr. Stephanie Bell, "African-American High Achievers: Developing Talented Leaders," 2000, pp. 41–60.

Ross, Ronald O., "Gaps, Traps and Lies: African-American Students and Test Scores," 2004, pp. 157–161.

Sharpe, Rhonda, "Preparing a Diverse and Competitive STEM Workforce," 2011, pp. 142–152.

Smith, Hal, "The Questions Before Us: Opportunity, Education and Equity," 2009, pp. 45–55.

Smith, Hal, Jacqueline Ayers, and Darlene Marlin, "Ready to Succeed: The National Urban League Project Ready: Post-Secondary Success Program," 2012, pp. 114–119.

Stokes, Patricia and Bush, Esther, "The Equity and Excellence Project: Community-Driven Education Reform," 2013, pp. 70–74.

Sudarkasa, Niara, "Black Enrollment in Higher Education: The Unfulfilled led Promise of Equality," 1988, pp. 7–22.

Thornton, Alvin, "The Nation's Higher Education Agenda: The Continuing Role of HBCUs," 2011, pp. 160–167.

Watson, Bernard C., with Fasaha M. Traylor, "Tomorrow's Teachers: Who Will They Be, What Will They Know?" 1988, pp. 23–37.

Willie, Charles V., "The Future of School Desegregation," 1987, pp. 37–47.

Wilson, Reginald, "Black Higher Education: Crisis and Promise," 1989, pp. 121–135.

Wilson, Valerie Rawlston, "On Equal Ground: Causes and Solutions for Lower College Completion Rates Among Black Males," 2007, pp. 123–135.

———, "Introduction to the 2011 Equality Index," 2011, pp. 14–22.

Wirschem, David, "Community Mobilization for Education in Rochester, New York: A Case Study," 1991, pp. 243–248.

EMERGING IDEAS

Clyburn, Mignon, "Challenges and Opportunities for African Americans in Communications Technology," 2014, pp. 192–195.

Huggins, Sheryl, "The Rules of the Game," 2001, pp. 65–66.

Shepherd, Dr. J. Marshall, "21st Century Jobs and Climate Change: A Curse and Blessing for African Americans," 2014, pp. 168–173.

Shumate, Jabar, "The Affordable Care Act and How It Can Fuel Entrepreneurism in Urban Communities," 2014, pp. 130–133.

EMPLOYMENT

Anderson, Bernard E., "The Black Worker: Continuing Quest for Economic Parity, 2002, pp. 51–67.

———, "William M. Rodgers III, Lucy J. Reuben, and Valerie Rawlston Wilson, "The New Normal? Opportunities for Prosperity in a 'Jobless Recovery,'" 2011, pp. 54–63.

Atlanta Highlight, "Economic Empowerment Tour," 2011, pp. 118–120.

Baker, Donna Jones, "Driving Economic Self-Sufficiency to Transform the Next Generation," 2014, pp. 178–181.

Burns, Ursula, "Leaving No Brains Behind," 2014, pp. 152–157.

Cleaver II, Emanuel, "Green Impact Zone of Kansas City, MO," 2011, pp. 88–93.

Coulter, Patricia, "Small Business Growth = Job Growth," 2010, pp. 118–124.

Dallas Highlight, "Urban Youth Empowerment Program," 2011, pp. 84–86.

Darity, Jr., William M., and Samuel L. Myers, Jr., "Racial Earnings Inequality into the 21st Century," 1992, pp. 119–139.

Dodd, Christopher, "Infrastructure as a Job Creation Mechanism," 2009, pp. 101–108.

Gillibrand, Kirsten, "A Dream Not Deferred," 2012, pp. 60–63.

Hamilton, Darrick, "The Racial Composition of American Jobs," 2006, pp. 77–115.

Hammond, Theresa A., "African Americans in White-Collar Professions," 2002, pp. 109–121.

Herman, Alexis, "African-American Women and Work: Still a Tale of Two Cities," 2008, pp. 109–113.

Marshall, Cynthia, "Digitizing the Dream: The Role of Technology in Empowering Communities," 2013, pp. 130–133.

McConduit-Diggs, Erika, "Winning TrifE3cta for Community Empowerment: Education, Employment, Entrepreneurship," 2014, pp. 164–167.

Morial, Marc H. and Hal Smith, "Education is a Jobs Issue," 2011, pp. 130–137.

National Urban League, "12 Point Urban Jobs Plan," 2011, pp. 46–52.

National Urban League Policy Institute, "Where Do We Go From Here? Projected Employment Growth Industries and Occupations," 2011, pp. 64–75.

———, The National Urban League 8-Point Education and Employment Plan: Employment and Education Empower the Nation, 2012, pp. 54–59.

Nightingale, Demetra S., "Intermediaries in the Workforce Development System," 2010, pp. 84–91.

Patrick, Deval L., "Growing an Innovative Economy in Massachusetts," 2011, pp. 154–158.

Reuben, Lucy J., "Make Room for the New 'She'EOs: An Analysis of Businesses Owned by Black Females," 2008, pp. 115–124.

Rivlin, Alice M., "Pay Now or Pay Later: Jobs, Fiscal Responsibility and the Future of Black America," 2011, pp. 202–206.

Rodgers, William, "Why Reduce African-American Male Unemployment?," 2009, pp. 109–121.

Sharpe, Rhonda, "Preparing a Diverse and Competitive STEM Workforce," 2011, pp. 142–152.

Shepherd, Dr. J. Marshall, "21st Century Jobs and Climate Change: A Curse and Blessing for African Americans," 2014, pp. 168–173.

Solis, Hilda, "Creating Good Jobs for Everyone," 2010, pp. 66–72.

Taylor, Barton, "Opening New Doors Through Volunteerism," 2010, pp. 126–131.

Thomas, Jr., R. Roosevelt, "Managing Employee Diversity: An Assessment," 1991, pp. 145–154.

Tidwell, Billy, J., "Parity Progress and Prospects: Racial Inequalities in Economic Well-Being," 2000, pp. 287–316.

———, "African Americans and the 21st-Century Labor Market: Improving the Fit," 1993, pp. 35–57.

———, "The Unemployment Experience of African Americans: Some Important Correlates and Consequences," 1990, pp. 213–223.

———, "A Profile of the Black Unemployed," 1987, pp. 223–237.

Wilkins, Ray, "Jobs, the Internet, and Our Exciting Future," 2011, pp. 94–99.

Wilson, Valerie Rawlston, "Introduction to the 2011 Equality Index," 2011, pp. 14–22.

ENVIRONMENT

Buckner, Marland and Chanelle P. Hardy, "Leveraging the Greening of America to Strengthen the Workforce Development System," 2011, pp. 76–83.

Cleaver II, Emanuel, "Green Impact Zone of Kansas City, MO," 2011, pp. 88–93.

McDuffie, Brenda, "The Strategic Alliances for Addressing the Skills Gap: The Buffalo Urban League Green Jobs Construction Training Program," 2013, pp. 158–161.

EQUALITY

Capehart, Jonathan, "Race Still Does Matter—A Lot," 2013, pp. 150–153.

Edelman, Marian Wright, "Time to Wake Up and Act: The State of Black America," 2013, pp. 68–69.

Fudge, Marcia L., "Unfinished Business," 2013, pp. 65.

Hardy, Chanelle P., "Introduction to Lift Ev'ry Voice: A Special Collection of Articles and Op-Eds.," 2013, pp. 60–61.

Holder, Jr., Eric H., "Civil Rights Enforcement in the 21st Century," 2013, pp. 144–148.

House, Tanya Clay, "The Evolving Fight to Protect the Vote," 2014, pp. 114–115.

Ifill, Sherrilyn, "Standing in the Breach: The Supreme Court and Shelby," 2014, pp. 118–123.

Jones-DeWeever, Avis A., "The Enduring Icon: Dr. Dorothy Height," 2013, pp. 64.

Lewis, John, "New Tactics, Same Old Taint," 2013, pp. 62–63.

Mack, John W., "Reflections on National Urban League's Legacy and Service," 2013, pp. 66.

Raines, Franklin D., "What Equality Would Look Like: Reflections on the Past, Present and Future, 2002, pp. 13–27.

Shapiro, Dr. Thomas, "Policies of Exclusion Perpetuate the Racial Wealth Gap" 2014, pp. 106–107.

Sharpton, Al, "Though We Have Achieved Much, the Battle Continues," 2013, pp. 63–64.

EQUALITY INDEX

Brown, Alvin, "Commentary on the Jacksonville Equality Index," 2014, pp. 71–72.

Christopher, Gail, "Commentary on 2013 Black–White Equality Index: Mobilizing our Nation toward Racial Healing and Equity," 2013, pp. 28–29.

Global Insight, Inc., "The National Urban League Equality Index," 2004, pp. 15–34.

———, "The National Urban League Equality Index," 2005, pp. 15–40.

———, "The National Urban League Equality Index," 2010, pp. 18–39.

———, "The National Urban League 2012 Equality Index," 2012, pp. 20–43.

Hancock, Michael, "Commentary on the Denver Equality Index," 2014, pp. 66–67.

IHS Global Insight, "The National Urban League 2013 1963 to Now Equality Index," 2013, pp. 26–27.

———, "The National Urban League 2013 Black–White Equality Index," 2013, pp. 32–43.

———, "The National Urban League 2013 Hispanic–White Equality Index," 2013, pp. 46–57.

IHS Global Insight, "The National Urban League 2014 Equality Index," 2014, pp. 28–61.

———, "The National Urban League 2014 Black–White Equality Index," 2014, pp. 26–45.

———, "The National Urban League 2014 Hispanic–White Equality Index," 2014, pp. 46–61.

———, "The National Urban League 2014 Metropolitan Areas Index," 2014 pp. 62–99.

Murguía, Janet, "Commentary on 2013 Hispanic–White Equality Index: Partners in a Shared Plight," 2013, pp. 44–45.

powell, john a., "Commentary on 2013 Black–White Equality Index: A Theory of Change," 2013, pp. 30–31.

Rawlings-Blake, Stephanie, "Commentary on the Baltimore Equality Index," 2014, pp. 62–63.

Thompson, Rondel and Sophia Parker of Global Insight, Inc., The National Urban League Equality Index, 2006, pp. 13–60.

Thompson, Rondel and Sophia Parker of Global Insight, Inc., The National Urban League Equality Index, 2007 pp. 17–58.

Wharton, AC, "Commentary on the Memphis Equality Index," 2014, pp. 74–75.

Wijewardena, Madura, "Understanding the Equality Index," 2013, pp. 22–25.

Wilson, Valerie Rawlston, "The National Urban League 2008 Equality Index: Analysis," 2008, pp. 15–24.

———, "The National Urban League 2008 Equality Index," 2009, pp. 15–24.

———, "Introduction to the 2013 Equality Index," 2013, pp. 12–21.

FAMILIES

Anderson, Maggie, "Facts Versus Fiction: Buying Black as an Economic Empowerment Strategy," 2014, pp. 182–187.

Battle, Juan, Cathy J. Cohen, Angelique Harris, and Beth E. Richie, "We Are Family: Embracing Our Lesbian, Gay, Bisexual, and Transgender (LGBT) Family Members," 2003, pp. 93–106.

Bell, William C., "Community Based Organizations and Child Welfare: Building Communities of Hope," 2013, pp. 166–169.

Billingsley, Andrew, "Black Families in a Changing Society," 1987, pp. 97–111.

———, "Understanding African-American Family Diversity," 1990, pp. 85–108.

Cox, Kenya L. Covington, "The Childcare Imbalance: Impact on Working Opportunities for Poor Mothers," 2003, pp. 197–224.

Drucker, Ernest M., "The Impact of Mass Incarceration on Public Health in Black Communities," 2003, pp. 151–168.

Dyson, Eric Michael, "Sexual Fault Lines: Robbing the Love Between Us," 2007, pp. 229–237.

Hanson, Renee R., "A Pathway to School Readiness: The Impact of Family on Early Childhood Education," 2008, pp. 89–98.

Hill, Robert B., "Critical Issues for Black Families by the Year 2000," 1989, pp. 41–61.

———, "The Strengths of Black Families' Revisited," 2003, pp. 107–149.

Ivory, Steven, "Universal Fatherhood: Black Men Sharing the Load," 2007, pp. 243–247.

Lorain County Highlight, "Save Our Sons," 2011, pp. 176–178.

Rawlston, Valerie A., "The Impact of Social Security on Child Poverty," 2000, pp. 317–331.

Scott, Kimberly A., "A Case Study: African-American Girls and Their Families," 2003, pp. 181–195.

Shapiro, Thomas M., "The Racial Wealth Gap," 2005, pp. 41–48.

Stafford, Walter, Angela Dews, Melissa Mendez, and Diana Salas, "Race, Gender and Welfare Reform: The Need for Targeted Support," 2003, pp. 41–92.

Stockard, Jr., Russell L. and M. Belinda Tucker, "Young African-American Men and Women: Separate Paths?," 2001, pp. 143–159.

Teele, James E., "E. Franklin Frazier: The Man and His Intellectual Legacy," 2003, pp. 29–40.

Thompson, Dr. Linda S. and Georgene Butler, "The Role of the Black Family in Promoting Healthy Child Development," 2000, pp. 227–241.

West, Carolyn M., "Feminism is a Black Thing?": Feminist Contribution to Black Family Life, 2003, pp. 13–27.

Willie, Charles V. "The Black Family: Striving Toward Freedom," 1988, pp. 71–80.

FOREWORD

Height, Dorothy I., "Awakenings," 2008, pp. 9–10.

Obama, Barack, Foreword, 2007, pp. 9–12.

King III, Martin Luther, Foreword, 2009, pp. 9–10.

Ribeau, Sidney, "A Competitive Foundation for the Future," 2011, pp. 8–9.

FROM THE PRESIDENT'S DESK

Morial, Marc H., "The State of Black America: The Complexity of Black Progress," 2004, pp. 11–14.

———, "The State of Black America 2012: Occupy the Vote to Educate, Employ & Empower," 2012, pp. 6–9.

———, "The State of Black America: Prescriptions for Change," 2005, pp. 11–14.

———, "The National Urban League Opportunity Compact," 2006, pp. 9–11.

———, "Empowering Black Males to Reach Their Full Potential," 2007, pp. 13–15.

———, From the President's Desk, 2008, pp. 11–14.

———, From the President's Desk, 2009, pp. 11–13.

———, From the President's Desk, 2010, pp. 6–7.

———, From the President's Desk, 2011, pp. 10–12.

———, From the President's Desk, 2012, pp. 6–9.

———, From the President's Desk, 2013, pp. 8–11.

———, From the President's Desk, 2014, pp. 8–13.

HEALTH

Browne, Doris, "The Impact of Health Disparities in African-American Women," 2008, pp. 163–171.

Carnethon, Mercedes R., "Black Male Life Expectancy in the United States: A Multi-Level Exploration of Causes," 2007, pp. 137–150.

Chávez, Anna Maria "Helping Girls Make Healthy Choices," 2012, pp. 124–126.

Christensen, Donna, "A Healthier Nation," 2014, pp. 115–117.

Christmas, June Jackson, "The Health of African Americans: Progress Toward Healthy People 2000," 1996, pp. 95–126.

Cooper, Maudine R., "The Invisibility Blues' of Black Women in America," 2008, pp. 83–87.

Gaskin, Darrell, "Improving African Americans Access to Quality Healthcare," 2009, pp. 73–86.

Gaskins, Darrell J., LaVeist, Thomas A. and Richard, Patrick, "The State of Urban Health: Eliminating Health Disparities to Save Lives and Cut Costs," 2013, pp. 108–128.

Hamilton, Darrick, Goldsmith, Arthur H., and Darity, William, "An Alternative 'Public Option'," 2010, pp. 98–110.

Johnston, Haile, and Tatiana Garcia-Granados, "Common Market: The New Black Farmer," 2012, pp. 100–105.

Leffall, Jr., LaSalle D., "Health Status of Black Americans," 1990, pp. 121–142.

Lorain County Highlight, "Save Our Sons," 2011, pp. 176–178.

McAlpine, Robert, "Toward Development of a National Drug Control Strategy," 1991, pp. 233–241.

Morris, Eboni D., "By the Numbers: Uninsured African-American Women," 2008, pp. 173–177.

——— and Lisa Bland Malone, "Healthy Housing," 2009, pp. 87–98.

Nobles, Wade W., and Lawford L. Goddard, "Drugs in the African-American Community: A Clear and Present Danger," 1989, pp. 161–181.

Obama, Michelle, "Let's Move Initiative on Healthier Schools," 2011, pp. 138–140.

Patrick, Deval L., "Growing an Innovative Economy in Massachusetts," 2011, pp. 154–158.

Primm, Annelle and Marisela B. Gomez, "The Impact of Mental Health on Chronic Disease," 2005, pp. 63–73.

Primm, Beny J., "AIDS: A Special Report," 1987, pp. 159–166.

———, "Drug Use: Special Implications for Black America," 1987, pp. 145–158.

Ribeau, Sidney, "Foreword: A Competitive Foundation for the Future," 2011, pp. 8–9.

Richard, Patrick, Gaskins, Darrell J. and LaVeist, Thomas A., "The State of Urban Health: Eliminating Health Disparities to Save Lives and Cut Costs," 2013, pp. 108–128.

Sebelius, Kathleen, "Affordable Health Care is a Civil Right," 2014, pp. 124–129.

Shaw, Jr., Lee, "Healthy Boys Stand SCOUTStrong™," 2012, pp. 126–128.

Shumate, Jabar, "The Affordable Care Act and How It Can Fuel Entrepreneurism in Urban Communities," 2014, pp. 130–133.

Smedley, Brian D., "In the Wake of National Health Reform: Will the Affordable Care Act Eliminate Health Inequities?" 2011, pp. 168–175.

———, "Race, Poverty, and Healthcare Disparities," 2006, pp. 155–164.

Watson, Elnora, "Urban League of Hudson County (ULOHC) Health Care Initiatives in a 'Sankofa' Moment," 2014, pp. 134–137.

Williams, David R., "Health and the Quality of Life Among African Americans," 2004, pp. 115–138.

Wilson, Valerie Rawlston, "Introduction to the 2011 Equality Index," 2011, pp. 14–22.

———, "Introduction to the 2012 Equality Index," 2012, pp. 10–15.

Wijewardena, Madura ,"Understanding the Equality Index," 2012, pp. 16–19.

HIGHLIGHTS

Allen, V., Brown, L., Ray, J., Slash, J., "Preparing Indiana's Children for College, Work and Life—Indiana Urban League Affiliates," 2014, pp. 148–151.

Atlanta, "Economic Empowerment Tour," 2011, pp. 118–120.

Braswell, Allie L., and James T. McLawhorn, Jr., "A Call to Advocate for America's Military Veterans," 2012, pp. 94–99.

Buffalo, McDuffie, Brenda, "The Strategic Alliances for Addressing the Skills Gap: The Buffalo Urban League Green Jobs Construction Training Program," 2013, pp. 158–161.

Dallas, "Urban Youth Empowerment Program," 2011, pp. 84–86.

Greater Stark County, Watts, Vincent and White, Edith, "Project Advocate: A Roadmap to Civic Engagement," 2013 pp. 140–143.

Hampton Roads, White, Edith and Watts, Vincent, "Project Advocate: A Roadmap to Civic Engagement," 2013 pp. 140–143.

Lorain County, "Save Our Sons," 2011, pp. 176–178.

McConduit-Diggs, Erika, "Winning TrifE3cta for Community Empowerment: Education, Employment, Entrepreneurship," 2014, pp. 164–167.

Middle Tennessee, Stokes, Patricia and Bush, Esther, "The Equity and Excellence Project: Community-Driven Education Reform," 2013, pp. 70–74.

Obama, Michelle, "Let's Move Initiative on Healthier Schools," 2011, pp. 138–140.

Pittsburgh, Bush, Esther and Stokes, Patricia, "The Equity and Excellence Project: Community-Driven Education Reform," 2013, pp. 70–74.

Rollins, Nolan V., "The Economic Winds of Change: New Markets for an Old Problem," 2012, pp. 90–93.

Runner, Shari, "Inspiring Innovation: The Chicago Urban League Youth Investor/Entrepreneurs Project (YIEP)," 2012, pp. 110–113.

Watson, Elnora, "Urban League of Hudson County (ULOHC) Health Care Initiatives in a 'Sankofa' Moment," 2014, pp. 134–137.

HOUSING

Calmore, John O., "To Make Wrong Right: The Necessary and Proper Aspirations of Fair Housing," 1989, pp. 77–109.

Clay, Phillip, "Housing Opportunity: A Dream Deferred," 1990, pp. 73–84.

Cooper, Maudine R., "The Invisibility Blues' of Black Women in America," 2008, pp. 83–87.

Corbett, Keith, "Economic Innovation: Finance and Lending Initiatives Point Paths to Prosperity for Underserved Communities," 2011, pp. 122–129.

Freeman, Lance, "Black Homeownership: A Dream No Longer Deferred?," 2006, pp. 63–75.

———, "Housing in the Post-Bubble Economy," 2010, pp. 74–83.

Harris, Andrea, "The Subprime Wipeout: Unsustainable Loans Erase Gains Made by African-American Women," 2008, pp. 125–133.

James, Angela, "Black Homeownership: Housing and Black Americans Under 35," 2001, pp. 115–129.

Jones, Stephanie J., "The Subprime Meltdown: Disarming the 'Weapons of Mass Deception,'" 2009, pp. 157–164.

Leigh, Wilhelmina A., "U.S. Housing Policy in 1996: The Outlook for Black Americans," 1996, pp. 188–218.

Morris, Eboni and Lisa Bland Malone, "Healthy Housing," 2009, pp. 87–98.

Richardson, Cy, "What Must Be Done: The Case for More Homeownership and Financial Education Counseling," 2009, pp. 145–155.

——— and Garrick Davis, "Rescue: The Case for Keeping Families in Their Homes by Confronting the Foreclosure Crisis," 2011, pp. 110–117.

Shapiro, Dr. Thomas, "Policies of Exclusion Perpetuate the Racial Wealth Gap" 2014, pp. 106–107.

Spriggs, William, "Nothing Trickled Down: Why Reaganomics Failed America," 2009. pp. 123–133.

Wilson, Valerie Rawlston, "Introduction to the 2011 Equality Index," 2011, pp. 14–22.

IN MEMORIAM

National Urban League, "William A. Bootle, Ray Charles, Margo T. Clarke, Ossie Davis, Herman C. Ewing, James Forman, Joanne Grant, Ann Kheel, Memphis Norman, Max Schmeling," 2005, pp. 139–152.

———, "Renaldo Benson, Shirley Chisholm, Johnnie Cochran, Jr., Shirley Horn, John H. Johnson, Vivian Malone Jones, Brock Peters, Richard Pryor, Bobby Short, C. Delores Tucker, August Wilson, Luther Vandross, and NUL members Clarence Lyle Barney, Jr., Manuel Augustus Romero;" 2006, pp. 279–287.

———, "Ossie Davis: Still Caught in the Dream," 2005, pp. 137–138.

———, "Ed Bradley, James Brown, Bebe Moore Campbell, Katherine Dunham, Mike Evans, Coretta Scott King, Gerald Levert, Gordon Parks, June Pointer, Lou Rawls, and Helen E. Harden," 2007, pp. 249–257.

———, "Effi Barry, Jane Bolin, Daniel A. Collins (NUL Member), Oliver Hill, Yolanda King, Calvin Lockhart, Mahlon Puryear (NUL Member), Max Roach, Eddie Robinson, William Simms (NUL Member), Darryl Stingley, and Ike Turner," 2008, pp. 205–217.

———, In Memoriam, 2009, pp. 225–241.

Jones, Stephanie J., "Rosa Parks: An Ordinary Woman, An Extraordinary Life," 2006, pp. 245–246.

MILITARY AFFAIRS

Braswell, Allie L., and James T. McLawhorn, Jr., "A Call to Advocate for America's Military Veterans," 2012, pp. 94–99.

Butler, John Sibley, "African Americans and the American Military," 2002, pp. 93–107.

MUSIC

Boles, Mark A., "Breaking the 'Hip Hop' Hold: Looking Beyond the Media Hype," 2007, pp. 239–241.

Brown, David W., "Their Characteristic Music: Thoughts on Rap Music and Hip-Hop Culture," 2001, pp. 189–201.

Bynoe, Yvonne, "The Roots of Rap Music and Hip-Hop Culture: One Perspective," 2001, pp. 175–187.

Marsalis, Wynton, "Making the Grade: Put the Arts Back in Education," 2014, pp. 158–163.

OP-ED/COMMENTARY

Archer, Dennis W., "Security Must Never Trump Liberty," 2004, pp. 139–142.

Bailey, Moya, "Going in Circles: The Struggle to Diversify Popular Images of Black Women," 2008, pp. 193–196.

Bernard, Michelle, "An Ode to Black America," 2009, pp. 203–207.

Boles, Mark A., "Breaking the 'Hip Hop' Hold: Looking Beyond the Media Hype," 2007, pp. 239–241.

Burnham, David, "The Fog of War," 2005, pp. 123–127.

Capehart, Jonathan, "Race Still Does Matter—A Lot," 2013, pp. 150–153.

Chappell, Kevin, " 'Realities' of Black America," 2011, pp. 192–195.

Cooke, Cassye, "The Game Changer: Are We Beyond What is Next to What is Now?," 2009, pp. 209–212.

Covington, Kenya L., "The Transformation of the Welfare Caseload," 2004, pp. 149–152.

Dyson, Eric Michael, "Sexual Fault Lines: Robbing the Love Between Us," 2007, pp. 229–237.

Edelman, Marian Wright, "Losing Our Children in America's Cradle to Prison Pipeline," 2007, pp. 219–227.

Emerson, Melinda F., "Five Things You Must Have to Run a Successful Business," 2004, pp. 153–156.

Fauntroy, Michael K., "The New Arithmetic of Black Political Power," 2013, pp. 154–157.

Hardy, Chanelle P., "Introduction to Lift Ev'ry Voice: A Special Collection of Articles and Op-Eds.," 2013, pp. 60–61.

Holder, Jr., Eric H., "Civil Rights Enforcement in the 21st Century," 2013, pp. 144–148.

Ivory, Steven, "Universal Fatherhood: Black Men Sharing the Load," 2007, pp. 243–247.

Jones, Nathaniel R., "Did I Ever? Yes I Did," 2009, pp. 213–219.

Journal of Blacks in Higher Education (reprint), "The 'Acting White' Myth," 2005, pp. 115–117.

Kirk, Ron, "Education: The Critical Link between Trade and Jobs," 2013, pp. 76–80.

Lanier, James R., "The Empowerment Movement and the Black Male," 2004, pp. 143–148.

Lee, Barbara, "President Obama and the CBC: Speaking with One Voice," 2009, pp. 193–197.

Lewis, John, "New Tactics, Same Old Taint," 2013, pp. 62–63.

Lindsay, Tiffany, "Weaving the Fabric: the Political Activism of Young African-American Women," 2008, pp. 187–192.

Malveaux, Julianne, "Black Women's Hands Can Rock the World: Global Involvement and Understanding," 2008, pp. 197–202.

Rivlin, Alice M., "Pay Now or Pay Later: Jobs, Fiscal Responsibility and the Future of Black America," 2011, pp. 202–206.

Ross, Ronald O., "Gaps, Traps and Lies: African-American Students and Test Scores," 2004, pp. 157–161.

Sharpton, Al, "Though We Have Achieved Much, the Battle Continues," 2013, pp. 63–64.

Taylor, Susan L., "Black Love Under Siege," 2008 pp. 179–186.

Taylor, Robert D., "Wealth Creation: The Next Leadership Challenge," 2005, pp. 119–122.

West, Cornel, "Democracy Matters," 2005, pp. 129–132.

Wijewardena, Madura and Kirk Clay, "Government with the Consent of All: Redistricting Strategies for Civil Rights Organizations," 2011, pp. 196–201.

Wilkins, Ray, "Jobs, the Internet, and Our Exciting Future," 2011, pp. 94–99.

OVERVIEW

Morial, Marc H., "Black America's Family Matters," 2003, pp. 9–12.

Price, Hugh B., "Still Worth Fighting For: America After 9/11," 2002, pp. 9–11.

POLITICS

Alton, Kimberley, "The State of Civil Rights 2008," 2008, pp. 157–161.

Brazile, Donna, "Fallout from the Mid-Term Elections: Making the Most of the Next Two Years," 2011, pp. 180–190.

Brown James, Stefanie, "Black Civic Engagement 2.0: In with the Old, in with the New," 2013, pp. 67–68.

Campbell, Melanie L., "Election Reform: Protecting Our Vote from the Enemy Who Never Sleeps," 2008, pp. 149–156.

Capehart, Jonathan, "Race Still Does Matter—A Lot," 2013, pp. 150–153.

Coleman, Henry A., "Interagency and Intergovernmental Coordination: New Demands for Domestic Policy Initiatives,"

1992, pp. 249–263.

Fauntroy, Michael K., "The New Arithmetic of Black Political Power," 2013, pp. 154–157.

Fudge, Marcia L., "Unfinished Business," 2013, pp. 65.

Hamilton, Charles V., "On Parity and Political Empowerment," 1989, pp. 111–120.

———, "Promoting Priorities: African-American Political Influence in the 1990s," 1993, pp. 59–69.

Henderson, Lenneal J., "Budgets, Taxes, and Politics: Options for the African-American Community," 1991, pp. 77–93.

Henderson, Wade, "A Watershed Year for Bipartisanship in Criminal Justice Reform," 2014, pp. 110–111.

Holden, Jr., Matthew, "The Rewards of Daring and the Ambiguity of Power: Perspectives on the Wilder Election of 1989," 1990, pp. 109–120.

Holder, Jr., Eric H., "Civil Rights Enforcement in the 21st Century," 2013, pp. 144–148.

House, Tanya Clay, "The Evolving Fight to Protect the Vote," 2014, pp. 114–115.

Kilson, Martin L., "African Americans and American Politics 2002: The Maturation Phase," 2002, pp. 147–180.

———, "Thinking About the Black Elite's Role: Yesterday and Today," 2005, pp. 85–106.

Lee, Silas, "Who's Going to Take the Weight? African Americans and Civic Engagement in the 21st Century," 2007, pp. 185–192.

Lewis, John, "New Tactics, Same Old Taint," 2013, pp. 62–63.

Lindsay, Tiffany, "Weaving the Fabric: The Political Activism of Young African-American Women," 2008, pp. 187–192.

Mack, John W., "Reflections on National Urban League's Legacy and Service," 2013, pp. 66.

McHenry, Donald F., "A Changing World Order: Implications for Black America," 1991, pp. 155–163.

Persons, Georgia A., "Blacks in State and Local Government: Progress and Constraints," 1987, pp. 187–192.

Pinderhughes, Dianne M., "Power and Progress: African-American Politics in the New Era of Diversity," 1992, pp. 265–280.

———, "The Renewal of the Voting Rights Act," 2005, pp. 49–61.

———, "Civil Rights and the Future of the American Presidency," 1988, pp. 39–60.

Price, Hugh B., "Black America's Challenge: The Re-Construction of Black Civil Society," 2001, pp. 13–18.

Rivlin, Alice M., "Pay Now or Pay Later: Jobs, Fiscal Responsibility and the Future of Black America," 2011, pp. 202–206.

Scott, Robert C. "Bobby," "Minority Voter Participation: Reviewing Past and Present Barriers to the Polls," 2012, pp. 44–47.

Tidwell, Billy J., "Serving the National Interest: A Marshall Plan for America," 1992, pp. 11–30.

Watts, Vincent and White, Edith, "Project Advocate: A Roadmap to Civic Engagement," 2013 pp. 140–143.

West, Cornel, "Democracy Matters," 2005, pp. 129–132.

White, Edith and Watts, Vincent, "Project Advocate: A Roadmap to Civic Engagement," 2013 pp. 140–143.

Wijewardena, Madura and Kirk Clay, "Government with the Consent of All: Redistricting Strategies for Civil Rights Organizations," 2011, pp. 196–201.

Williams, Eddie N., "The Evolution of Black Political Power," 2000, pp. 91–102.

Yearwood, Jr., Lennox, "The Rise and Fall and Rise Again of Jim Crow Laws," 2012, pp. 48–53.

POVERTY

Baker, Donna Jones, "Driving Economic Self-Sufficiency to Transform the Next Generation," 2014, pp. 178–181.

Cooper, Maudine R., "The Invisibility Blues' of Black Women in America," 2008, pp. 83–87.

Edelman, Marian Wright, "The State of Our Children," 2006, pp. 133–141.

McConduit-Diggs, Erika, "Winning TrifE3cta for Community Empowerment. Education, Employment, Entrepreneurship," 2014, pp. 164–167.

Shapiro, Dr. Thomas, "Policies of Exclusion Perpetuate the Racial Wealth Gap" 2014, pp. 106–107.

PRESCRIPTIONS FOR CHANGE

Bell, William C., "Community Based Organizations and Child Welfare: Building Communities of Hope," 2013, pp. 166–169.

Burns, Ursula, "Leaving No Brains Behind," 2014, pp. 152–157.

Capehart, Jonathan, "Race Still Does Matter—A Lot," 2013, pp. 150–153.

Clyburn, Mignon, "Challenges and Opportunities for African Americans In Communications Technology," 2014, pp. 192–195.

Fauntroy, Michael K., "The New Arithmetic of Black Political Power," 2013, pp. 154–157.

Lomax, Dr. Michael, "Getting Kids To and Through College: Our Kids, Our Jobs," 2014, pp. 142–147.

Lombard, Tanya, "Transforming Futures for a Daring Tech Tomorrow—African-American Entrepreneurs, Broadband and the Coming Community Benefits," 2014, pp. 188–191.

Marshall, Cynthia, "Digitizing the Dream: The Role of Technology in Empowering Communities," 2013, pp. 130–133.

McGhee, David, "Mentoring Matters: Why Young Professionals and Others Must Mentor," 2013, pp. 162–165.

National Urban League, "Prescriptions for Change," 2005, pp. 133–135.

Pinkett, Dr. Randal, Robinson, Dr. Jeffrey, "Entrepreneurship and Economic Development," 2014, pp. 174–177.

Shepherd, Dr. J. Marshall, "21st Century Jobs and Climate Change: A Curse and Blessing for African Americans," 2014, pp. 168–173.

Shumate, Jabar, "The Affordable Care Act and How It Can Fuel Entrepreneurism in Urban Communities," 2014, pp. 130–133.

RELATIONSHIPS

Taylor, Susan L., "Black Love Under Siege," 2008, pp. 179–186.

RELIGION

Lincoln, C. Eric, "Knowing the Black Church: What It Is and Why," 1989, pp. 137–149.

Richardson, W. Franklyn, "Mission to Mandate: Self-Development through the Black Church," 1994, pp. 113–126.

Smith, Dr. Drew, "The Evolving Political Priorities of African-American Churches: An Empirical View," 2000, pp. 171–197.

Taylor, Mark V.C., "Young Adults and Religion," 2001, pp. 161–174.

REPORTS FROM THE NATIONAL URBAN LEAGUE

Gaskins, Darrell J., LaVeist, Thomas A. and Richard, Patrick, "The State of Urban Health: Eliminating Health Disparities to Save Lives and Cut Costs," 2013, pp. 108–128.

Hanson, Renee, Mark McArdle, and Valerie Rawlston Wilson, "Invisible Men: The Urgent Problems of Low-Income African-American Males," 2007, pp. 209–216.

Hardy, Chanelle P., Dr. Valerie Rawlston Wilson, Madura Wijewardena, and Garrick T. Davis, "At Risk: The State of the Black Middle Class," 2012, pp. 74–83.

Jones, Stephanie J., "Sunday Morning Apartheid: A Diversity Study of the Sunday Morning Talk Shows" 2006, pp. 189–228.

Lanier, James, "The National Urban League's Commission on the Black Male: Renewal, Revival and Resurrection Feasibility and Strategic Planning Study," 2005, pp. 107–109.

LaVeist, Thomas A., Richard, Patrick and Gaskins, Darrell J., "The State of Urban Health: Eliminating Health Disparities to Save Lives and Cut Costs," 2013, pp. 108–128.

National Urban League, "12 Point Urban Jobs Plan," 2011, pp. 46–52.

National Urban League Council of Economic Advisors, Bernard E. Anderson, William M. Rodgers III, Lucy J. Reuben, and Valerie Rawlston Wilson, "The New Normal? Opportunities for Prosperity in a 'Jobless Recovery,'" 2011, pp. 54–63.

National Urban League Policy Institute, The Opportunity Compact: A Blueprint for Economic Equality, 2008, pp. 43–74.

———, "Putting Americans Back to Work: The National Urban League's Plan for Creating Jobs" 2010, pp. 40–44.

———, "African Americans and the Green Revolution" 2010, pp. 46–59.

———, "Where Do We Go From Here? Projected Employment Growth Industries and Occupations," 2011, pp. 64–75.

———, "The 2012 National Urban League 8-Point Education and Employment Plan: Employment and Education Empower the Nation" 2012, pp. 54–59.

———, "The National Urban League Introduces New Reports on the State of Urban Business" 2012, pp. 64–69.

National Urban League Policy Institute, LaVeist, Thomas A., Richard, Patrick and Gaskins, Darrell J., "The State of Urban Health: Eliminating Health Disparities to Save Lives and Cut Costs," 2013, pp. 108–128.

Richard, Patrick, Gaskins, Darrell J. and LaVeist, Thomas A., "The State of Urban Health: Eliminating Health Disparities to Save Lives and Cut Costs," 2013, pp. 108–128.

REPORTS

Joint Center for Political and Economic Studies, A Way Out: Creating Partners for Our Nation's Prosperity by Expanding Life Paths for Young Men of Color—Final Report of the Dellums Commission, 2007, pp. 193–207.

Reed, James and Aaron Thomas, The National Urban League: Empowering Black Males to Meet Their Full Potential, 2007, pp. 217–218.

Wilson, Valerie Rawlston, "Introduction to the 2011 Equality Index," 2011, pp. 14–22.

SEXUAL IDENTITY

Bailey, Moya, "Going in Circles: The Struggle to Diversify Popular Images of Black Women," 2008, pp. 193–196.

Battle, Juan, Cathy J. Cohen, Angelique Harris, and Beth E. Richie, "We Are Family: Embracing Our Lesbian, Gay, Bisexual, and Transgender (LGBT) Family Members," 2003, pp. 95–106.

Taylor, Susan L., "Black Love Under Siege," 2008, pp. 179–186.

SOCIOLOGY

Cooper, Maudine R., "The Invisibility Blues' of Black Women in America," 2008, pp. 83–87.

Taylor, Susan L., "Black Love Under Siege," 2008, pp. 179–186.

Teele, James E., "E. Franklin Frazier: The Man and His Intellectual Legacy," 2003, pp. 29–40.

SPECIAL SECTION: 21ST AGENDA FOR JOBS AND FREEDOM

Christensen, Donna, "A Healthier Nation," 2014, pp. 115–117.

Hardy, Chanelle P., "Introduction to the Special Section," 2014, pp. 102–103.

Harper, Hill, "America Incarcerated: Who Pays and Who Profits," 2014, pp. 112–113.

Henderson, Wade, "A Watershed Year for Bipartisanship in Criminal Justice Reform," 2014, pp. 110–111.

Hinojosa, Ruben, "Financial Literacy: Investing to Empower," 2014, pp. 108–109.

Honda, Mike, "Equity and Excellence Lead to Opportunity," 2014, pp. 104–105.

House, Tanya Clay, "The Evolving Fight to Protect the Vote," 2014, pp. 114–115.

Shapiro, Dr. Thomas, "Policies of Exclusion Perpetuate the Racial Wealth Gap" 2014, pp. 106–107.

SPECIAL SECTION: BLACK WOMEN'S HEALTH

Browne, Doris, "The Impact of Health Disparities in African-American Women," 2008, pp. 163–171.

Morris, Eboni D., "By the Numbers: Uninsured African-American Women," 2008, pp. 173–177.

SPECIAL SECTION: KATRINA AND BEYOND

Brazile, Donna L., "New Orleans: Next Steps on the Road to Recovery," 2006, pp. 233–237.

Morial, Marc H., "New Orleans Revisited," 2006, pp. 229–232.

National Urban League, "The National Urban League Katrina Bill of Rights," 2006, pp. 239–243.

SPECIAL SECTION: LIFT EV'RY VOICE

Brown James, Stefanie, "Black Civic Engagement 2.0: In with the Old, in with the New," 2013, pp. 67–68.

Edelman, Marian Wright, "Time to Wake Up and Act: The State of Black America," 2013, pp. 68–69.

Fudge, Marcia L., "Unfinished Business," 2013, pp. 65.

Hardy, Chanelle P., "Introduction to Lift Ev'ry Voice: A Special Collection of Articles and Op-Eds.," 2013, pp. 60–61.

Jones-DeWeever, Avis A., "The Enduring Icon: Dr. Dorothy Height," 2013, pp. 64.

Lewis, John, "New Tactics, Same Old Taint," 2013, pp. 62–63.

Mack, John W., "Reflections on National Urban League's Legacy and Service," 2013, pp. 66.

Sharpton, Al, "Though We Have Achieved Much, the Battle Continues," 2013, pp. 63–64.

SURVEYS

The National Urban League Survey, 2004, pp. 35–51.

Stafford, Walter S., "The National Urban League Survey: Black America's Under-35 Generation," 2001, pp. 19–63.

———, "The New York Urban League Survey: Black New York—On Edge, But Optimistic," 2001, pp. 203–219.

TECHNOLOGY

Clyburn, Mignon, "Challenges and Opportunities for African Americans In Communications Technology," 2014, pp. 192–195.

Dreyfuss, Joel, "Black Americans and the Internet: The Technological Imperative," 2001, pp. 131–141.

Lombard, Tanya, "Transforming Futures for a Daring Tech Tomorrow—African-American Entrepreneurs, Broadband and the Coming Community Benefits," 2014, pp. 188–191.

Patrick, Deval L., "Growing an Innovative Economy in Massachusetts," 2011, pp. 154–158.

Pinkett, Dr. Randal, Robinson, Dr. Jeffrey, "Entrepreneurship and Economic Development," 2014, pp. 174–177.

Ramsey, Rey, "Broadband Matters to All of Us," 2010, pp. 112–116.

Ribeau, Sidney, "A Competitive Foundation for the Future," 2011, pp. 8–9.

Wilkins, Ray, "Jobs, the Internet, and Our Exciting Future," 2011, pp. 94–99.

Wilson III, Ernest J., "Technological Convergence, Media Ownership and Content Diversity," 2000, pp. 147–170.

URBAN AFFAIRS

Allen, Antoine, and Leland Ware, "The Geography of Discrimination: Hypersegregation, Isolation and Fragmentation Within the African-American Community," 2002, pp. 69–92.

Bates, Timothy, "The Paradox of Urban Poverty," 1996, pp. 144–163.

Bell, Carl C., with Esther J. Jenkins, "Preventing Black Homicide," 1990, pp. 143–155.

Bell, William C., "Community Based Organizations and Child Welfare: Building Communities of Hope," 2013, pp. 166–169.

Bryant Solomon, Barbara, "Social Welfare Reform," 1987, pp. 113–127.

Brown, Lee P., "Crime in the Black Community," 1988, pp. 95–113.

Bryant, John Hope, "Financial Dignity in an Economic Age," 2013, pp. 134–138.

Bullard, Robert D. "Urban Infrastructure: Social, Environmental, and Health Risks to African Americans," 1992, pp. 183–196.

Chambers, Julius L., "The Law and Black Americans: Retreat from Civil Rights," 1987, pp. 15–30.

———, "Black Americans and the Courts: Has the Clock Been Turned Back Permanently?" 1990, pp. 9–24.

Edelin, Ramona H., "Toward an African-American Agenda: An Inward Look," 1990, pp. 173–183.

Fair, T. Willard, "Coordinated Community Empowerment: Experiences of the Urban League of Greater Miami," 1993, pp. 217–233.

Gaskins, Darrell J., LaVeist, Thomas A. and Richard, Patrick, "The State of Urban Health: Eliminating Health Disparities to Save Lives and Cut Costs," 2013, pp. 108–128.

Gray, Sandra T., "Public-Private Partnerships: Prospects for America...Promise for African Americans," 1992, pp. 231–247.

Harris, David, "'Driving While Black' and Other African-American Crimes: The Continuing Relevance of Race to American Criminal Justice," 2000, pp. 259–285.

Harris, Dot, "Diversity in STEM: An Economic Imperative," 2013, pp. 92–95.

Henderson, Lenneal J., "African Americans in the Urban Milieu: Conditions, Trends, and Development Needs," 1994, pp. 11–29.

Hill, Robert B., "Urban Redevelopment: Developing Effective Targeting Strategies," 1992, pp. 197–211.

Johnston, Haile, and Tatiana Garcia-Granados, "Common Market: The New Black Farmer," 2012, pp. 100–105.

Jones, Dionne J., with Greg Harrison of the National Urban League Research Department, "Fast Facts: Comparative Views of African-American Status and Progress," 1994, pp. 213–236.

Jones, Shirley J., "Silent Suffering: The Plight of Rural Black America," 1994, pp. 171–188.

LaVeist, Thomas A., Richard, Patrick and Gaskins, Darrell J., "The State of Urban Health: Eliminating Health Disparities to Save Lives and Cut Costs," 2013, pp. 108–128.

Mack, John W., "Reflections on National Urban League's Legacy and Service," 2013, pp. 66.

Massey, Walter E. "Science, Technology, and Human Resources: Preparing for the 21st Century," 1992, pp. 157–169.

Mendez, Jr., Garry A., "Crime Is Not a Part of Our Black Heritage: A Theoretical Essay," 1988, pp. 211–216.

Miller, Jr., Warren F., "Developing Untapped Talent: A National Call for African-American Technologists," 1991, pp. 111–127.

Murray, Sylvester, "Clear and Present Danger: The Decay of America's Physical Infrastructure," 1992, pp. 171–182.

Pemberton, Gayle, "It's the Thing That Counts, Or Reflections on the Legacy of W.E.B. Du Bois," 1991, pp. 129–143.

Pinderhughes, Dianne M., "The Case of African-Americans in the Persian Gulf: The Intersection of American Foreign and Military Policy with Domestic Employment Policy in the United States," 1991, pp. 165–186.

Richard, Patrick, Gaskins, Darrell J. and LaVeist, Thomas A., "The State of Urban Health: Eliminating Health Disparities to Save Lives and Cut Costs," 2013, pp. 108–128.

Robinson, Gene S. "Television Advertising and Its Impact on Black America," 1990, pp. 157–171.

Sawyers, Dr. Andrew and Dr. Lenneal Henderson, "Race, Space and Justice: Cities and Growth in the 21st Century," 2000, pp. 243–258.

Schneider, Alvin J., "Blacks in the Military: The Victory and the Challenge," 1988, pp. 115–128.

Shepherd, Dr. J. Marshall, "21st Century Jobs and Climate Change: A Curse and Blessing for African Americans," 2014, pp. 168–173.

Smedley, Brian, "Race, Poverty, and Healthcare Disparities," 2006, pp. 155–164.

Stafford, Walter, Angela Dews, Melissa Mendez, and Diana Salas, "Race, Gender and Welfare Reform: The Need for Targeted Support," 2003, pp. 41–92.

Stewart, James B., "Developing Black and Latino Survival Strategies: The Future of Urban Areas," 1996, pp. 164–187.

Stone, Christopher E., "Crime and Justice in Black America," 1996, pp. 78–94.

Tidwell, Billy J., with Monica B. Kuumba, Dionne J. Jones, and Betty C. Watson, "Fast Facts: African Americans in the 1990s," 1993, pp. 243–265.

Wallace-Benjamin, Joan, "Organizing African-American Self-Development: The Role of Community-Based Organizations," 1994, pp. 189–205.

Walters, Ronald, "Serving the People: African-American Leadership and the Challenge of Empowerment," 1994, pp. 153–170.

Allen, Antoine, and Leland Ware, "The Geography of Discrimination: Hypersegregation, Isolation and Fragmentation within the African-American Community," 2002, pp. 69–92.

Wiley, Maya, "Hurricane Katrina Exposed the Face of Poverty," 2006, pp. 143–153.

WELFARE

Bell, William C., "Community Based Organizations and Child Welfare: Building Communities of Hope," 2013, pp. 166–169.

Bergeron, Suzanne, and William E. Spriggs, "Welfare Reform and Black America," 2002, pp. 29–50.

Cooper, Maudine R., "The Invisibility Blues' of Black Women in America," 2008, pp. 83–87.

Covington, Kenya L., "The Transformation of the Welfare Caseload," 2004, pp. 149–152.

Spriggs, William E., and Suzanne Bergeron, "Welfare Reform and Black America," 2002, pp. 29–50.

Stafford, Walter, Angela Dews, Melissa Mendez, and Diana Salas, "Race, Gender and Welfare Reform: The Need for Targeted Support," 2003, pp. 41–92.

WOMEN'S ISSUES

Bailey, Moya, "Going In Circles: The Struggle to Diversify Popular Images of Black Women," 2008, pp. 193–196.

Browne, Doris, "The Impact of Health Disparities in African-American Women," 2008, pp. 163–171.

Cooper, Maudine R., "The Invisibility Blues' of Black Women in America," 2008, pp. 83–87.

Harris, Andrea, "The Subprime Wipeout: Unsustainable Loans Erase Gains Made by African-American Women," 2008, pp. 125–133.

Herman, Alexis, "African-American Women and Work: Still a Tale of Two Cities," 2008, pp. 109–113.

Lindsay, Tiffany, "Weaving the Fabric: The Political Activism of Young African-American Women," 2008, pp. 187–192.

Malveaux, Julianne, "Black Women's Hands Can Rock the World: Global Involvement and Understanding," 2008, pp. 197–202.

———, "Shouldering the Third Burden: The Status of African-American Women," 2008, pp. 75–81.

Mensah, Lisa, "Putting Homeownership Back Within Our Reach," 2008, pp. 135–142.

Morris, Eboni D., "By the Numbers: Uninsured African-American Women," 2008, pp. 173–177.

Reuben, Lucy J., "Make Room for the New 'She'EOs: An Analysis of Businesses Owned by Black Females," 2008, pp. 115–124.

Stafford, Walter, Angela Dews, Melissa Mendez, and Diana Salas, "Race, Gender and Welfare Reform: The Need for Targeted Support," 2003, pp. 41–92.

Taylor, Susan L., "Black Love Under Siege," 2008, pp. 179–186.

West, Carolyn M., "Feminism is a Black Thing?": Feminist Contribution to Black Family Life, 2003, pp. 13–27.

WORLD AFFAIRS

Malveaux, Julianne, "Black Women's Hands Can Rock the World: Global Involvement and Understanding," 2008, pp. 197–202.

NATIONAL URBAN LEAGUE
STAFF

// HEADQUARTERS EXECUTIVE STAFF

PRESIDENT & CHIEF EXECUTIVE OFFICER
Marc H. Morial

SENIOR VICE PRESIDENT
Marketing & Communications
Rhonda Spears Bell

SENIOR VICE PRESIDENT & EXECUTIVE DIRECTOR
Washington Bureau
Chanelle P. Hardy, Esq.

SENIOR VICE PRESIDENT & CHIEF TALENT OFFICER
Wanda H. Jackson

GENERAL COUNSEL
Nicolaine M. Lazarre

SENIOR VICE PRESIDENT
Affiliate Services
Herman L. Lessard

SENIOR VICE PRESIDENT
& CHIEF TECHNOLOGY OFFICER
Strategy & Innovation
Michael E. Miller

SENIOR VICE PRESIDENT
Economics & Housing
Cy Richardson

SENIOR VICE PRESIDENT
Development
Dennis Serrette

SENIOR VICE PRESIDENT
Education, Youth Development & Health
Hal Smith

SENIOR ADVISOR
Latraviette D. Smith-Wilson

SENIOR VICE PRESIDENT & CFO
Finance & Operations
Paul Wycisk

PRESIDENT & CEO
Urban Empowerment Fund,
a subsidiary of the National Urban League
Donald E. Bowen

// WASHINGTON BUREAU STAFF

SENIOR VICE PRESIDENT & EXECUTIVE DIRECTOR
Chanelle P. Hardy, Esq.

SENIOR DIRECTOR, OPERATIONS & CHIEF OF STAFF
Cara M. McKinley

VICE PRESIDENT, COMMUNICATION
& EXTERNAL RELATIONS
Pamela Rucker Springs

VICE PRESIDENT, RESEARCH & ECONOMIST
Valerie Rawlston Wilson, Ph.D.

SENIOR LEGISLATIVE DIRECTOR, WORKFORCE,
CIVIL RIGHTS & SOCIAL SERVICES
Suzanne M. Bergeron, MSW

SENIOR LEGISLATIVE DIRECTOR,
EDUCATION & HEALTH POLICY
Susie Saavedra

LEGISLATIVE DIRECTOR, RESEARCH & POLICY
Hazeen Y. Ashby, Esq.

LEGISLATIVE DIRECTOR,
FINANCIAL & HOUSING POLICY
Kyle R. Williams, Esq.

SENIOR LEGISLATIVE MANAGER,
EDUCATION & HEALTH POLICY
Shree Chauhan

SPECIAL ASSISTANT TO THE EXECUTIVE DIRECTOR
Courtney R. O'Neal

BROADBAND & TECHNOLOGY FELLOW
Sean E. Mickens

NATIONAL URBAN LEAGUE
AFFILIATES

AKRON, OHIO
Akron Community Service Center and Urban League

ALEXANDRIA, VIRGINIA
Northern Virginia Urban League

ALTON, ILLINOIS
Madison County Urban League

ANDERSON, INDIANA
Urban League of Madison County, Inc.

ATLANTA, GEORGIA
Urban League of Greater Atlanta

AURORA, ILLINOIS
Quad County Urban League

AUSTIN, TEXAS
Austin Area Urban League

BALTIMORE, MARYLAND
Greater Baltimore Urban League

BATTLE CREEK, MICHIGAN
Southwestern Michigan Urban League

BINGHAMTON, NEW YORK
Broome County Urban League

BIRMINGHAM, ALABAMA
Birmingham Urban League

BOSTON, MASSACHUSETTS
Urban League of Eastern Massachusetts

BUFFALO, NEW YORK
Buffalo Urban League

CANTON, OHIO
Greater Stark County Urban League, Inc.

CHARLESTON, SOUTH CAROLINA
Charleston Trident Urban League

CHARLOTTE, NORTH CAROLINA
Urban League of Central Carolinas, Inc.

CHATTANOOGA, TENNESSEE
Urban League Greater Chattanooga, Inc.

CHICAGO, ILLINOIS
Chicago Urban League

CINCINNATI, OHIO
Urban League of Greater Southwestern Ohio

CLEVELAND, OHIO
Urban League of Greater Cleveland

COLUMBIA, SOUTH CAROLINA
Columbia Urban League

COLUMBUS, GEORGIA
Urban League of Greater Columbus, Inc.

COLUMBUS, OHIO
Columbus Urban League

DALLAS, TEXAS
Urban League of Greater Dallas and North Central Texas

DENVER, COLORADO
Urban League of Metropolitan Denver

DETROIT, MICHIGAN
Urban League of Detroit and Southeastern Michigan

ELIZABETH, NEW JERSEY
Urban League of Union County

ELYRIA, OHIO
Lorain County Urban League

ENGLEWOOD, NEW JERSEY
Urban League for Bergen County

FARRELL, PENNSYLVANIA
Urban League of Shenango Valley

FLINT, MICHIGAN
Urban League of Flint

FORT LAUDERDALE, FLORIDA
Urban League of Broward County

FORT WAYNE, INDIANA
Fort Wayne Urban League

GARY, INDIANA
Urban League of Northwest Indiana, Inc.

GRAND RAPIDS, MICHIGAN
Grand Rapids Urban League

GREENVILLE, SOUTH CAROLINA
Urban League of the Upstate, Inc.

HARTFORD, CONNECTICUT
Urban League of Greater Hartford

HOUSTON, TEXAS
Houston Area Urban League

INDIANAPOLIS, INDIANA
Indianapolis Urban League

JACKSON, MISSISSIPPI
Urban League of Greater Jackson

JACKSONVILLE, FLORIDA
Jacksonville Urban League

JERSEY CITY, NEW JERSEY
Urban League of Hudson County

KANSAS CITY, MISSOURI
Urban League of Kansas City

KNOXVILLE, TENNESSEE
Knoxville Area Urban League

LANCASTER, PENNSYLVANIA
Urban League of Lancaster County

LAS VEGAS, NEVADA
Las Vegas–Clark County
Urban League

LEXINGTON, KENTUCKY
Urban League of Lexington-
Fayette County

LONG ISLAND, NEW YORK
Urban League of Long Island

LOS ANGELES, CALIFORNIA
Los Angeles Urban League

LOUISVILLE, KENTUCKY
Louisville Urban League

MADISON, WISCONSIN
Urban League of Greater Madison

MEMPHIS, TENNESSEE
Memphis Urban League

MIAMI, FLORIDA
Urban League of Greater Miami

MILWAUKEE, WISCONSIN
Milwaukee Urban League

MINNEAPOLIS, MINNESOTA
Minneapolis Urban League

MORRISTOWN, NEW JERSEY
Morris County Urban League

NASHVILLE, TENNESSEE
Urban League of Middle Tennessee

NEW ORLEANS, LOUISIANA
Urban League of Greater
New Orleans

NEW YORK, NEW YORK
New York Urban League

NEWARK, NEW JERSEY
Urban League of Essex County

NORFOLK, VIRGINIA
Urban League of Hampton Roads

OKLAHOMA CITY, OKLAHOMA
Urban League of Greater
Oklahoma City

OMAHA, NEBRASKA
Urban League of Nebraska, Inc.

ORLANDO, FLORIDA
Central Florida Urban League

PEORIA, ILLINOIS
Tri-County Urban League

PHILADELPHIA, PENNSYLVANIA
Urban League of Philadelphia

PHOENIX, ARIZONA
Greater Phoenix Urban League

PITTSBURGH, PENNSYLVANIA
Urban League of Greater
Pittsburgh

PORTLAND, OREGON
Urban League of Portland

PROVIDENCE, RHODE ISLAND
Urban League of Rhode Island

RACINE, WISCONSIN
Urban League of Racine &
Kenosha, Inc.

RICHMOND, VIRGINIA
Urban League of Greater
Richmond, Inc.

ROCHESTER, NEW YORK
Urban League of Rochester

SACRAMENTO, CALIFORNIA
Greater Sacramento Urban League

SAINT LOUIS, MISSOURI
Urban League Metropolitan
St. Louis

SAINT PETERSBURG, FLORIDA
Pinellas County Urban League

SAN DIEGO, CALIFORNIA
Urban League of
San Diego County

SEATTLE, WASHINGTON
Urban League of
Metropolitan Seattle

SPRINGFIELD, ILLINOIS
Springfield Urban League, Inc.

SPRINGFIELD, MASSACHUSETTS
Urban League of Springfield

STAMFORD, CONNECTICUT
Urban League of Southern
Connecticut

TACOMA, WASHINGTON
Tacoma Urban League

TALLAHASSEE, FLORDIA
Tallahassee Urban League

TOLEDO, OHIO
Greater Toledo Urban League

TUCSON, ARIZONA
Tucson Urban League

TULSA, OKLAHOMA
Metropolitan Tulsa Urban League

WARREN, OHIO
Greater Warren-Youngstown
Urban League

WASHINGTON, D.C.
Greater Washington Urban League

WEST PALM BEACH, FLORIDA
Urban League of Palm Beach
County, Inc.

WHITE PLAINS, NEW YORK
Urban League of
Westchester County

WICHITA, KANSAS
Urban League of Kansas, Inc.

WILMINGTON, DELAWARE
Metropolitan Wilmington
Urban League

**WINSTON-SALEM,
NORTH CAROLINA**
Winston-Salem Urban League

**2014 STATE OF BLACK AMERICA
WEBSERIES DIGITAL EVENT TEAM**

Rhonda Spears Bell

Zuhirah Khaldun-Diarra

Kristian Buchanan

Simone Jordan

Beatriz Mota

Will Ashley

Candece Monteil